Matthew Zajac grew up in Inverness and studied drama at Bristol University. He has worked as an actor for 30 years, appearing in theatres throughout the UK, and in numerous film, TV and radio productions. He has worked as a director and producer for several theatre companies and has also produced two films. He is currently Joint Artistic Director of Dogstar Theatre Company which tours its productions in Scotland and abroad. In 2009, he was named Best Actor in the Critics' Awards for Theatre in Scotland for his performance in his play The Tailor of Inverness. The play has won several other awards and has toured extensively in Scotland and to Poland, Ukraine, Germany, Sweden, Australia and the USA. Further touring to Denmark, Sweden, Ireland, Wales and Ukraine will take place in 2013.

D1428521

Praise for this book

'Matthew Zajac's breathtaking investigation of his father's mysterious past has taken him into the darkest corners of Central Europe's 20th century history. Out of a merely curious son develops a forensic investigator who peels back the lies hiding truths not just about Nazism and Stalinism but also the puzzling but energetic mendacity of his own father. Zajac's winning personality, however, turns what might have been a sustained exploration of pessimism into a revelatory and uplifting examination of self, family and national identity. Matthew's final discovery is heart-stopping and sincerely moving. This book ploughs a parallel furrow to *The Hare with Amber Eyes*.'

Misha Glenny, author of *The Balkans*, *McMafia*, and *Dark Market*, writing of this book

Praise for the play *The Tailor of Inverness* by Matthew Zajac
'... a beautifully realised tale of the reality of survival in war-torn Eastern Europe ... Matthew Zajac's moving performance is a triumph of evocative staging and storytelling.'

Katie Toms, *Observer*

'...brilliantly encapsulates the effects of war on individuals, families and societies... As the truth becomes less and less certain, so the fracturing impact of the war grows more tangible, lending this touching personal story the grand metaphorical weight of 20th-century history. All this and live fiddle too.'

Mark Fisher, *The List*

'This is a towering piece of work with a glorious performance by the author.'

Emer O'Kelly, *Sunday Independent Ireland*

THE TAILOR OF INVERNESS

Matthew Zajac

SANDSTONEPRESS
HIGHLAND | SCOTLAND

First published in Great Britain by
Sandstone Press Ltd
PO Box 5725
One High Street
Dingwall
Ross-shire
IV15 9WJ
Scotland.

www.sandstonepress.com

Editor: Robert Davidson

The publisher acknowledges subsidy from Creative Scotland towards
publication of this volume.

ISBN: 978-1-908737-45-8
ISBN e: 978-1-908737-46-5

Cover design by Graham Thew, Dublin.
Front cover photograph of Matthew Zajac by Laurence Winram.

Typeset by Raspberryhmac Creative Type.
Printed and bound by Totem, Poland.

For Virginia, Ruby & Iona
For my mother
For Anna Kotek
For Irena

The dress you gave me
Was a butterfly
Blown by the wind
I pinned it to my heart

The dress you gave me
Squeezed through the rubble
And the air between the censor's hands
Its creases match mine

The dress you gave me
Is my bitter sister
I pinch and tear at her absence
Though she was never born

Your stitching is strong
Closed up, impenetrable
Your fear folds in the shadows of the skirt
I wear it and watch
As you run
Into
The Distance

Matthew Zajac

Contents

List of Illustrations

Poland and its borders

PROLOGUE

I've got this thing inside me which I need to get out. It has been there since I was born and it has grown as I've grown. When I was a child, a teenager, a young man, I wasn't aware that I would feel a compulsion to purge it, but that changed around the age of 30. I'm 49 now, and I've reached the point where I start to write this book, where the purge begins. Purge. A word with negative connotations in modern times, when associated with politics. Not for me though, as I begin my personal purge, my clearing out.

Although a purge can suggest atonement, a spiritual cleansing, mine won't have that effect. It won't have a moral dimension. Perhaps purge is the wrong word. Perhaps the full meaning of this exercise, its payback, will remain elusive.

This purge is about self-expression and although I'm confident of the therapeutic power of the process of self-expression, for me anyway, which this book represents, I don't wish to express everything. Indeed, I can't. Some of the history is incomplete, unknown in spite of my best efforts. I present this story to you in the knowledge that questions will remain.

The thing I need to get out is my father's story. His name was Mateusz Zajac. He was a Pole. I inherited his name, with

13

the English form Matthew, which he also adopted when he settled in Scotland. He was a tailor. He started his own business in Inverness, the main town of the Scottish Highlands, in 1956.

So that's what this book is: a striving for an understanding of where I've come from, of the past which has produced me, of places, of myself, of my father. Of a farm in Ukraine, formerly the Ukrainian Soviet Socialist Republic of the Union of Soviet Socialist Republics (USSR), formerly Poland, formerly the Galician region of the Austro-Hungarian Empire, formerly Poland. It's a journey, both physical and – what? – psycho-logical, spiritual, rational? All of these, I suppose, although I wouldn't describe myself as religious at all.

I want to make contact with my origins, with my father's origins, to open a route which was closed to him in September 1939 with the German and then Soviet invasions and partition of Poland. A route to his home in the village of Gnilowody, near the town of Podhajce in the Tarnopol region or, as one should say today now that these places are Ukrainian, not Polish, a route to Hnilowody, near the town of Pidhaitsi in the Ternopil region. A route to his parents. He told me that after September 1939, he never saw them again. That informa-tion is contained in Part Three of this book, edited transcripts of conversations I recorded with him in 1988, the year before the Berlin Wall came down.

My generation had grown into adulthood as Soviet Communism ossified and then stumbled towards relinquishing its power over its satellites. In adulthood, I had begun to be more conscious of the pain caused by the wrenching apart of my father's family and the impossibility of him ever seeing his birthplace. So much was unknown, censored, oppressed. I began to feel a need to unlock it all. That's why I made the recordings with him. They were my starting point, but it took me a long time to go any further. I was hampered by the preoccupations of my work, by my lack of Polish, by my own urge, inherited or learned, to live in the moment and look forward.

My father's energetic, single-minded drive to create his new life in Scotland, to 'never look back' had been a success in many ways. He had brought up well-educated Scottish children. He was highly respected and well known in Inverness and the Highlands for his work, producing beautiful suits, coats, Inverness capes, skirts, kilts, plus fours and hunting jackets and making alterations to everything from evening dresses to jeans. He had a long-running contract with the RAF base at Kinloss. As an important mark of his integration into Highland life, he had been accepted into the Freemasons. His life, and ours, was orientated towards succeeding in the world we were in. There was no going back. Except for the holidays.

When I made the recordings, I had an idea that I might want to write about him one day. I envisaged a book, what you now have before you. But when I first started to think seriously about writing it, it was a daunting prospect as I had never written a book and didn't consider myself to be a writer. I had dabbled in writing from time to time, experimenting with a couple of screenplays and short stories and the occasional poem and song, but I had never felt the compulsion which I think is common to true writers. I guess that has changed now.

During the years of my discoveries about my father, I remained unable to find my way into writing this story. Then one day, I think in 2006, I saw what was staring me in the face. I had spent a large part of my professional life working with new plays, acting in them, commissioning and producing them, and I had my own theatre company, Dogstar, started in Inverness in 1999 by my friend and colleague Hamish MacDonald. I joined him to run the company in 2003. I knew a lot more about plays than I did about prose writing, so why not try writing a play about my father first? And that's what

I did, though it's not a conventional drama. I sometimes wonder if you can even describe it as a play.

The Tailor of Inverness opened at the 2008 Edinburgh Fringe Festival at the Assembly Rooms and to my great joy and surprise, it was an instant hit. Eighteen of its twenty four performances sold out. Hundreds of people failed to get a ticket. The production won a clutch of awards. Since then, it has toured three times in Scotland and to Poland, Ukraine, Germany, Sweden, Denmark, Ireland, Australia and the USA. The response of audiences in each of these countries has been quite overwhelming.

The success of the play gave me the confidence and the motivation to get on with writing the book.

Here it is at last.

PART ONE
Inverness to Lesna

1: The Poles of Inverness

In 1956, three years before I was born, my parents moved to the electric flats in Dalneigh, a neat new council estate on the west side of Inverness. We stayed in the flats until 1967, moving just around the corner to a semi-detached house. Dalneigh was populated then with many young families making a new start. Most of these families, like mine, were incomers to Inverness, from Scotland's Central Belt or rural parts of the Highlands, attracted to the growing town by jobs, new houses, clean air and the stunning surrounding landscape. The estate had an assertively modern new primary school which housed 600 children, baby-boomers smartly turned out by proud parents in their red and black uniforms, a peaceful, democratic re-appropriation of that dangerous colour combination. Dalneigh encapsulated the relief and optimism of post-war, post-rationing Britain, where ordinary people could aspire to, and began to achieve higher standards of living, where, for the first time, ordinary people could actually afford TVs, cars, washing machines and refrigerators. It was a new community in a new world, a perfect place for strangers to re-invent themselves.

There weren't many Poles in Inverness then. Maybe twenty, each one a survivor of the Second World War from a country

Me and my father Mateusz, the electric flats, Dalneigh 1961

which had lost one quarter of its total population. Twenty wasn't enough for a community, for a club and a Saturday Polish school like they had in Glasgow and Edinburgh. There was a bigger group in Easter Ross around Invergordon, where Polish soldiers had been stationed during the war. We went to a couple of Polish cultural events there in the '60s which featured Polish food and a traditional dancing group, some local daughters dressed in colourful costumes: black velvet sequinned waistcoats, skirts, boots and ribboned headdresses.

Dad didn't go to the Catholic church in Inverness, which must have curtailed his contact with some of the local Poles. We all went to my mother's church, the Scottish Episcopalian St. Andrew's Cathedral. I don't think my dad was ever very religious, but he was observant. He went with the flow and followed the form. When I learned of his parents' separate creeds and their attendance at his father's Catholic and his mother's Orthodox church services, I understood his pragmatic attitude, even more so when I took into account the fact that my Scottish grandparents followed different creeds too. Granny was the Episcopalian, Grampa was Church of Scotland. There was also an anti-Catholic streak on that side of the family, as was the case in thousands of Scottish Protestant families at the time (and, sadly, even to this day), so life could have been more difficult for my parents if my dad had declared himself a 'papist'. His pragmatism when it came to religion was just one aspect of his adaptability.

In his old age, my father regretted the fact that he hadn't taught us Polish. He worked very long hours when I was young, so it would have been difficult for him. He also explained that someone had persuaded him that it would confuse us. I think that 'someone' was probably my mother. In her defence, I think this was a common view at the time. I've met many second-generation Poles like me who were never taught the language by their fathers.

Polish was spoken at home, though, when dad was visited by his Polish friends. I always loved hearing it. There was a sense of joy about it, as the men were released from the restrictions of their second language, and the Polish flowed out of them, animated, relieved, fully engaged with each other. I often wished I could join in, but satisfied myself with mimicking the sounds and the song of it, happy to recognise the few words and phrases I understood, happy because they were happy.

These visits usually took place at the weekend and they got progressively happier as the drink flowed with the talk. My father's closest Polish friends in Inverness were John Bloczynski and Rura, and they were regular visitors to the house, especially Rura. Rura's first name was Wladyslaw, but everyone knew him as Rura. It was simpler for the Highlanders to get their tongues round his surname. Rura worked for the Forestry Commission and lived alone in a single room which reeked of tobacco in the Commission's hostel in Cannich, a small village deep in the Highlands about 50 kilometres west of Inverness.

He was an energetic and immensely strong wee man with a quiff of reddish-brown hair and tanned, leathery skin. He had been a member of the Commandos during the war and now he spent his life in the forestry plantations of Glen Affric, Glenurquhart and Mullardoch. His English was poor, so my parents would help him with form-filling and officialdom. In return, he would help my father in the garden. He was a prodigious worker and would happily dig the potato patch at an incredible rate and chop logs which he'd bring from Cannich in his mini-van. He also had a carpentry workshop at the hostel where he spent much of his spare time. He made us many wooden objects: a couple of coffee tables, lampshades, ashtrays, a meat safe before we had a fridge, which still stands in my mother's garden, forty-five years after he made it; a sledge and even a pair of cross-country skis for my sister, which she never used because they were far too heavy. He built our large garden shed, also still standing and watertight. He just couldn't stop making things. They were always solid, built to last.

Rura would turn up on a Saturday, sometimes bearing his latest creation and always bearing whisky, rum or vodka, sometimes all three. Mum and Dad would go with him to the British Legion Club or entertain him and a few neighbours at home. Rura loved the socialising. His life in Cannich was lonely, so he was always ready to have fun when he got to Inverness. He laughed and joked a lot and made up for his poor English with his sheer energy and personality. He also communicated with his mouth organ and, later on, his accordion. He wasn't a great player, but he loved playing and had enough talent to drive through his tunes with gusto. He never read music, he just learned tunes he liked by ear, popular Scottish tunes of the time and the odd Polish tune: 'Lovely Stornoway,' 'Sto Lat,' 'Donald Where's Your Troosers,' 'March, March, Dabrowski,' 'The Dashing White Sergeant'.

After I began piano lessons at the age of eight, my mother would usher me into the living room in my pyjamas to give the adults a tune. I always found this a strangely lonely experience, with my back to everyone, facing my music and the piano keys and feeling the weight of expectation bearing down on me. It always seemed to go quite well, though. The adults were indulgent and delighted, but I was still relieved to finish, smiling in response to the clapping and words of encouragement and scurrying out of the room with my glass of lemonade, away from the chatter and the smell of cigarettes and alcohol. Rura's applause was always the loudest. He simply embodied *joie de vivre*.

After I passed my driving test, when I was seventeen, I would sometimes drive Rura back to Cannich. By then, I had decided to become an actor and he would always delight in acting out a High Noon scenario with me when we met, drawing his imaginary six-shooters and exploding into laughter. On one of the last occasions when we met, at the hostel in Cannich, he gave me the skull and antlers of a dead stag he had found. The beast had been wounded by hunters and had managed to escape into the forest, to die there. Rura died up there himself, struck down by a massive heart attack in 1985, when he was out working on his beloved hills. I guess the combination of his intense work rate and heavy smoking finished him. Perhaps the stressful effects of his desperate wrench away from Poland in 1939 and his lonely life in Scotland played their part too. He hadn't reached sixty, which means he couldn't have been more than fourteen when the war broke out.

I never found out how he'd managed to get to Britain then,

though I do know he trained as a Commando during the war at their base near Spean Bridge in Lochaber. Maybe he'd lied about his age in 1939 to join up with the Polish Army and was one of those Polish soldiers, like the ones in Invergordon, who managed to escape from both the Soviets and the Nazis at the beginning of the war, making their way to Britain.

Paul Makajewski, known in Inverness as Paul Mackay, was another Pole who lived alone, in a small council flat in Inverness. Like Rura, he never returned to Poland. Like Rura, he was a carpenter. He had been a member of the Polish Olympic team at the 1936 Berlin games, the Jesse Owen games. I think Paul was a hurdler. He had left a wife behind in Poland, but he would have been afraid to return after the war.

Those who did go back after service with the Polish Forces in the British army were treated by the Communist authorities as dangerous elements, contaminated by the West, potential spies or subversives. They were arrested. Some were summarily executed, most were sent to penal colonies in the Siberian Gulag, which could also be a death sentence.

Paul was a regular drinker at the men-only bar of the British Legion Club, where I worked for a few months when I was eighteen. I remember him as a sad figure in his later years. He used to visit my dad in his shop, always with a quarter- or half-bottle in the pocket of his long, shabby coat. Lonely and alcoholic, he craved company and some Polish conversation. He was soft-spoken, articulate, sensitive and, when I think of him now, deeply homesick.

The other Poles we knew in Inverness coped more success-fully with their exile. Jan Bloczynski, or John Blo, the mechanic, made a modest success of his car repair business. He was a hard worker, ruddy-faced and rotund. He and my dad were quite close. They supported each other as they made their way in Inverness as small businessmen. John was from Pomerania in north-west Poland. Like a number of the Highland Poles, and like many Poles from Pomerania, he had been conscripted into the Wehrmacht during the war and was captured by the Allies. He was still admitted as a member to the Legion Club, though.

Jan Orfin worked as a labourer and, unusually, he had a Polish wife. They were a diminutive couple, both dark-haired. Jan's was slicked back like my dad's and he had a little moustache which made us think of Hitler, but that's as far as it went, for he was a kind man. The Orfins lived in a tiny cottage on Celt Street in the oldest part of the town by the river. The walls and furniture in their cramped living room were covered in embroidered cloths and crocheted rugs made by Mrs. Orfin. I was only there a few times during the 60s and early 70s, but that room made a strong impression on me as I had never seen one decorated in such a style. I never saw one quite like that again until I visited my father's birthplace in 2003.

Mr. Sieczarek was an accomplished violinist who led the Inverness schools' orchestra. He was born in France, of Polish parents. His wife ran a community centre and they had two sons who were excellent athletes. The younger son, Mark, went off to study with the Royal Ballet from the age of 11 and now has a very successful career as a dancer and choreographer in Germany. There was Richard the baker, Mr. Miller the key-cutter and Mr. Dow the shopkeeper. These last two had changed their names to British ones, for convenience.

That was about it. Polishness was far from ever-present in my life as a boy in Inverness. It was there, exotic, attractive, somehow a part of me, but distant too. We went to Glasgow a couple of times a year to visit Granny and my dad's brother Kazik, and Dad had a couple of other Polish friends there, Kazik Kerr the tailor and Josef Samson the photographer. But apart from attending one or two of the Invergordon gatherings in the '60s, and a couple of dinners at the restaurant of the

24

Polish club in Glasgow, our contact with other Poles was very limited. With no community organisation, the Inverness Poles led lives which were quite isolated from their native culture, unless they made exceptional efforts. There was one way in which my father did make an exceptional effort. Beginning in 1957, when he received his British Passport, and ending in 1990, he saved and planned for what became biennial trips for him and his family to visit his younger brother Adam in Poland.

2: The Journey

We'd travel to Poland by car from our house in Inverness. In the weeks leading up to our departure, my parents would buy gifts and luxuries which were either unobtainable or too expensive for my relatives in Poland: nylons, Cadbury's drinking chocolate, whisky, even Kellog's Corn Flakes. My father took great care in packing the suitcases and the car, filling every available nook and cranny, a shoe here, a hairbrush there. We'd drive down the winding old A9, filled with landmarks: the lonely white church on the hillside at Daviot, always a welcome sight as we neared Inverness on our return; the German soldier's head in the rock wall at Slochd, a knobbly accident of nature, which we fired imaginary machine guns at as we passed in our bus on school and cub scout trips, da-da-da-da-da-da-da-da-da-da!; the bleak high pass of Drumochter where deer grazed close to the road in winter; the tall, white Blair Castle, the only place in Britain where a private army is allowed; that tricky stretch of winding road at Killiecrankie.

We'd stop a night in Newcastle or Carlisle, at my Aunt Cathy's, and sail on the overnight ferry from Harwich to the Hook of Holland, stopping to buy huge, juicy peaches in a market in Cambridge. This was in the early days of the A1, a few years before the M6 and ro-ro ferries. Our lovely red Vauxhall Cresta, with its leatherette seats and a speedometer which moved in a line from green to orange to red as it reached top speed, always fascinating for the boyish me, would be lifted into the ferry hold by crane. The car would be carefully driven onto two metal planks, the wheels rolling into snug cups. Four thick chains, dangling from the crane hook, were clipped to each end of the planks. The car would then be lifted, its weight ensuring stability. They did this with each car and truck, one by one. It was very exciting to my 6-year-old eyes. I marvelled at the gigantic structures around me: the cranes, the railway terminal, the quay and the ship, all to carry us to a foreign place, another home.

The holiday was one big adventure. I remember thrilling at the toy compactness of the ferry cabin, its turquoise and orange bedcovers and starched sheets, how we fitted ourselves and our overnight bags into the little bunks, us boys topping and tailing. I remember an overnight in Arnhem and a doubly exotic meal because 1) it was in a restaurant and 2) it was Malaysian, with dishes kept hot on metal stands with little candles burning underneath. My mother always loved being in Holland. She loved its neatness and industry and, to a degree, its liberalism. It was also the home of Arie and Hank, two former Dutch servicemen she and her sister had dated happily for a while in Glasgow around 1946. They were *en route* to what was then the Dutch East Indies, now Indonesia.

My mother tells me that I rarely expressed boredom during the long days in the car. My own memories are quite vivid and I recall an endless fascination for place-names as we drove over the millions of concrete blocks that formed the autosnelweg/autobahn: Delft, Gouda, Utrecht, Oosterbeek. This was aided by an impressively detailed route plan provided by the

AA's Five Star Travel Service whose sticker was proudly displayed on our windscreen. It charted every town, village, junction, road number and the distances in between from Inverness to our destination, the village of Lesna in the south-west corner of Poland. It had been compiled specially for us and it contributed to the feeling that this was our special adventure. There was no one else in the world who would make our journey, Inverness to Lesna. Emmerich, Wesel, Bottrop, Essen, Recklinghausen, Gutersloh, Bielefeld, Hannover, Braunschweig, Helmstedt.

There was a three-hour wait at Helmstedt, the border between West and East Germany. The Bundesrepublik Deutschland (BRD) and the Deutsch Demokratische Republik (DDR). The People's Republic of Germany and the German Democratic Republic. Which was which? Each name could have applied to either side, their difference lying only in their stress on the People and Democracy. They vied for legitimacy, each claiming true and just representation of their populations. I remember Berlin in the '80s, the two sides of that divided city straining at each other over the Wall with the monumental products of their propaganda war, there at the epicentre of the Cold War: capitalist and socialist super-buildings; giant communist slogans and capitalist advertising icons; the consumerist paradise of Kurfurstendamm and the gigantic brutalism of Alexanderplatz. The People's Republic of Germany (Social Democratic) and the German Democratic Republic (Socialist). Such similar names, but how different they were. Even at the age of six, and even by simply driving across the partitioned nation on its autobahn, never seeing a town or city close up, the differences were obvious.

At Helmstedt, it was always hot and it was always stressful. As we drove the last few kilometres towards the border which split Germany, there was a palpable change in the atmosphere of our journey. Like carefree children suddenly brought to book by a stern schoolmaster, we became quiet and attentive as my parents fished out documents and checked that they were in order. Speed limits were progressively reduced. The low buildings of the border crossing came into view. Our eyes were immediately drawn to the machine gun turrets, sitting above and behind them. In the distance to the right and left, more lookout towers were spaced alongside the high barbed wire fences. Queues of vehicles formed, moving slowly through the West German crossing and into the large transit area. We parked. I imagine my father taking a deep breath as he stopped and gathered the papers and passports, before setting off for the transit hall. There were numerous forms to fill in, in spite of our transit visas, procured from the East German Embassy in London months before.

Queueing was at best haphazard, so queues were jumped and formless crowds, rather than queues, pressed in towards the perennially rude, surly and sweaty border officials. Often there were minor errors on our forms and the officer would insist on my father completing a fresh form, which meant another period of queueing and pressing. My mother would go to the transit hall every so often to check on progress, to bring him a drink or perhaps take his place in the queue for a while, and she had to make sure she was there when dad finally reached the counter, to be seen and checked. We would stay close to the car, visit the toilet and spend long periods staring at other British Polish children and their families before plucking up the courage to carry out the odd awkward conversation with them.

The seriousness of this border always discouraged the development of play. Anxiety pervaded the place. Waiting at Helmstedt was always tense for my parents, for my father in particular. Here was the strongest possibility of being turned back. We never were, but there was always the underlying threat that we might be. We were seeking admission to a world of secret police and aluminium coins, of vodka and censorship, of political prisoners and peasants: Communist Europe.

It was at Helmstedt that the still unhealed wounds of the war were most clearly exposed. The partition of Germany was one of the most stark manifestations of the Cold War, but it was also a physical realisation of all the fear, paranoia and distrust engendered by the war itself. The greatest fear had been engendered by the monstrously effective Nazi war machine, so there was a logic for the Allies in splitting Germany, ensuring that it could not unite and rekindle its threat. In the early 1960s and, one might argue, right up to the end of the Cold War and beyond, the shock of World War Two was still very strongly felt. For many, it still is.

Only a few years ago, the Polish Sejm (parliament) voted for a tally to be made of the cost of damage inflicted on Poland by Germany during the conflagration. The wounds are still healing. The war came to a shuddering halt and the victorious powers were determined to impose their new order, to dragoon and control the shell-shocked European masses, to build a new peace, a disfigured peace, but a peace nevertheless. The Iron Curtain was part of that peace. Mass trauma creates mass inarticulacy: so few of the war generation were willing to speak of it. Aside from the pain that remembering could bring on themselves, they didn't want to burden their children with it. Their new world would be one free from blood and death.

It's only in my maturity that I've come to realise how short a time 20 years is. I was born less than 14 years after the war ended, in 1959. Then, everything was looking forward, it was an age of optimism and plenty in Britain. We read *Commando* comics full of war stories and watched 'All Our Yesterdays' on TV, but all that history and *Donner und Blitzen* seemed to us children to be in the distant past. Fourteen years is an eternity when you're six. Now, of course, 1998 seems to me today to be very recent. Our journeys through Northern Europe in the

1960s really were journeys through a recovering continent.

The economic miracle fostered by the Marshall Plan and Common Market membership in West Germany, made travelling through there seem like a breeze. There were no border controls to speak of from the Netherlands into West Germany and comforting signs of prosperity were everywhere. The miracle had taken place: a devastated land had been rebuilt into Europe's most prosperous in less than 20 years. My mother's open admiration for the German recovery, which she put down less to the massive aid from the US and its victorious partners, and more to the popularly-held belief that Germans were intrinsically more industrious and efficient than anyone else, was symbolised by her purchase of pairs of *lederhosen* for me and my brother, which we dutifully wore. It never occurred to me that this might be viewed as a provocative act in Poland or Britain in 1965. I don't think it occurred to her either.

When we had finally delivered the forms with all the answers in the right order, when they had been processed and approved and our 15 Deutschmarks had been paid and our transit visa stamped, when the car had been thoroughly searched, as it usually was, we would slowly pass the machine-gun turrets and electrified fence manned by East German and Soviet soldiers. We had entered the DDR. The transit visa was simply that: we were allowed to travel by a specified route through the country and we had to do it within a specified period, 12 or 24 hours, I can't remember which. The speed limit was lower and now we really were on Hitler's autobahn: there had been little resurfacing on the road, the original concrete blocks were patched up and settlement often made the joins uneven. Each block was the width of one carriageway and about 5 metres long, so vehicles would clunk-a-clunk-a-clunk-a through the quiet countryside. The traffic on this side was much thinner. Sometimes we'd see hardly any vehicles.

The border experience, the gun turrets and the quietness of the autobahn, save for the thudding clunk-a-clunk-a-clunk-a, made for a sense of loneliness and vulnerability.

Marienborn, Uhrsleben, Magdeburg. We broke down near Magdeburg once, at some roadworks. It was baking hot, that 1967 trip, I think, the year when all six of us went, Angela, Catherine, Graeme and I on the back seat. Graeme and I in our khaki shorts and white vests, treating ourselves in the sweltering heat to glasses of tomato juice from huge tins of the stuff my father had bought in anticipation of this long day's journey. The car had overheated, or the fan belt had broken, the radiator was leaking, a circulation pipe was holed, something like that.

We pulled over to the verge. Lines of traffic slowly passed as workmen dug away in the distance. Patches of tarmac were melting, fields of wheat stood still and parched. My father had attended a night class in car mechanics in Inverness, so he could identify the problem. He didn't have the means to fix it though. We were stuck. As Dad scratched his head and we wondered what was to become of us, a man pulled up on a motorbike. It had a side-car which contained two little girls.

They were from Magdeburg. They'd been swimming at a lake in the country. He was a mechanic. He was very friendly, handsome with black wavy hair, a round, open face with prominent cheekbones. He made a temporary repair, using tools he was carrying. It was done in half an hour. My father gave him some Deutschmarks, which he refused at first. We set off, with the man and his girls following for a few kilometres to see that the car was functioning properly, until they parted from us with a wave at the Magdeburg junction. I remember waving to them, knowing we'd never see them again, but feeling that a veil had been lifted, that the mystery and threat of being in this country guarded by gun turrets had been diminished, that the place had become humanised. We had friends here, they were ordinary people. I wished that I could go to their house and play with the little girls. But we had a transit visa.

Burg, Wollin, Brandenburg. The Berliner Ring was tantalising. I wanted to see Berlin! The city seemed to be guarded by thick forests, so all I saw were trees. Trees, the occasional *rastplatz*, and the signs. Michendorf, Ludwigsfelde, Konigs-Wusterhausen, Friedrsdorf, Storkow, Furstenwalde. Their slip roads curved into the forest, large *Ausfahrt* (exit) signs at their bends drawing me towards them. I imagined myself speeding along and separating from the car, following the slip roads into the forest and on to these forbidden towns and villages. Finally, Frankfurt-am-Oder and Swiecko, the Polish border. We'd get there in the late afternoon or early evening, the two countries' border stations on either side of the Oder, linked by a high bridge, the river cut into the deep gorge which had proved such a formidable obstacle for the advancing Soviet armies in 1945.

There were gun turrets here too, of course, but this border always seemed less threatening. The crossing usually took about an hour rather than the three hours of Helmstedt. We were leaving the DDR, and we'd successfully kept within the time limit of our transit visa, so the German officials weren't required to apply the same degree of scrutiny as their Helmstedt colleagues. Then we'd be on the bridge, moving at a crawl, observing the 20km-an-hour speed limit, knowing we were being watched from the towers on either side, neither in East Germany nor Poland. I wondered at the freedom of the anonymous water below me, flowing unhindered towards the Baltic, indifferent to nations and borders. I wondered about this gap we were in, this no man's land. While we were here, did it mean that we were nowhere? For those few moments on that bridge, did we somehow cease to exist? I felt a strange mixture of claustrophobia and freedom; that we were in a peculiar state of suspension. I almost felt weightless. I liked it.

I don't think it was a suspension bridge. Perhaps these strange feelings were also due to the relief of leaving the DDR behind and the happy fact that we were about to enter Poland. My father became cheerful and relaxed, even in the knowledge that we still had to negotiate the Polish border post. Here, his halting, basic German was replaced with his mother tongue. We were scrutinised by the Poles. A couple of times, we even had the car searched, but it didn't seem to matter so much. My father cheerfully conversed with the Polish border officials and usually there was some laughter. They recognised him as an exiled soldier and were usually disposed to leniency, even friendliness towards him. They were amused by his Polish, with its Galician accent and old-fashioned turns of phrase.

On my last childhood crossing at the Oder, in 1974, there was a slightly longer delay than normal. A neighbour of my uncle's (so I was told) had requested that my father bring him some porn magazines from the West. My father had agreed, much to my mother's disgust. They didn't have porn in Communist Poland, at least not openly, it was banned. My father hadn't bothered with concealment, they were on the shelf behind the rear passenger seat and duly picked up with much guffawing by the border guards. They took them into their office for a thorough examination, which took about twenty minutes, before they were returned. My mother was silent, but her embarrassment was obvious. My father joked with the guards as they handed the magazines back.

I was bemused, sympathetic to my mother's view that the magazines were degrading but also to the idea that my father was striking a little blow for free speech, albeit a sleazy one.

We entered Poland. As we left the border behind, we looked forward to reaching our destination, just 250 kilometres to the south, but it was slow going.

No longer on the autobahn, the road surface deteriorated. My father had to be alert for pot-holes and subsidence as the light began to fade. We drove through settlements: Cybinka, Krosno Odrzanskie, Dabie, Kosierz, Bogaczow, Silesian villages which had been German before the war. Many of the buildings we passed bore the scars of the war, peppered with bullet holes, sometimes missing chunks of masonry. The road surface alternated between cobbles and asphalt, with numerous bumpy traverses of railway lines. We passed the odd car and truck, and farmers returning home from the fields on their long horse-drawn carts. People in the villages would stop and gaze at us, fascinated by our exotic car, our strangeness. We would gaze back as we passed, conscious of our difference. Dad had fixed a little Union Jack to the extended aerial on the bonnet, which seemed to emphasise this. Asserting our Britishness in this way seemed to provide us with a little more security too.

Zary, Zagan, Wegliniec. There was a large garrison of the Soviet Army at Zagan. We passed long barrack blocks in the night, the yellow light of low-watt bulbs seeping through thin curtains in blank square window frames, glimpsed sentries lighting cigarettes. I was aware even then that all the East German and Polish military personnel and installations which we had seen on our journey were subservient to this power, Soviet power. With this knowledge, these banal blocks became giant concrete boots always threatening to crush the Polish countryside.

In the surrounding forests lay the sites of a former network of Nazi prisoner-of-war camps, one of which, Stalag Luft III, was the scene of an escape by eighty allied prisoners in March 1944. This escape, led by the British Major Roger Bushell, became the subject of the 1960s film 'The Great Escape'. Of the eighty, all but three were caught. Fifty were executed by firing squad. There were much larger camps at Zagan than Stalag Luft III, which held over 10,000. In 1942, Stalag VIIIE held over 100,000, mainly Soviet prisoners. These prisoners received extremely harsh treatment. Starvation, epidemics, beating and ill treatment took a heavy toll of lives. After its victory, the Red Army used the camps to hold German P.O.W.s and repatriated Polish soldiers, most of whom would eventually be sent to labour camps in the Soviet Union.

We didn't see much more of the Soviet or Polish Armies on our Polish holidays until 1967. Uncle Adam's home in Lesna was only a few kilometres from the Czech border. During that holiday, we often encountered Soviet military vehicles, and even tanks on the country roads around Lesna. In retrospect, it seems that this activity was taking place in preparation for what came in summer 1968, the invasion of Czechoslovakia by Warsaw Pact forces led by the Soviets. Although the reforming leader of the Prague Spring, Alexander Dubcek, didn't become First Secretary of the Communist Party of Czechoslovakia until January 1968, Moscow's armies were ready to remove him and his government long before then. We were oblivious to all that in 1967. We were simply curious, intimidated tourists on a family visit.

Czerwona Woda and Luban Slask. The roads grew dark and quiet as we approached. Road signs were usually small and infrequent and more than once, we'd miss them or spot them too late, so that Dad would have to reverse the car to check we were on the right track. Excitement was high as we entered Luban, the small town only 12 kilometres from Lesna. The road and the railway line criss-crossed each other I think eight times on those 12 kilometres, so we had to take them slowly.

These were the last obstacles on our journey, after the form-filling of months before for the Polish and East German Embassies, the booking of ferries, the three-day drive, the punctures and mechanical breakdowns, the negotiation of the Iron Curtain. These steel railway lines on the road, not level crossings, but lines which usually simply sat on the road surface, perhaps with little ramps on either side of each track in an effort to ease the stress on a vehicle's suspension, were irritating reminders that we were there on sufferance. Miniature rigid steel barriers poking us from below, telling us 'OK, so you're nearly there, but it hasn't been easy for you and it's going to stay that way. Don't forget us. We're not far away.'

I think even in my childish mind it wasn't difficult to reach an understanding of how easily paranoia can be induced. Steel railway lines, the Iron Curtain, barbed wire, gun turrets. It seemed as if Communism's rulers had produced a shape-changing metallic monster to control us. But we had our own little metallic monster to protect us, our red Vauxhall Cresta, our capitalist V-sign. Up yours, Brezhnev, look at us! We never felt quite so gung-ho then as we travelled inside the Iron Curtain, but the sight of us and our relative wealth probably had that effect on some. We were quiet, respectful and curious, and sometimes I felt a little guilty to have come from a luckier part of the world.

And then we were there, Lesna.

3: Arrival

We trundled along the long straight Ulica Baworowo into the village, turning left at the little pink-painted bar into a narrow driveway which led to three houses set back from the road. The middle house was Uncle Adam's, a neat, solid, two-storeyed pre-war German-built dwelling. The lights were on and they were standing in the drive as if they'd been waiting there all day: Adam, his wife Aniela, and their children, Jurek and Ula. In spite of stiff bodies, we sprang from the car to be greeted. My father immediately hugged Adam, laughing and crying, and they planted three kisses on each other's cheeks, left, right, left. We followed suit, struggling with our Scottish reserve and our lack of Polish, while my father, after a 14-hour drive, found a new energy, full of animation and good humour, chatting away and translating for us as we were led into the living room where a great spread awaited us: soup, *placki*, cold meats, *kielbasa,* salads, bread, *kompot,* tea and vodka.

Adam was shorter and stockier than my father. He was barrel-chested, with thick, brown wavy hair which infringed over his shirt collar at the back, Teddy Boy sideburns, and a square, open face, big working hands and a twinkle in his blue eyes. He had an infectious sense of humour, which he used constantly during our stays, always happy times for him and us. He was a good-time guy, a bit of a tearaway in his youth and five years younger than my father. Fourteen years old when the war broke out, he had remained in Gnilowody with his parents until the Germans occupied it in 1941. He was taken 500 miles east by them to work as a forced labourer in a Silesian quarry, not far from Lesna. He worked there until the Soviet liberation of 1945.

When he realised, a few months after the war had finished, that the ground he was standing on was no longer German, but Polish, and that returning to Gnilowody wasn't an option, he occupied an empty flat, a former German home. He met and married Aniela, herself a former forced labourer. Jurek was born and they needed a bigger house. Adam learned of the house on Ulica Baworowo which was occupied by a couple of Soviet officers. One night, the officers were drinking and playing cards in the house when Adam burst in like a madman, wielding an axe. The officers fled. He had been there ever since. That's the story I was told. I expect the truth was less dramatic, but you never know.

Aniela ran a neat general store in the town square. It wasn't hers, of course. All shops belonged to the state. She was a dark-haired, dark-eyed woman, kind and conscientious, sober and watchful. She drank very little and cooked wonderful Polish food. She never mastered any English beyond yes, no and thank you, but then neither did my mother with Polish. She often persisted with the daft idea that if you say something loudly enough in English, it will be understood. 'In Scotland, we drink tea with milk. IN SCOTLAND, WE DRINK TEA WITH MILK! WITH MILK! MILK! Matt, tell them what milk is.' At least she kept trying. She must have experienced a great deal of frustration at her inability to communicate and her reliance on my father as a translator. There was never any question about coming though. I'm sure she understood how important these visits were for him, and for us, so she always supported him and although she sometimes complained about the extent of my father's generosity, she recognised that it would always be necessary for a significant proportion of the family's income to be spent on the biennial Polish trip and on Adam's family and on the brothers' mother, Zofia.

Zofia was the grandmother I never met. A fairytale figure in a thatched cottage in a fertile land. A farmer's wife surrounded by ducks, geese and hens, haystacks and horses. A weatherbeaten *Babcha* in a scarf, staring out at us with a defiant look from the only picture I'd ever seen of her, taken during the '60s, I guess. She looked strong, determined and worn. She called silently from a beautiful, inaccessible place. The old country, the former Polish lands in the east, in eastern Galicia, lost to the Soviets when they invaded in September 1939, only 17 days after the German invasion from the west, now in the Ukrainian Soviet Socialist Republic. If we were inside the Iron Curtain, there was an even thicker Iron Curtain beyond, at the eastern Polish border, impenetrable, protecting the monolithic power, the Soviet Union.

Zofia had survived the Soviet invasion, the German onslaught and the Soviets' vengeful reconquering of her land. And she was still there in Gnilowdy when I was a boy, but barely present in our consciousness, barely mentioned. Spectral, yet alive, red-blooded, living in the real world. Feeding her hens, meeting her neighbours, going to her church, picking her apples. In that frightening, fairytale place, so green and yet so grey. I recall no letters from her. I don't think they were allowed. As a child, I didn't understand how I could have a living, breathing grandmother who I would never meet. I didn't try to understand. As a child, I simply accepted that this was the way things were. She was on the other side of the border. We weren't allowed to go there.

One or two letters did come from Ukraine. They were sent

by my father's cousin, Bogdan Baldys. I understand now that Bogdan would only have been allowed the privilege of sending a letter to the West because he was a Communist official, a party member. I think the letter or letters arrived around the time of Zofia's death, in 1971. Beyond news of her illness and death, my father didn't tell us anything about their contents. They were exotic to us, words written with the Cyrillic alphabet. We were told it was Russian. It might have been Ukrainian, Bogdan's native tongue, but then Ukrainian may have been suppressed and disapproved of. If so, Bogdan would have written in Russian. I didn't even know there *was* a Ukrainian language until I went there in 2003. My father certainly never told us, even though he could speak it. He always described it as 'Russian'. I only began to understand all this in the light of the new history I would learn in my middle age.

I also learned in later life that my father sent money regularly to Adam, which he would then send on to Zofia, via Moscow. The Soviet system made small concessions to compassion, often only if it was advantageous, as in this case, where my father's hard currency would enter the coffers of the Communist banking system while providing a little stimulus to a local economy. So Zofia was more comfortable than most of her neighbours in Gnilowody, but money would never compensate for the complete inaccessibility of her sons. Adam was eventually granted a visa to visit Zofia when she became ill, and again when she died, to attend her funeral. Every detail of his journey, including precise train and bus times, exactly where he would be staying, who he would be visiting and when these visits would take place had to be submitted prior to the granting of his visa. He was kept under surveillance the whole time he was in Ukraine.

Adam worked as a foreman in a local textile factory. He had never risen higher because he refused to join the Party, which would have encouraged the spooks to keep an eye on him in Ukraine. He had succeeded in teaching himself quite a sophisticated level of conversational English by listening to the CIA-funded Radio Free Europe, a subversive act. While Adam was interested in listening to a Western perspective on the world's news and political developments, his priority was to learn English from RFE. He was happy to bring up his family, have fun with his friends and tend his large garden and his bees. He had around twenty hives and produced a substantial quantity of honey every year, most of which he sold or bartered. This kind of free-market activity was much more common in the country than in the cities. Country folk produced more by themselves and were under less surveillance.

Like most apiarists, Adam had developed an immunity to bee stings. We hadn't, so it was unfortunate when, during my first visit, in 1961 at the age of two, I took against the bees and started kicking away at their hives. The bees didn't like that, so they attacked. I was rescued by my mother and my sister. I'm told they received far more stings than I did.

Adam had also supplemented his income by engaging in a smuggling operation across the Czech border. I don't know the extent of his activities, but I do remember being shown a suitcase in his attic once. I think Jurek must have taken us up there. He claimed it was full of banknotes, his father's smuggling profits. I don't know if it really was full of banknotes. If Adam was secretly rich, he couldn't spend his money in large amounts as it would attract suspicion. How could a factory foreman have so much money? But his was the first house in the neighbourhood to have a modern bathroom installed, with a bath and a flushing toilet. This was in the early '70s. Prior to that, we used an outside toilet, a cubicle next to the henhouse with a wooden platform seat above a hole in the ground. I always approached a visit there as a test, to see how long I could hold my breath.

Later in the '70s, Adam and Aniela bought a car for Ula, a rare luxury for Polish families. It was a 600cc Polski Fiat 126, the most common private car on Polish roads during that period. The Polish government, under Edward Gierek, wanted to gain popular support by increasing consumption, pumping money into the economy and making more consumer durables available following the austerity of the '50s and '60s. It revived a pre-war licensing agreement with Fiat and built a new car plant to produce the 126. What was a city runabout in the West became a family car in Poland, for those lucky enough to own one. Sometimes we would see these tiny cars packed with four, five or even six family members, with luggage piled on a roof rack, off on their holidays, just like us.

Adam, Aniela, Mateusz, Ula, my sister Angela and Jurek, Lesna 1959

43

4: Our Polish Summers

We stayed in Lesna for nearly a month. The town lies in the foothills of the Karkonosze Mountains, a western offshoot of the huge Carpathian arc. We went on day trips to Swieradow Zdroj, a small mountain spa, and Szklarska Poreba, the main ski resort, pretty places, full of ornate wooden buildings, cafés and souvenir shops. The big chairlift at Szklarska took us up to 1300 metres and within a kilometre of the Czech border.

The weather was normally hot and sunny. We spent a lot of our time at Czocha, a man-made lake located only three kilometres from Lesna. Often we would walk there, making our way through the undergrowth at the back of the long garden, up the bank and onto a path which led through fields and then a forest in a deep gorge. We passed abandoned factory buildings, the workplace of slave labourers during World War Two, connected to a sub-camp of the huge Gross-Rosen concentration camp network. Eventually we came to the foot of a dam built in the late 19th century, part of an early hydro-electric scheme. Aware of the great wall of water behind it, I was always a little apprehensive at the sight and was eager to scurry up the 300-odd steps to the top. I was in awe of the fact that this curved construction of blackened stone blocks could actually remain solid, but not entirely convinced that it would stay that way. Despite the fact that the dam had stood resolutely for seventy-five years, my faith in those who built it and my understanding of its engineering remained incomplete. I needn't have worried. It's still there today.

The lake was surrounded by woods. It was about five kilometres long, wide at either end with a narrow bend in the middle, entrenched by rock walls. On the heights above the bend stood the round towers and halls of the 13th century Castle Czocha, imposing and mysterious, especially from the water below. We often hired pedalos or kayaks and would look up at the castle's battlements rising out of the rock as we paddled, imagining princesses and cannons, archers and coloured pennants, vampires and wicked barons.

On the flatter shore, by the field which became a car park in the summer, there was a swimming area marked by ropes and buoys, a campsite and rows of little summer houses, a café and a youth camp. Large groups of children would holiday there, the sons and daughters of railway workers, miners and such-like, from Poland's industrial and urban centres. They'd walk in a crocodile from the camp, wearing headscarves and neckerchiefs, sometimes with the insignia of some youth organisation. Officially-sanctioned Trades Unions, Government and Party organisations would fund and promote these camps. There were groups of communist youths there too.

During my last childhood visit to Poland. In 1974, I went to a disco at the young communists' camp. I was asked for my passport at the gate but was too young for a passport in those days. You only got one in the UK when you reached sixteen. This caused some consternation, and the fledgling Party official was forced to consult his superiors. My companion, Wladek Limont, a neighbour's son, persuaded them I wasn't a spy. Wladek and I were the same age, fifteen. We didn't have much language in common, but we liked each other nonetheless and kicked about together quite a lot that summer. Wladek's father was an Argentinian communist, a political exile who had come to Poland to live a life which agreed with his ideology. I don't know if Lesna met his expectations. My father told me that during his early visits to Lesna, in 1957 and '59 especially, Mr. Limont had taken care to avoid any contact with him. He didn't want to be seen fraternising with a visitor from the capitalist West. Memories of indiscriminate mass deportations to the death-ridden labour camps of Siberia were still fresh in those days. You could be accused and sentenced on a whim, without anyone having seen you do anything wrong. Talking to a westerner could be viewed as a highly suspicious act.

Maybe the person who spots you covets your job or your apartment or bears a grudge against you, and so you would be reported, denounced. You might survive this time, but a black mark now exists by your name and it only takes a minor change in the political temperature, a ripple of paranoia in the high reaches of the party, for a new purge to take place. Mr. Limont would have been seen by the two not-so-secret policemen who were always parked outside Uncle Adam's house during those early visits, while inside the brothers mocked them and celebrated their reunion in one long private festival of love and vodka.

The disco was in a hall decorated with posters glorifying the Party, communist youth and industrial and sporting achievement. Most of the kids were too shy to dance. Wladek and I danced together and looked at the girls, as they looked at us. We had been listening to Radio Luxemburg that summer and Wladek had been recording some of the songs. His favourite was Hot Chocolate's 'Brother Louie'. He'd brought his recording of the song with him and managed to persuade the comrade DJ to play it. This was quite daring as the only western songs played up to that point were a couple of the

46

Beatles' earlier, tamer tunes. We danced, happily ignoring the quizzical stares of a few young ideologues.

Although he was the son of a Party member, I don't think Wladek was ever going to buy into the Soviet myth. I think by then, his father wasn't really buying into it either. He seemed to actively encourage our friendship and enjoyed visiting Adam, Aniela and my parents for a seat in the garden and a glass or two, happy to chew over the failings of the regime and enquire about conditions in the West. I suppose it could have been a more subtle form of spying, but I don't think so.

Wladek's thirst for Western Pop was an example of another side to young Poland at that time, another side to conformism, a place where young people were eager to break out, to embrace a freer life. Gierek's new consumerism and the student radicalism of 1968 had bred a strong desire for self-expression and independence from communist orthodoxy. The state made efforts to contain these impulses by sanctioning a few Polish rock bands, the most famous being the blues rock band with the defiantly English slogan-name, Breakout. The band's long hair, its leanings towards the rocking lifestyle of the west, its flouting of convention and, most importantly, its music, were loved by hundreds of thousands of young Poles. Breakout's gigs became a rallying point for disaffected youth. It all got too much for the state, though, and in 1970 a broadcasting ban was imposed on them, but their popularity grew and they kept on playing throughout the '70s.

My cousin Jurek was a Breakout fan. He was a student of mechanical engineering. He had long black hair and a leather jacket and a mate called Bogdan who rode a big motorbike. Jurek wanted nothing to do with Communism and I expect the Communists wanted nothing to do with him.

Poland was not the Soviet Union. Due to its size and perhaps the fact that it had achieved military victories over Russia in the past, the Polish Communist state was allowed a little more latitude by Moscow than its other satellites. I guess Moscow recognised the need to appease Polish popular opinion, that the violent suppression of the Poles would be more difficult than that of Hungary in 1956 and Czechoslovakia in 1968. No doubt the Soviets closely monitored the Polish political climate and didn't hesitate to put pressure on the Polish government when it felt necessary, but they left their Polish comrades in government to deal with protest themselves, which they did, with volence, imprisonment and killing, in 1956, 1970, 1976 and 1981.

Jurek wanted to get out of Poland, and in 1971 he came to Inverness on a tourist visa, ostensibly for a three-week holiday. He stayed a year. My father got him an illegal job as a mechanic with John Bloczynski, whose garage was in a backstreet near the town centre. Jurek's English was virtually non-existent when he arrived and he quickly became lonely and homesick. He drank heavily at the weekends during that year and would regularly fall out of a taxi and into our house on Saturday nights, usually around 10.30pm after an all-day binge. The pubs in Scotland closed at 10.00pm in those days. My parents would usually be out at the Legion, so I would help him up the stairs and into bed. My mother got so fed up she suggested he move into the shed. By the end of the year, Jurek had succeeded in gaining an entry visa to Australia and had saved enough money to get there. He emigrated to Sydney and got a job with ICI in Papua New Guinea and, after a few years, opened a Russian restaurant called *Rasputin*. He returned to Inverness once, in 1978. I was about to start university and Jurek gave me £100, which was a lot then. I think he felt guilty about his bad behaviour. Jurek's still in Sydney, having spent the latter part of his working life as a hospital catering manager. Now retired, he rarely returns to Poland.

In Lesna, Elzbieta Czupek, who would eventually emigrate to Denmark, became a friend of my sisters. She took me out in a kayak on Czocha once, when I was ten and she was about seventeen, on a baking hot day. We paddled to the other side of the lake to visit a friend she knew was camping there. As we beached the kayak, Elzbieta and her friend exclaimed how hot it was, and her friend pulled off her T-shirt in one swift movement, to cool down. She was naked from the waist up. I was agog. I had never seen such careless abandon before! It was long before my puberty, so there was nothing sexual in it for me. It shocked me to see the young woman's breasts though, and fascinated me. Coming from Presbyterian Scotland, it embarrassed me too. How could she do this and behave as if it was the most natural thing in the world? How could she so casually admit me into what I had been brought up to believe was a very private and shameful world? Why wasn't she ashamed? Why was *I*? I think I felt a certain envy at her complete lack of self-consciousness, but concluded that what she'd done was perfectly logical in the circumstances and that this young woman was neither shameful nor wicked, merely free.

We had lunch with Elzbieta's friend then kayaked the length of the lake, all the way to the stagnant swamp at the western end and back. We returned to be met by the ire of my parents. I had been out in the blazing sun for three hours with no protection. I knew I was sunburned, but didn't realise how much. On the way home, I began to feel sick. By the time we got to Uncle Adam's, I was delirious. I was in bed, shivering, sweating and covered from head to toe in an extremely uncomfortable sticky ointment for three days.

My second view of a woman's breasts was equally eye-popping. One afternoon, my parents were entertaining with Adam and Aniela round a table in the garden, as they often did and, as usual, they had company. Adam's best friend was Jan the Butcher, a man after his own heart: garrulous, playful, anarchic, a flouter of authority; a hard worker and a lover of vodka. He loved it too much. It would kill him before he was fifty. Jan was easily ten years younger than Adam. He had an attractive young wife, Danuta, short, shapely and strong. Jan and Danuta had come to show off their new baby. I was sitting at the table in the living room, probably playing patience or building a house of cards, when Danuta came in from the garden with her baby, sat in an armchair and fished out one of her full breasts for the child.

As with the young woman at the lake, this was clearly nothing out of the ordinary, but again, I was momentarily transfixed before coming to my senses and looking away. Women in Scotland just didn't do this in the '60s. Most of my generation had been bottle fed. I remember even in the '90s being in a café in Pitlochry when my partner Virginia was asked to leave because she had begun to breastfeed. It was true that Danuta had left the revellers at the garden table for some privacy, but it was also clear that my presence wasn't a problem and the wide open living room door she'd ignored when she entered suggested anyone else's presence wouldn't have troubled her either.

Uncle Adam's garden was always a place of abundance during our summers there. There were the beehives. He grew huge beef tomatoes in the open, the best tomatoes I've ever tasted: cabbages, courgettes, onions, beetroot, potatoes and carrots. He grew raspberries, redcurrants and blackcurrants. He had apple trees and pear trees and two big cherry trees. We spent many an hour up in the cherry trees, picking and eating juicy cherries until our stomachs ached. Adam would make a kind of cherry wine. Ula and Aniela would make cherry cakes and sweet *pierogi* with cherries, sugar and cream. There were lots of hens with their chicks and pullets, which we'd delight in chasing. Every so often, Adam or Jurek would select a hen for the pot, scurry after it, axe in hand, grab it and decapitate it on the wood block. It was an appalling and fascinating sight to see the headless chicken scrabbling about, twitching and dying. Aniela would pluck it and then make delicious chicken consommé with parsley and home-made egg noodles. The hens roamed freely behind a high fence, in front of which was the yard and the steps leading up to the door. We'd sometimes sit on those steps in the evening and play cards while the adults sat around the garden table chatting, singing and toasting.

The vodka flowed freely. They drank it in the classic Eastern European style. The table was covered with little plates of food: slices of salami and tomato, gherkins, peppers, bread, carrot salad and cheese. The little glasses were filled, a toast was made and the vodka was knocked back. They'd shudder and gasp as the vodka thrilled through them and their hands would reach for some food and they'd continue their chat, always animated and expressive, with lots of gesturing and drama. After fifteen minutes or so, they'd repeat the routine. They could sustain this for hours. Sometimes we'd take a break from playing cards on the stoop to wait on them, replenishing the plates of food, supplying water and *kompot* to help them pace themselves or fetching another bottle. If the weather turned cooler, they'd move into the house and sit at the round table in the living room. They always preferred sitting at a table rather than in armchairs. The table provided a focal point which sustained an energy to their socialising. They'd get drunk, of course, but it was rare to see anyone legless. I only remember seeing my father in that condition once.

He was tanned and handsome, and seemed quite coherent when he was sitting at the table, but as soon as he rose, he swayed and staggered towards us, a look of calm, distant concentration on his face. He knew he'd gone too far. We scrambled clear as he made for the steps into the house, grabbing the stone balustrade and hauling himself up and past us, mumbling an apology, hurling himself into the hall and into his bedroom to collapse onto bed. I was surprised and a little embarrassed, but the other adults sympathetically laughed it off, as did my father the next morning as we took him cups of tea to help him recover from his hangover. He was contrite too and I respected him for the frankness of his admission that he'd lost control. I'm sure there were other times when he was as drunk as that in Lesna, but I didn't see them.

Adam, my parents and their friends boozed away, way beyond the recommended medical levels we're so familiar with today, but there's no doubt in my mind that they thoroughly enjoyed themselves. Adam would take delight in opening a new bottle of 'good medicine', and on the celebration would go. That's what our visit really was, one long celebration of the brothers' reunion, of their survival, of their relative prosperity, of our modest piercing of the Iron Curtain and the fact that the Polish Communist state, for all its repression and subservience to Moscow, could accommodate our visit. My parents certainly had no interest in actively subverting the People's Republic. They understood that we were there on sufferance and that any action which could be construed as subversive would result in the refusal of any future visas.

The simple fact of our presence in Poland, along with the hundreds of other British Polish families who made these summer journeys, presented the many curious Poles who met us with an impression of life in the West. The Poles in Lesna and Silesia weren't so different from my father. They had survived the maelstrom and had settled in a new land too, albeit one where nearly everyone was Polish.

Once, after the guests had gone and my mother had retired early, Adam and my father moved to the little table in the kitchen. They had drunk a sackful, but they kept going, deep in conversation, and decided that they fancied mixing their vodka with raw eggs. They drank a shot, then tapped an egg each with a knife and sucked it down. They kept on talking and talking, becoming more and more agitated. Then they both began to cry. Through flowing tears, they talked and drank and sucked raw eggs. Hearing them cry we gingerly approached the kitchen door and watched. They seemed oblivious. 'What are you talking about, Dad?'

He turned to me and ushered me over, smiling. He stroked my head. 'Ach, Matthew, we're just remembering the friends we lost in the war. You should go to bed. On you go. To bed.' He turned back to Adam and their memories.

I'd never seen my father in such a state. I'd never heard him talk in such a way. I'd never heard him talk about the war, except in general terms, not about specific things that had happened to *him*. I wished I could understand his Polish. I wanted to know everything he said. I did pick up quite a lot of Polish vocabulary in Lesna, but I had no grammar. I couldn't string together anything other than the most basic sentences.

The depth of the emotions my father and Adam were expressing, the simple explanation he had given me, the length and intensity of their conversation, the fact that it could only happen here in Lesna after so much vodka, all contributed to present me with a tantalising glimpse of his terrible experience, of the pain and fear, the horror, the hunger and loss he had learned to live with and suppress. Who were these friends? Were they schoolfriends, or were they with him in the army? How had they died? How many of them were there and were any still alive? I wanted to know everything, but I knew nothing. I was shocked, moved and frustrated. This would be the first and only time I'd witness him talking in this way and I didn't understand any of it.

5: The Persecution of the Flies

The days in Lesna would pass with the happy routines of visits to Czocha, cherry picking, garden parties and big meals. A girl would turn up every morning at the house with a little enamelled bucket full of fresh, unpasteurised milk, straight from the cow. On days when we didn't visit Czocha, we'd walk to the town square to buy *lody* – ice cream. It amused me that this was the word my Scottish granny used to address me in her musical Lanarkshire accent – 'You're a fine wee loddie, Matthew'.

One summer, during *longeurs* in the house, I made it my mission to rid the kitchen of flies and became adept at catching them, placing the side of my open hand gently on the wall near my prey and then whipping my hand forward as it closed into a fatal fist. Initially, I got a thrill out of perfecting my killing technique, of having the power of life and death over the flies, but after a few days I grew tired of it and a little uneasy. My persecution of the flies had become both banal and a challenge to my conscience. I gave it up.

I played numerous card games and built houses of cards. Jurek taught me a slick way to shuffle them. Ula, who was three years older than me, would often be found in the kitchen between meals, surreptitiously spooning Cadbury's drinking chocolate into her mouth or munching a bowl of Corn Flakes. During the '70s, the Polish government established a network of luxury goods shops in the towns and cities which only accepted US dollars. The dollars were sent into the country by relatives in the US and other western countries. These shops stocked a lot of western goods, including the drinking chocolate which Ula loved. There was one in Luban, so we'd go there to satisfy Ula's craving, always taking a supply of dollars. It was a condition of our visit that we exchange a stipulated amount of money at the official rate, which we did through the Polish Consulate in Edinburgh or at the border, I can't remember which. My father gave some of his additional dollars to Adam and exchanged the rest on the black market, receiving many times the official rate and enabling him to treat our friends and relatives with even greater largesse.

We befriended Ella and Ryszard Wraga, the fair-haired friendly children of a vet who lived a couple of houses away, and we'd go with them to swim in the river which ran through the town. English had recently been introduced in Polish schools and Ella enjoyed practicing hers on us as we swung from a tree on the riverbank and released ourselves into the water. Jurek once took us to a disused quarry on the edge of the town. I wondered if it had been the quarry where Adam had been put to work during the war. It had filled with water, so we swam there. There was no shore, just sheer rock walls to dive from into the black depths of the quarry. I found the place unnerving, especially when I surfaced and found myself staring into the eyes of a large frog, just inches from my nose. When we returned, Jurek was severely reprimanded by his father. The quarry was a dangerous place. A child had dived too deep during the previous summer and drowned after becoming entangled in the submerged wreckage of machinery.

We didn't watch much TV, though I do have two strong

TV memories from those times, both epic. We watched the Apollo 11 moon landing of 1969 in Lesna. Communist TV was gracious enough to accept the American triumph in the space race. The second memory is the screening of the 1960 Polish medieval romance *Krzyzacy* ('Knights of the Teutonic Order'), a three-hour Polish blockbuster about the titanic conflict between the Poles and the Teutonic Knights which culminated in the Battle of Grunwald (1410). The film is akin to the Hollywood historical epics of the period, such as *Spartacus* and *El Cid*. The charging massed ranks of knights and a harrowing torture scene where one of the Polish heroes is blinded with a red-hot knife remain with me. There was also a *kino* (cinema) in Lesna's town square. The political relaxation of the '70s allowed the screening of approved western films. I think the censors must have been quite liberal, because I remember going to the Lesna *kino* with Ula in 1974 to watch Clint Eastwood's 1971 erotic Gothic Western *The Beguiled*. Maybe they viewed it as an educative example of capitalist degeneracy, but we were entertained.

Aniela would make more wonderful soups, *barszcz* and *zurek*, creamy cauliflower soups with eggs, and she'd cook joints of meat which were delivered every week by Jan the Butcher. We visited Jan's slaughterhouse once to fetch some meat. It was a hot day and I remember standing by my father holding his hand as he chatted briefly with Jan. It was a high roofed building. The air was moist with steam and the odour of warm, freshly killed animals. The sun streamed through a high window creating shafts of light. A few of his colleagues worked behind him, skinning and butchering. Piles of guts and offal lay on a sloping table which had a little gutter in its centre where blood and juices ran off into a bucket. Jan stood with a huge knife in his right hand, gripping the neck of a calf in his left. His hands and apron were splashed with blood and there were flecks of it on his sweating face. The calf whimpered, while another was led to its fate. I was transfixed, horrified and curious. Jan observed my wide eyes and joked with my dad that it was good for me to see where my dinner came from. But it was time to go. I'd seen enough. He had to get on with his work and I think they both felt that it would be too much for me to witness the killing of the calf.

I did learn a lot about killing in Poland. On more than one occasion, we'd be out on an excursion and we'd stop at a war cemetery. I remember a huge Soviet one on a hill covered with seemingly endless rows of graves. There was a track leading from the main road straight up the hill to a tapering stone column topped with a big five-pointed red star. The inscription at its base commemorated the Soviets' Great Patriotic War and gave its dates: 1941-45. 1941 was the year the Nazis invaded the Soviet Union. This prompted a bitter response from my father, Aniela and Adam, which was only tempered by the presence of so many dead Soviet soldiers. They felt insulted by the Soviets willfully ignoring the fact that the war had started here in Poland in 1939 with the almost simultaneous invasions by the Nazi and Soviet armies. The Poles were allowed to remember the Nazi invasion, but not the Soviet one.

On a few occasions, we passed a farmhouse in the country near Lesna. It was empty, which was unusual. It looked like a reasonably sound building. I listened as my father translated the story of the house. A peacable German family had lived there. It was said that they had harboured Jews during the war, but they were brutally murdered just after the war ended. A Polish family had taken possession of the house but, after a few years, they abandoned it, terrified by the ghosts of the murdered Germans. No one wanted to live there now. There appeared to be a collective sense of guilt about this family among the local population. It seemed strange to me that in a region where so many murders had been committed, where the worst excesses of the Nazi regime were given free rein and where eventually almost the entire German population had been supplanted by Poles, there was this one house which had become sacrosanct. The existence of the empty farmhouse helped me to understand that in the midst of all the killing and destruction, and in its aftermath, those who survived had to grapple with their morality.

And then there was Auschwitz. We drove there and back on a long, hot summer's day in 1969, a 650-kilometre round trip. Some of the journey was on the only stretch of motorway in Poland at the time, Hitler's Silesian autobahn. It took us past Wroclaw, ending halfway from there to Opole, the pre-war capital of Upper Silesia. Opole was unusual because its German population was allowed to remain after the war. Most of the Opole Germans spoke a Silesian dialect, *wasserpolnisch*, and were considered to qualify as Polish. Miroslav Klose, a striker in the German national football team in recent years, was born and raised in Opole. My memory of passing through was that of a busy, grimy city where the leaves of the trees were covered in a white dust.

Opole was the gateway to the heavy industrial heartland of Silesia. We passed through Gliwice, which had a huge tank factory then, and then by-passed Katowice. The biggest of Silesia's industrial cities, the Polish Communist government changed Katowice's name to Stalinogrod in 1953, to mark the death of the great dictator, but the people of Katowice refused to accept this. Stalinogrod lasted three years before the Communists admitted defeat and the city reverted to Katowice. There were around five million people in this region living in a forest of industrial chimneys which belched out black smoke. The whole region was an inferno of industrial production. Steelworks, car plants, coachworks, military factories and power stations fuelled primarily by coal. There are huge coal mines in Walbrzych to the west. They yield vast quantities of low-grade brown coal which produces much higher carbon emissions than black coal. It wasn't surprising to find that, by the 1980s, acid rain was eroding the stonework of historic buildings and destroying the forests in the mountains to the south.

We arrived at Auschwitz in the heat of the midday sun. Graeme and I weren't allowed in. We were too young. So my parents, Adam and Aniela left us on a bench close to the gate and its infamous 'Arbeit Macht Frei' arch, eating ice cream. We sat there in our shorts and blue polo shirts for two hours, watching the visitors come and go. My experience of Auschwitz that day was gleaned from the mood of these visitors, quiet, sombre, stony-faced, and from the conversations of the adults in the car on the way home. They were quiet and preoccupied. My father expressed surprise that so much of the place was still intact, that so much evidence was still there. They grappled with the question of how it could have happened. They understood the words of Nazi racial policy, but they couldn't grasp how its followers could act upon it by building and operating such a place as Auschwitz. This came out in sighs and exclamations followed by silences. They were overwhelmed by the negation of humanity which Auschwitz represents and it depressed them. 'How could they have done this....?' 'The children too....' 'You have to see it with your own eyes.' They described the mounds of suitcases, spectacles and clothes, the piles of watches, jewellery and gold teeth which had been stripped from the victims. I pictured them, and as we passed through the nearby town of Oswiecim (Auschwitz in Polish), I wondered at the fact that the busy activity of everyday life could exist simultaneously with the place we'd just visited. I was only ten, but I felt cheated. I felt I had an understanding of what Auschwitz was but I needed to know more.

My parents had bought a book, in English, which contained photographs and a history of the camp. When we got back to Lesna, I spent the following day reading it from cover to cover, examining every detail of every photograph. The book was horribly fascinating, although one could argue that it was wrong to expose a child of ten to the horror of Auschwitz. The revelations of the book, the scale of the slaughter, the mounds of corpses, the gas chambers, the torture, the disgusting medical 'experiments' didn't give me nightmares or visibly upset me in any way. Perhaps this was due to my callowness, the immature child's ability to simply accept the world which adults construct for him or her. But I was deeply affected in another way. I had been presented with a factual account of the *Shoah* and I had visited the gates of its epicentre. It became indisputably real to me. I realised the absolute necessity of ensuring that such a crime was never to be repeated. I understood that it was possible for a whole nation to be manipulated, indoctrinated and brutalised by organised political criminals and that that nation could then acquiesce or collaborate in the murder of millions of people.

The cartoon Nazis of my Hotspur and Commando comics became absurdities, the cartoon killing ridiculously clean. Witnessing the bomb-damaged buildings of Poland, its war graves and the ghastly pinnacle of industrialised murder that was Auschwitz, Belzec, Treblinka, revealed to me the death-filled reality of Nazi Europe, and the monumental folly of war. At the age of ten, this new understanding was primarily an objective one. I *felt* very little about it. No anger or terror. Perhaps, a certain numbness. Perhaps it was necessary for me to protect myself unconsciously by reacting with a degree of detachment. I don't know, but it was only with maturity that I gained the ability to empathise with the individual and collective suffering of the victims of the war.

In 1974, we went on a trip to Warsaw. We stayed for a night or two in the city centre flat of friends of Adam's, Mr. & Mrs. Stefaniak. We walked by the banks of the Vistula and in the beautiful Lazienki Gardens. We visited the amazingly convincing *Stare Miasto* (Old Town), replicated from the rubble of the razed city after the war, and saw 'Stalin's Gift,' the monolithic Palace of Culture and Science, built by the Soviets after the war. It was nearly pulled down after the fall of the Berlin Wall and there's an old joke in Warsaw that you get the best view of the city from its terraces because then you're not looking at it.

Mr and Mrs Stefaniak were a warm, friendly couple in their late fifties. He was a caretaker in a museum in the *Stare Miasto*. He was also a concentration camp survivor. Amazingly, he'd succeeded in taking a few photographs in the camp, which he showed us: surreptitious, sometimes blurred grey pictures of prisoners sorting clothes, being marched to work, a beating. Little square black and white images of crushed lives, bent, tired bodies in striped camp uniforms. They were images filled with danger and hopelessness. Mr. Stefaniak explained how the camera had been smuggled into the camp, passed to him by a Pole who lived nearby when he was outside the camp perimeter on a work detail and then returned to him in the same way. He would have been shot for taking these pictures, if he had been caught.

By 1976, I was seventeen and full of the narcissistic preoccupations of a British teenager. During the previous year, I had been on an exchange trip with my school to Augsburg, the Bavarian city which was twinned with Inverness. The exchange was with a girls' convent school and I'd carried out a postal romance with one of the girls ever since. As usual every two years, my parents planned to drive to Poland, but I was eager to return to Augsburg with my friend, Tom Morrison. They agreed to give Tom and me a lift to Germany, taking a more southern route to Poland in order to leave us closer to Bavaria. They dropped us off in Mannheim on the river Rhine and carried on to the West-East German border at Herleshausen near Eisenach and on through Thuringia and Lower Saxony to Lesna. I wasn't aware of it at the time, but I wouldn't return to Poland until 1989. From the late '70s until then, I was occupied with the business of becoming an adult, going to university and immersing myself in the world of my chosen profession, trying to make my way as an actor.

PART TWO
Mateusz

[Extracted from tape recordings made in 1988]

6: Childhood

*There was one time, ach aye, I was just wee, was in the winter,
and we went into town, it was not far, just a few kilometres.
We were on the sleigh. Sleigh and the horses. Two horses and
the sleigh, you see. And at night on the way back I heard a
wolf howl.*

'Did you hear the wolf, Dad?'

'Don't worry about it,' he said.

*A few minutes later, a pack of wolves came running out of
the darkness behind us. It was very frightening.*

'I can see them, Dad! They're chasing us!'

*We usually had torches, pitch torches, flaming torches to
ward them away. But that time we didn't have any.*

'Take the shovel!'

*We had a shovel for the snow on the sleigh, so I took it in
both hands, ready to clout any wolf that caught up with us.
Father stung the backs of the horses with his crop. The horses
pulled very fast.*

'Faster dad, faster! Come on! Come on!'

*He kept at the horses with the crop. The wolves were closing,
clouds of steam from them, panting away. Closer, and closer.
I gripped the shovel and shivered. The nearest one was only*

about five or six metres from us. But he couldn't get any closer, stayed with the others, racing after us, for maybe half a minute. Felt like half an hour! The horses pounding on, the snow flying up. Then the wolves began to tire and we pulling away. 'They're giving up!' And they did. They knew they couldn't catch us. They slowed down and were swallowed up in the darkness. Outran the wolves. I didn't have to use the shovel.

The wolf would never attack you when he's alone, just always in the pack. One or two would never attack you but when he's in the pack, would attack, you see. They were hungry of course. Lots of sheep been carried away by the wolves, even wee calf been attacked you know, yes. By Jove we charged home fast! Aye.

The village was small, I don't know, maybe four, five hundred of us. Gnilowody. Not far from the town. The town of Podhajce. School start from seven years of age, and before that I was always on the farm, have various things to do. Maybe to look after the chicken or geese or ducks and ting like that.

It was a reasonably big farm ...ten, twelve heads of cattle, four working horses and two riding horses you see. A mass of geese and ducks. I don't know how many... geese chasing me many a times because geese quite vicious sometimes, oh chase you! Many times I been bitten by the geese...the hens... about a hundred anyway...and land, it was about two hundred and fifty hectares. And, well, we children, it was nothing like a modern music nowadays, cinema or any thing like that, we have to make our own entertainment.

Used to make swings from the trees, from the rafters in the barns and ting like that. And make our own toys, like a man jumping up and down when you press the wee ladder on the bottom you know. I still know how to make it. Even playing cards we made from a piece of cardboard. One time, Kazik – Kazik was a bit older and he decided to make a set of dominoes and he cut the bits of wood and now to get the eyes on, so we burned the eyes on with a piece of wire, heat it in the stove and burn the eyes on. Took about a week but we have a set of dominoes!

Father always got a weekly gazette, the Citizen, Obywatel and sometime he bought magazine and that was where we got to know the various way of playing cards or the dominoes and ting like that.

Marvellous summers we had, it was always very hot. We grow tomatoes outside and all sorts of vegetable that doesn't grow here in Inverness grow there. Grow prolific. Nobody looked after them. Father used to plant them and they just grow and a mass of tomatoes without any care because the ground was very fertile you see, not need much manuring because the black earth you see?

There was a burn running through the village and in the middle of it, there was a mill. The wheat and barley was all ground on a great big stone driven from the water wheel, and we used to watch how it was, slowly, slowly and grind and grind. Sometime a hundred kilogram sack of wheat took a day to grind! Ground non-stop all the time you see?

Reasonably good life we had, you know. We never went hungry in those days. To sell our produce father had to travel quite a few kilometres to different towns to see where the price is better. We were self-sufficient, so we didn't need to go to town to buy this, buy another. We didn't need to do that, were self-sufficient completely.

We ate all sorts of things. There was some meat. We used to kill a pig or a bullock you know, it was salted and cured and all that. I was involved in the curing yes, but the killing no, father used to done that with some friends and made the sausages from the pork and things like that. But mainly it was vegetables and floury ting like noodles, like macaroni. Mother made herself of course. And potatoes, turnip, beetroot, cabbage. Was barrels of cabbage, pickled cabbage.

Polenta was often cooked, you know, the cornflour. And it was very tasty, mother used to make it with cream and sometime even with the fried bacon. We drank milk, the children and the adults. But sometime father made beer. He tried to make vodka once, but didn't come out right, and he abandoned the idea 'cos they weren't drinkers. He says I'd rather buy a bottle. Juices, from a brambles, blackcurrant, redcurrant and cherry. Into the jars with sugar and just left there to ferment in big containers, about 25 litres. Sugar was expensive, comparison with other tings. The juice was quite strong. One time when I was wee I took a cup and I slept for about two days yes, I did. I didn't realise it was so strong. Mother and father, they give me a row like anything. If you misbehaving you got a belting and that was that. Here! Lie down! One time, how was it...och we nearly set the house on fire.

During the First World War, there was a front in our area, you see? And each time you dug anywhere you always found a bullet or a grenade or an artillery cartridge. And they were still perfectly sound. So one time, me and my brothers dismantled them. We had quite a heap of gunpowder and started hammerin' with a hammer to make a spark. And the damn ting made a spark all right. And it went off with a bang! Adam was wounded in the hand that time, he still have a scar there.

Oh, I gotta such a belting. Father was chasing and pulling and I got a battering like anything you know. A lot of boys in that area were blinded, lost the arms, lost the fingers because of that you see?/ Somehow I was lucky. I know a chap, he become a musician, he play a violin, lost his eyes because of that. Marcin, Marcin something, I just don't remember his surname you know? Blinded, but he still played the violin, you know, played with the band, travelling band.

There was organised maybe once a month in the summer, a barn dance on somebody's farm. Round dances, waltzes an' polkas. Songs and storytellers from the village. There was a specially old woman there, Laska was her second name, she was a great storyteller. We used to gather around her an' she tell you such a stories. About the eagles and a princess and the giant and the princess again and the man that turned into the frog, those kinds of things. Fairy tales.

Every village had characters. Like Stefan Bobik. He was supposed to be village idiot, but he wasn't that daft, he just played the goat. He got a good laugh wherever he went. There was a sort of general store where they sold drink too. He always got a drink for nothing, for telling a joke or make some stunt. Sleight of hand. He would make things disappear, and they say he was daft! He wasn't daft at all!

He told us once that in the fields near Kotusow, 'I seen such a big cabbage, they had to use oxen to pull it from the field! They made enough sauerkraut to fill five thousand jars and from the centre of it, the joiners made a new wheel for the mill!'

And of course, we went to the school. Of course the teachers were disciplinarians. We always got a cane if we not done anything right, or a ruler on the hand. But I quite liked school. One time I burned the hand of one boy. You know you not realise these things when you small. The stove burning to heat the school and I grabbed the poker and say to the boy, here, pull, to see who would pull each other over, you know? Didn't realise that poker was hot the other end! Never think, you see?

The teachers was man and wife. Very nice people. He was an officer from the First World War, he fought with Pilsudski's army. He have no leg, lost his leg in the war. They been in the village for years. When the Russian came in the Second World War, they were deported to Siberia because they weren't desirable characters, according to the Russians. I don't know what happened to them at all.

I have plenty friends. Everyone was a friend. There was one Wladyslaw Zajac, no relation at all. There would have been some connection very very far back. He was the same age as me, a tall, strong boy. We always went together, sung the songs, climbed the trees, trapped the rabbits, chased the fox in the winter, oh what a chase it was. You see the fox, and you round with the horse and the sleigh. Circle it, fox, all around and join the circle. If fox not run away before you close the circle, you have him because he would not cross the circle. And you go smaller and smaller circle and smaller circle and then bang, you got the fox. Aye. We caught a few that way. Need to be mighty fast because the fox they are clever trying to get out of the circle before you join it. He's out of the circle, its finished, he's got away.

Heaps of girls in the village, of course. Och, I have number of girlfriends! There was Milanja, there was Michalina, and Maria... they just lived a couple of houses from us... Oh, Saucuk! Maria Saucuk. They were Ukrainians, Greek Orthodox, you know. The village was mixed, Greek Orthodox, Roman Catholic and the odd Lutheran. The school was mixed too. There was a family of Jews who went to school too, was two boys, Lipko and Muinka, that's Menachem and Lippe in the Hebrew.

There was no religious conflict in the village. Everyone treated the same! We grew up with Jews, we grew up with Ukrainians, was no animosity between anybody! When they appeared, when all the conflict start to show its ugly head – when Hitler came into power in Germany – it spread so quick, there start discriminate against this religion, against that, oh he's a Jew and he's a Ukrainian and he's a Pole! Don't buy from him because he's a Jew. We never heard that before. There was no such a Nazi movement or anything like that. There was in the west of Poland, but in the east of Poland, no. Not until after Hitler came into power. The propaganda, it spread like a wildfire you see? You see?

But with us there was not even think of that er, any discrimination, you know. Like, with us, was all services in one church! The Greek Orthodox priest was having a service, the Roman Catholic was having a service in the same church, alternative Sunday.

And we celebrated two Christmases! The Catholic and the Orthodox. Perfectly in order! Oh Christmas, tremendous celebration it was. The preparation went on for a week beforehand. The great pleated doughnut been made, the special kolacz, and when Christmas come, we have Christmas Eve supper after the sun set. Usually carp and kucza, the poppy seed and wheat boiled so that it opens up, very tasty. And a poppy seed and a honey, about half a dozen courses, and then father used to have a bottle of vodka and that home made wine so we got a wine and they got a vodka. It was, oh tremendous and the celebration went on for about three days.

I remember when I was little my older sister got married, the man that played the trumpet was blind and the man that played the violin was blind. Two blind men. I was four years old and I remember that to this day. And the preparation for the wedding went on for weeks. Baking, cooking and preserving and when the wedding day came in it was so many people! I never seen so many people before in one spot! Nobody took much notice of me and I cried most of the time!

My sister. Of course she is dead now, aye. Milanja. She was the oldest. 1906 she was born. That's where my mother was, living with her in Gnilowody, behind the Iron Curtain where we come from you know. Milanja got married to another farmer. And she moved about kilometre or two away. Smaller farm than ours. But we didn't know she had a heart condition. She died of a heart trouble, she was quite young, about 50-odds when she died and Pawel, her husand, och he lived about twenty years after that, looked after mother of course. And well he's dead now too. There you are. They had a boy, exactly the same age as Adam, but during the war, he disappeared, don't know what happened to him...he was too young to fight, just like Adam. What happened there, nobody knows, he might have got mixed up with some underground organisation. Some people say that he was shot, by the Germans. Some people say that he was shot by the Russians. So there you are.

He was their only boy, so there's nobody from that side now. He was very very clever boy. He was so bloomin' good he practically spoke German before the war! You know, when he was little, there was a village of Beckersdorf, not far from us, German village from the time of Czarina Katerina. They were Polish citizens but they still retain German language, German culture you see? And he got mixed up with those boys from there. Well, they spoke German obviously. So did he! He spoke German just like them! Before he was twelve! Very clever boy he was.

There was a lot of jealousy because if you see the village, I'm picturing now. When you enter that German village, the building were sort of symmetrically built, they were so clean, there was a gates and a hedges and this and that. And you got other village was everything sort of a haphazard you know? Was not any discipline or symmetry to anything but with them it was. Discipline was there, you see! So there was a lot of jealousy towards the Germans. I wouldn't say they were richer but they were more efficient to make use of what they had. Better than the Poles or the Ukrainians or the...so. And a, well, I don't know...

We have the family of Hutsuls, they come from the Carpathian mountains, they always come in the summer to help with the harvest. Those mountain people, all they have was just some goats and sheep. They not have any arable land to have crops, you see? They come the second week of July and they stayed till harvest finished, till August. After harvest was in, wheat was threshed on the machines and a father

71

apportioned their due, so many sacks of wheat, barley and oats. And that was loaded onto the carts and taken to the railway station and they were taking that all home! Naturally they mill the wheat to flour to last them for the winter. Oh I enjoyed the harvest because it was very hot, and we enjoyed romping in the straw and hay!

And after the Hutsuls went away, potato harvest came in. There was again, number of people come to help. They been paid for it, daily. Potatoes were dug, we didn't have machines. Men been digging them and right behind, women and children been picking them up into the heaps. They sort of a crofters, subsistence farmers. They always got paid for it however they want, sometimes with wheat, sometimes with money. Maybe they had too small a croft they didn't have enough potatoes so they made agreement with father he give them a ton of potato for the winter.

Was not many farms the size of ours. That was ours and a my Uncle Anton and Uncle Michal. It was bigger farm one time and was divided in three, between the three brothers. Just before the second world war, it was decreed to stop that subdividing. Because you see, what would happen? Was three of us. Now our farm would have been divided again on three! You would end up with very little. You wouldn't be able to make a living. So now one would inherit the farm and the rest have to get the job somewhere else, in towns or whatever. So I went to do tailoring. And Kazik didn't want the farm. I think Adam would have been left with it. I had ideas about making lots of money!

Kazik had a civil service job. He was sort of a tax inspector. I don't know what I was going to do but I had my eye on Warsaw, because my cousins were there you see. To go there and make some sort of a fortune there. But it never came anything to it because war broke out.

Was no police in our village. We never have any trouble,

any vandalism or anything. If anything sprung like that the people dealt themselves with it and that's that! There was feuds between neighbours. About most irrelevant tings. Like maybe the neighbour's sheep went over the fence and tramp the onion bed or eat their flowers. And they yell at each other ...keep your animal at your place, look at the damage its made I'll sue you for it! There was one family, two brothers, and they always been fighting. They lived just next door to each other. They have a wee crofts. The Kuszpisz brothers. And they fight nearly every week. Nobody took much notice, though there was a number of times father was called and my uncle to settle what they been fighting over.

One brother accused the other that he stole his chickens. And one accuse the other that he stole his bullock. He say, 'If I stole the bullock, he would be somewhere here! You think I put him in my pocket?!'

'Ah you stole him you b so-and-so, you went to the market and sold him to the slaughterhouse!'

And father and uncle try to pacify them by saying to one you must have stolen it.

'Oh, I didn't steal it.'

'Well, you give him so much.'

'I'm not giving him anyting, because I didn't steal it.'

'Well, who did?'

And so on. And they were father's age! Old men, yes!

There was one woman who lived on her own, they call her a witch. She was no more witch than anybody else! But we were afraid of her. We teased her and she usually chased us with a broom. Wawolka we call her.

'Wawolka, tell us a story!'

'Come on, I'll tell you the story, come over here, I'll give you skelp on the ass!'

But sometime if there was just few of us: 'Sit down and I'll tell you a story.' She was good at making cures. Even my mother been gathering various herbs. A lot of people went to her for cures. Cos there was no doctors. And that's how they call Wawolka a witch because she was sort of a medicine woman.

I still remember my granny on mother's side. She was about ninety when she died. Karolina was her name. She always give me 50 groszy or a zloty, you know? For 50 groszy was heaps of sweeties! She lived about three kilometres from us. Another settlement. I think it was about '37 when she died. And a mother's brothers, was Michal and Roman, always with each other too and father was quite friendly with them all. So there is that chap in Tarnopol, I still get postcards from him, that was the son of Roman. Nicholas, Mykola, the teacher.

Somewhat a haphazard. I should have made some sort of a ...diary but you know I never did. Some people, those diary writers they put everything so meticulous. If I did that I probably would have a big book to write!

Wouldn't be any point to go back there, aye. No, no. I would go back if it was free passage and see what happened. But to stay there, no! Adam say you wouldn't recognise it at all. Nothing, nothing, nothing would resemble what you would know. So there you are, aye.

7: War

My father's brother Kazik 1939

I'd been in about 9 months. That army you know how it is, there's a lot of square-bashing, there's a lot of bullying going on. But on the whole I quite liked it.

Rumour of the war been going on for a while and then latterly it did happen, the war broke out and there was a flood of reservist to our regiment, 51st Infantry Regiment, based in Brzezany.

I was surprised and I wasn't. You see, war was anticipated for a number of years but everyone thought that as we had strong alliance with France and Britain; they were not going to violate that. And especially nobody expected that Russia would come from the other side. We didn't expect to be hit as quick and as hard as that.

We were in the south-east of Poland. You know, the territory called Galicia. We were quite near Russia to the east and Romania and Hungary to the south.

Many a time when I snatch a weekend pass, went home. Was not far. The last time I was home for the weekend about a month before the war broke out. We just did the usual thing you know. And father ask how it is in the army, they hear anyting? I say we don't hear anyting in the army, nobody tell you anyting there! And that was end of it. That was the last time I saw them. Never saw them again.

We headed somewhat north-west. For a week. We didn't move very far because the transportation was horse and cart! Everyting was carried on horses, machine guns, cannons and heavy equipment. After that it was obvious that German advance is very fast and there is no established front line. So we were ordered back and head for, head south to Romania or Hungary, to get across there. And the commanders themselves were in disarray because the High Command was away from Warsaw already! On their way to London. Who was left to order anyting? We were dispersed into smaller units. Because was no use travel by the convoy, there was no way of getting

76

over the frontier that way. Anyway. A lot of them made it.

And then, and then *we know that Russians are across the eastern frontier. They were supposed to be the great liberators or something. Who asked them there to do, nobody know! After they caught us they said: 'We are the liberators from the tyranny of capitalism, and that crap you know?' So I didn't make it.*

We were cut off and gathered to certain points and in the cattle truck and away. To Russia. We went to Kiev and then east. And from time to time when the train stop, so many was taken off and somehow I arrived about three weeks after on the other side of the world!

Everyone was starved to, half dead practically. We were dispersed to various collectives, collective farm you know?

And the Russians, they been so, beautifying everything. 'You are going to the collective farm to help build socialism. You are not prisoners as such, sort of a free workers from Europe. Free workers from the oppressed western capitalism.' Ha-ha.

So we end up beyond Ural practically. Er, what do you call the area? Forgot – Uzb...Uzbe...Uzbekistan. *Of all places, the damn ting you know? We revived a little from the starvation there because the food was reasonably good. We have the same as the other people there. A lot of vegetables like a cabbage and fish, a lot of fish, salted fish.*

What was the name of the place? Aaah...see that's again...I forgot again...where was it now?...Pr-...no,no...It was smaller than a village. A couple of hours from the station. 2-3 hours. We marched of course. Eh... Halenka, Halenka... Halenka *it was* called, *I tink.* Halenka, *yeah. It was Uzbek village, but was a lot of White Russians too. Criminals in the eyes of the regime! Psha! I come across people they serve 5 years, 7 years, and none of them know what for. They told they been part of some conspiracy against the state, and that's that. And not even that, they used to uproot whole villages, and shift them* thousands of miles and leave them with nothing in the middle of nowhere. Maybe in the middle of a forest and they have to build shelters, huts or holes in the ground and they have to eat whatever they could find and if they were strong, they might survive the first winter. The Russian have such a vast country that they have room to manipulate it that way. Not only villages, sometimes whole shire was uprooted and shifted to Siberia. The Communist must have been tinking that people might organise some resistance against them. If they start shifting them about, they have no chance, which was true. When you are uprooted like that, you have no chance to organise anyting!

The Uzbek people were suspicious of strangers but once they got to know our group, that we are not Russians or Communists at all, they were quite open. They hated the regime. They got on fine with some of the Russians there, but the bosses....well the bosses were doing their job. If they not doing it somebody else would because they would be replaced and they might end up in the labour camp.

But those Uzbeks, they didn't like the system at all. They expected the Germans to come and they would welcome them with open arms as far as we understood. And that happen that way in Russia, in a lot of places. Till the Germans start their atrocity. Till they got to know what the German all about, they not any better.

So I was on the farm. Looking after pigs, tilling and ploughing the field. Tings like that. Slept in a sort of a barn, plenty straw for bed and plenty straw to cover yourself. And in the winter, very very cold. Snows were 2-3 metres deep sometime.

I was not that long there, about year and a half.

The Uzbeks sometime offer you tea with a lump of butter, a lump of fat in it you know? Mm-hm. Which uh...I didn't like it in the beginning but you have to drink it 'cos they don't like you not to take it. And of course, there were members of the NKVD in the place. Four in the village, and their spies too, of course. You afraid. As they say in Russia, 'the walls have ears'.

The Uzbeks, they are Muslims. Strict Muslims. They still had their mosque. But the authority in Russia, they been trying to replace religion with their doctrine of Communism. All religion. The NKVD man would stand at the door of the mosque and peer in, who going there? Supposing a job came in, a promotion for a man. He wouldn't be promoted if he went to the mosque. They been trying to get the people to believe in just Communism, nothing else...nothing else exists... you pray to Stalin!

When was it, the amnesty? Was '42, aye beginning of '42 the amnesty was declared for the Polish prisoners. They never tell us officially. Nothing said! I found out about it the round-about way.

A lady doctor was on her weekly round and said, 'You know that there is a points that Poles gathered, forming the Polish army again.'

I say 'Where?!' 'Somewhere in the region.'

Doctor Halinka, Doctor Halina, that was all we know her by. Helena Rostropovich. Was it not Nadia? No. Helena, now I remember. Helena Rostropovich, that's what it was.

After that, we gather together and say 'Here, we must leave and find our people because nobody tellin' us anything.' And then we two by two, two by two, we just...kind of escape.

We knew that train is just passing at such and such a time. Cattle train or passenger whatever it was, you just hang on to it and went on. I travelled myself about for a couple of months, hundreds of miles back and forth.

I was with that chap from Warsaw. Jankowski. We have some money, because we been getting a little pay. But that wasn't much. The rest of the food you beg or steal! One time

I got a loaf of bread from the army unit. I found out where the bread was stored and I went there at night and stole another two! Through the window. It was a fortune! And around the bend I found another two Russians with a chunk of pig's fat, about two or three kilogrammes of it.

I say 'Where the hell you got that?'

They say, 'Well you got the bread.'

So we bartered, I give him half a loaf and he gave me a chunk of the fat. That's the way you survive, you just couldn't survive any other way, just steal and jump from train to train. And we met Poles like ourselves yes!

'An' a which way you travel?'

'Oh, we travel that way.'

'I been that way!'

'Oh. Did you meet any, any of our people?'

'No.'

'No?! They bound to be there, they must be there!'

And one time I was on one of the station lookin' for something to eat and I spotted the uniform of the Polish officer.

I say, 'What you doing here?'

'Well that what we look for, people like you. On every station we have the duty officer.'

'On every station!? I been on a hundred of station!'

Proskurov....I tink it was Proskurov...yeah Proskurov station. Er, the names, I never looked at. You just travelled, you see?

Naturally, we thought that we would go back to fight for Poland. Hundreds of Poles gathered there and the NKVD was still checking everything, because some of the Russian been trying to latch on to us. Most of them been pulled out. NKVD been always alert. But some got out, pretending to be Poles. There is one in Inverness. He runs the Queensgate Hotel. He latched on the same way and he managed to get out.

Was everyone in all sorts of ting, dressed, how they can.

Most of them everyting is torn, bashed, all sorts, you see? And I hear hair-raising stories. Just the same as us, sometime worse, sometime better. Some of them tangled with the NKVD and been shot. I was lucky, a few of us came out unscathed.

We were at Proskurov station for, I don't know, maybe a month... we got reasonably regular food then but not very much of it. Mainly black bread, cabbage soup and kasha. We didn't hear much about the war at all. The paper been a month old before we get hold of it you know? Maybe the officers know a bit more but never told us much.

That time when we managed to get out of Russia, that was the last transport. Because that was the time when Katyn came out. When those graves were discovered where the Russians massacred 24,000 Polish officers. Sikorski, our leader, he been twice to Moscow to see Stalin and demanded the officers. He says 'Well there is my men I'm gatherin,' but no officers, where is my officers?' 'Oh, they must be in the very far north, takes long time to come down or maybe they escaped to Manchuria.' They damn well know what happen to them.

We were lucky because after Katyn was discovered, the Polish Government in Exile in London demanded the International Enquiry. And the Russian been trying to plant that on Germans. But they couldn't succeed because it was the Germans who found them! And after the Polish Authorities insisted on the International Commission, the Russians broke their diplomatic ties with the Poles. Closed the frontier and not let any more Poles to Persia. All the other Poles that were gathered were drafted into Soviet Army...and those Polish units became the so called Koscziusko's Army. They went into Poland after the Russians. That was the basis of the Polish Army after the war.

So we were the last batch. We were embarked on to the boats on to the Caspian Sea and on to Persia, to Tehran. So in Tehran, I didn't bide there very long, maybe two months, *till we got organised and revived from a hunger and all that. No much time to mix with a local population. Language barrier and all that. We just nodded to people. Were taken on the sightseeing, tings like a mosques. Which I didn't take somehow much into heart because always been tinking about the war and going back home. How we going to get there?*

And there was no way to get in touch with the family or anyting. The officers were trying to establish some contact through the Red Cross, but there was none, not at that time. German kept clamp on and the Russian on the other side and that was that. No way contact anybody you see...

The men with some, higher education, degree or under-graduates, they went to the officers' school on the drastic courses to get trained because there was no officers to command! And rest of us were transported by Iraq and Syria, by hair-raising transport over that mountainous terrain to Egypt. Those drivers, they been driving so fast and roads so narrow and the drops hundreds of feet down, oh dear! It makes you dizzy looking at it you know? And the stones falling from under the wheels and cascading down! And we ended up in Cairo. Near Cairo, yes.

There was a huge camp there, tents, various regiments... that's where we were properly organised into battalions. Proper drill was done. It was a Polish camp, and a British camp there too. Couldn't do that all on our own because the British rule! We were there six months or so, training. Fattened up nicely. But was not our fight! Was nothing to do with a Poland! Was a bit of resentment, but ach, we still went and done our job there to get the Nazis out. That was the main fight. To get them out. To get them beaten.

Germans held the Tobruk and it was tremendous losses on the British that time. But the second assault, our corps, the 2nd corps went into battle with the British and Australians, Canadians. We managed to take Tobruk.

And by then we had learned a lot more about what had been going on in these two years. We knew about the concentration camps, the atrocities there. We knew about the Home Army, that had been in existence in Warsaw. There was a lot of a resentment about that. When the Home Army were rising in Warsaw with a few guns and home made bombs but nobody came to help them. Just a few air drops of supplies from the British planes and there was a massive Russian Army sitting on the other side of the river Vistula just watching, doing nothing! Watching the Home Army running out of ammunition. Komorowski, the Home army leader told the allies that he had enough to fight for 8 days. They lasted nearly two months. Russian want them to be defeated so its easier to rule Poland.

We talked to our officers about it but what could they say? They were on the directive from London anyway. And Sikorski was killed in that supposed accident. That was tremendous blow to the morale of Poles, that Sikorski died. On that plane crash. From Gibraltar.

It is a bit dubious. Story about his death. A lot of people think he was set up for that. Because he demanded too much. From the British and Americans. He was on the way from Middle East. I saw him there, I saw him in Egypt in that camp. He spoke to us with General Anders. He had been in India to see Ghandi and from India he stopped in Egypt. And a Polish crew been flying him all the time. It was a converted Liberator. He and his entourage been flying all the time in that plane. Now. They flying from Middle East they landed in Gibraltar to refuel. That's all. Refuel. Immediately after they landed, they were told that the plane is not safe to take off. They would have to transfer to different plane. And a Polish engineers on board, Polish mechanics, they checked it. Nothing wrong with the plane! But they still were ordered to leave the plane and go to another plane. The whole crew was left behind.

Sikorski and his entourage, his daughter, couple of generals, couple of colonels, was about a dozen of them went on another plane. British crew and a Czech pilot. They took off from Gibraltar. And a mile after they take off, they fell to the sea. Pilot escaped. Pilot escapes nicely. The crew from the Liberator, the Polish crew took off the next day with their plane to Britain. No repair was done to it, was nothing wrong with it. Why were they ordered to another plane? Was it not planned assassination? The Polish troops, they were not even allowed to talk about it. After Sikorski died. That was the command.

To this day, most of us think that it was all planned. By Churchill and Roosevelt. To appease Stalin. Because Sikorski was demanding too much. He wanted Poles to fight on Polish soil, nowhere else. And he wanted Polish sovereignty guaranteed.

I was made a sergeant but I got a field commission. So I was the first lieutenant, in charge of a company. One time I got lost in the desert. The certain point have to be taken, certain height on that desert. And when we very cautiously went in, there was nobody there! So I thought I'm in the wrong place! But I was in the right place. I should have stayed there. Thought I was in the wrong place, so I went on. To other position you know, but that was nothing there either, so we just got lost. We wander about for two days till divide the company in three and then, one party found our unit. We run out of food, we run out of water you see and everyone could hardly walk. So I got a quite a bollocking.

I never had the misfortune to be in hand-to-hand combat, 'cos it is a misfortune, you know.

And when we took a prisoners, we come across quite a few Poles that were in German Wehrmacht, from Upper Silesia and that. We just weed them out and into the Polish Units. They weren't considered to be traitors. Unless they were SS. But Wehrmacht, no, because they were just drafted into

Wehrmacht, in Upper Silesia and in Pomerania. Nazis regarded them as Germans, as Volksdeutsch, *you see?*

But I come across some Poles who were in SS. We come across one in Italy. He have the highest German decorations, ritterkreuz even, the knight's cross, he still had it with him! Well he was naturally taken away, probably been killed.

After that cleaning up after Tobruk, all the units prepared to land in Italy. The Anzio Landing. The Americans went first and then we went second. We weren't long in Sicily. The British Units came as the occupying force and we went to mainland. The British landed there already and we just went second. It was some fierce fighting in Sicily and on the mainland.

Civilian population receive us with open arms, oh they were very very friendly. It seem in Italy, Poles were somehow more friendly with the civilian population than anybody else.

So we pushin on to Rome, and that's when the Monte Cassino halted us. Up to then, there was not much resistance. Italians, they just gave up, they didn't bother fighting much. But the Germans did at that monastery at Monte Cassino. We were held back there for three or four months

Tremendous a lot died there. It was a such a fortress and there was no other way to get through...you would have to make another landing. It was out of the question, to prepare another landing. So we have to go through there, through that pass at Monte Cassino to get to Rome. Unit after unit went but the machine gun and artillery emplacements were all in caves you see? The bombs fallin on a top of them and not doing them any harm. Well, the command thought that all the heavy guns and the heavy artillery is where the monastery is, but it wasn't anything at all there! The monastery was completely devastated. Oh was fierce fighting you know, bit by bit...bunker by bunker, with a flamethrowers and grenades. I was in the supply unit. So we were not at the very front.

And then I was on the wing of Adriatic. We plod on until

Bologna. *And then after that, we hold it and the Americans and British took that wing and then we were sent back to Ancona.*

It was there at some point that it was over. It was announced at morning parade that the war is finished. Everybody hooray, now you going home soon! Felt quite happy more or less! Plenty vino and cognac oh...it wasn't that plentiful, but it was! The Italians been hiding it somewhere.

It was quite a, sort of a unbelievable jubilation.

But as it aspired, we didn't manage to go home because of the agreement between Churchill and Roosevelt and Stalin regarding division of Poland you see? So we couldn't go back. We couldnae go back in force as we had planned. Of course we were not forbidden to go. A lot of them did go. But not for a while after because as things stood our units, our regiment, our battalion, stood as part of the occupying force of Italy.

Americans were next to us in Ancona but we didn't mix much. A few fights with them over the blacks. The first time I ever met black man, it was amazing. I couldn't take my eyes off him. Oh, he's so black! You know? He say someting, I don't know what they say, I didn't speak English that time! And later I found out they were segregated in the American Army, the blacks and the whites. I have a few pints with the buggers, the Americans.

In the café you know, we came in and was no much room and a two black soldiers sittin' there and, and er, others standing, the white Americans and nobody sitting beside the blacks, so I just sit there with another chap and we just start drinking away and talkin' a hand talk and Italian a few words and a vino and a vino and a vino and that was talk you see! And white American comes to me and says that I shouldn't be sitting there.

I say, 'Why shouldn't I be sitting there, what the hell is wrong with it?'

86

'Because he's black!'

'I say, 'I know he's black. Whats wrong with that? And you soldier and he soldier and you fight together and you can't sit beside him, what the hell is that?'

I never knew such segregation. Daft, completely, but there you are. It still to this day exist, I'm sure. Or is it? Maybe no.

We just maintained the peace and order in the country. The part that we patrolled that was on the Adriatic coast, Ancona, Porto Ascoli, Porto Civitanova, Porto San Giorgio. We never had that much trouble. The mafia, I didn't know what it was! I thought it was some sort of a business ting you know. We sold a lot of surplus stuff to them. We have to hand it over when the occupation ceased. Trucks, blankets, various thing that the army have all been brought to one dump and we handed that over to the Italians. We couldn't take all the trucks and equipment we had back to Britain. And you barter sometime. A box of blankets for a case of cognac. We sold half of it at least, but we didn't know we were selling to the mafia. Some wise ones made a lot of money, but I was not wise enough regarding that. I had a chance to do it but it was a time that one loses the value of things you know? Monetary value was lost to me and to a lot of people. But ach, I not regret that, I lived quite well and drunk river of wine and a river of cognac!

I spoke Italian reasonably good but you know what, I'm forgetting, comes very difficult now.

I nearly got married in Rome you know! One time I been tearin' to Rome from Ancona on the motorbike and I met the old man standing outside his car and looking at it so I knew it was something wrong there, so I stopped and say Quescosa? Say that its car no going. So I say maybe its no petrol, so I put a little petrol. Still car won't start. I'm no much of a mechanic but found a loose wire sticking out so I say 'Where ta devil it go, maybe it go there,' so I stick it there. Started!

And oh, he thanked me and invited me to come to see, when I'm in Rome. So next time when I was in Rome, I went there. And it apparently transpires, he was a very wealthy man! Oh I got a surprise of my life!

A huge villa just outside Rome and I know right away it's quite a wealthy people you know? Greet me like a long lost brother, aye! Meal right away and everything. So I stayed a night there. So that er -Vittorio...Bolognese, Vittorio Bolognese! He come from Bologna, so he called Vittorio Bolognese. Introduce his daughter to me. She was quite a nice girl, but I somehow didn't care that much...Aeola. Aeola was her name. Vittorio say 'Next time you in Rome, come here.' So I went there, oh I stay there number of times and he took me to show his property. He owned three huge hotels in Rome. Two of them were in operation, one was not in operation, damaged by the war and was being rebuilt. He was wealthy man and she was his only child. For about a year of that time I was visiting Vittorio and Aeola. He been at me to marry Aeola and help him in the hotels business. What ta hell I knew about the hotel business but, nonetheless, I would have learned.

But somehow I didn't want to stop in Italy. Not sure if I like the country or someting I just don't know. Don't know what I didn't like that time! I was very confused, oh very confused! You didn't know what to do for the best, where you going to stay or anything like that. I tried to explain, I just couldn't stay in Italy, I must go to England to get demobbed first. 'Och, I'll, I'll get you demobbed here!' he said. Probably bribe and who knows what. But I was just determined to go. To tell you the truth, I didn't fall in love with her. Oh, they wrote to me no end, number of letters I got from them, 'cos I kept contact with them when I was in England. He was sorry that I not coming back to Rome, well...I probably would be better off if I'd stayed in Rome, who knows? Who knows?

I was always trying to contact mother and father. Was never

any way. And so latterly I contacted America – Anna Buhai, my cousin – and she writes that Kazik's in Glasgow! I didn't know Kazik was alive or not!

As soon as I heard from Anna, contacted Kazik. He come to see me. I stayed in Bury, near Manchester. Met Kazik for the first time since '39.

Och, many a time we talk about what we went through the war and all that, all the hope go to Poland, back to Poland, back to there, back another bugger all, we didn't get back to Poland. We could have went, of course a number of us went back. Like my friend Jerzy, George from Katowice. And another Jerzy, was two Georges, he was from Upper Silesia, he went back. But lost touch. Jankowski, I was right through war with him. He was older than I. He might not be around. Very nice man. When we parted, I stayed that time in Bury. He says, 'Well, I think I'll stay here.' He was planning to go to Wrexham, in Wales. I kept in touch with him for a while and then, och, you lose touch, so that's that.

And I just somehow didn't want to go to Poland because you see, our home was now, well the Russia, so there was no point going back . There was nothing to go back for because I know the system. I know the system! If I went back, you would be going to jail! Was 5 years at least, or maybe more. For being away to the west. To get 'rehabilitated' as thay call it. Probably 5 years wouldn't be enough, would be 10! As soon as I left Russia I would never go back because if I go back I would by the scruff of the neck into jail!

It's not necessary to be against the state. You could say that you didn't like that man in the kolkhoz, or you don't like that horse! Then you accused of being against the state! That's the case! It's a fact! And to hell with you. Because you must remember that all the work, necessary work like a railway, the canals, even the mines, they were all done by prisoners in Russia. They never paid anything for any work! If they require say 2 or 3 thousand people on certain project, they mass-arrested. Five years for you,10 for you, 7 for you then away... you against the state, that was the fact, people told me, and I believe it! And I would go back to that?! Never! Huh-huh, that's how it is.

Even those Polish soldiers that were whole wartime fighting against the Nazis, when they went back, they were not even allowed to write a letter to the west! For years! Like those two Georges. Faithfully promised to let me know how they get on. Not a peach, not a thing. And I knew afterwards, they were not allowed. Simple as that. Most of them were sent to jail for at least a year or two, to get 'rehabilitated'.

I don't know, when we get contact with Adam, I tink after I was demobbed. Again through America. Adam explained everything in the letters you see.

We know that all the Poles from the Eastern side of the new border was movin' west. So I was sure mother and father would be movin' west! And when I contacted Adam, where is father and mother?

'Oh, they still in Gnilowody.'

I say, 'Everybody come out, why didn't they come out?'

'They waited there because they thought you and Kazik will be coming home.'

You know the carry on, the old people. They should realise that we not be coming home. By then it was, '47 or '48, it was too late, they couldn't get out! It was too late! The Russian wouldn't let them go! Well, father died shortly afterwards. Father died, beginning '48... So mother stopped with her daughter there, she was married to one of the Ukrainian chap there, Pawel. I told you about the wedding. So there you are.

8: The Tailor of Inverness

I never knew there was such a thing as Scotland. It was all England! As far as we were taught in school, was England, British Isles! There was nothing to tell us there is Scotland, there is Wales. Kazik wrote that address was Scotland. Where's that!? And when I seen it on the map I thought for goodness' sake, that is London here and a Scotland? Up there. Ha-ha. So... just shortly after New Year in '47 we arrived in Dover actually and we went through London, then we went to Manchester. It was shrouded in mist. Foggy England. We liked the freedom of movement. Nobody bothered where you went.

I been in uniform for about a year before I got demobbed. I been attached to the British military police to help the Poles in the patrol. 'Cos there were a lot of Poles there, regiments of them. We did a few raids. Usually hunted deserters. Amnesty didn't come for them till about 1950.

The first time I went to Glasgow to see Kazik, we went to the Locarno dance hall and I met Anna there. I danced with her and she was very nice and yap, yap, yap, I don't know what she been talking about, but nonetheless – I begin to pick up English because we went to school, we have the classes there in Manchester.

I seen her about three times in the Locarno dance hall. Cup of coffee there, cup of tea here an' the band. That time, that's all it was at the dances, no drinks or anything. The old jazz, the old time waltzes, tangos, very nice. Very orderly, there was no rowdiness or anything. I don't know where I learned to dance, it just come. I didn't learn specially. Danced quite a lot in Italy. And then we made the arrangement for Sunday, to go to the carnival in Kelvin Hall. First we arranged to meet at the Kelvin Hall. And then she changed it to the Locarno, but I didn't understand that. So I'm waiting and waiting for her outside the Kelvin Hall. And she waited and waited for me outside the Locarno. And next day I went away.

About 2 or 3 months later I started workin' in Glasgow. Kazik, he know a few tailors. I was demobbed but we still had the army pay till we get the job. And we have to report to the police, as an alien, you've got alien book, you have to report change of address, change of job. Anyway...tailors, tailors, tailors, tailors...walking on Buchanan Street and we see a sign. 'Tailor Wanted'. And as it aspired, the manager was a Major Forbes and he was Liaison Officer with Polish troops in North Africa. He took me up to the workshop and intro-duced me to a Polish cutter called Bark who was working there. Zajac means hare in English. So Forbes say 'Mr. Bark! This is Mr. Hare!' So it was Bark and Hare! And everyone laughed! I had never heard of Burke and Hare!

And that was the first job I got. They take you on for a trial period first but to tell you the truth, I forgot all about how to do it. I just sat beside a good old tailor, Mr. Penman he was, come from Ballachulish, very nice man, he says 'I'll show you how to go about it.' I picked up from him, mass of, mass of things. It was five pound a week and Forbes say 'You be getting six, but don't tell anybody.' Maybe'cos of being a soldier or something you know? I was quite grateful for it till about a year after it was found out and what a ballahoo

92

it was about it, so everybody got a rise after that!

I was working in Buchanan Street for about two or three months and I went to the Locarno. I'm sittin' there lookin' at the girls and then she's standing there. 'Here! Where you been?!' So after that I meet her father and went to the house and all that carry on and, there you are, mm-hm.

She was cashier in fruitmarket. You know that big fruit-market, it was the wholesalers. In Candleriggs. That's where the fruitmarkets were one time.

Well going together and going to get married and father found out that I'm much older. He didn't like it. Her mother talked ten to the dozen or twenty. I think she liked me. Anna's father was a chef in the Athenaeum. Davey Graham. Anna and I went one time for lunch. It was quite dear. Half a crown! And after, we went for a drink with father and I discovered that father like a good snoot! So I met him quite often in the bar after that, in Horseshoe, in West Nile Street. He used to go to Horseshoe.

Her uncles on her mother's side, the Steins, were in Hamilton and in Blantyre an' granny an' grampa, they still were alive. An' a Grampa Graham, I met him about about two or three times. But I didn't go to his house. The Steins, I been a number of times in their house up in Blantyre. The Grahams were a bit better off. They were more of a gentlemen lookin' people, all bowler-hatted, but the Steins were entirely different, workmen. Miners. And the Grahams they were gentlemen farmers. Big farms they had. One family was Episcopalian and the other Church of Scotland, I don't know which was which. But as far as I concerned, there is no difference, a Protestant's a Protestant! But there is some difference. Aye.

I was living with Kazik's father-in-law on Berkeley Street just off Argyll Street, near Kelvingrove Park. Kelvin Hall. Then I decided to go on my own. Och, I stayed in so many places , always movin, always movin'. I stayed in Watt Street, in

Ibrox, in Townhead for a while. And then I stayed in Royston Road, then Alexandra, Alexandra Parade for a pound! Very cheap. And then I stayed in Maryhill on Homburg Street. After that, we got married, so we stayed on Bollan Street. And then we stayed with granny. For about six months, Angela was just little. And then I spoke to the boss, man's name Shearer, where I work, about the house. How to get the house? To get some permanent address. And he knew some factors for town houses to rent and next day or day after, there is a house on a Dumbarton Road, small house, a room and a kitchen. So hotfoot it to Dumbarton Road, see the place, no bad. Nice house, nice district, the trams going that way for a penny or two. So we got that house. And a rent was very very cheap. It was pound a month.

So we stayed there for a few years. And then I seen the advert for the tailor and cutter to take charge of the shop in Inverness. And the interview is in one of the hotels on Queen Street you know? So I went for the interview and got the job! So I went to Forbes, I say well, sorry to say but I have to say cheerio to you. He say how? Why? Where you going? Going to Inverness you know and that time the wages went up and up, I had 8 pound, or 9 pound that time, was quite good wages that time.

And Forbes say, 'We give you a rise, we give you 12 pound.'

'I'm sorry, I offered 16 in Inverness.'

'Oh, we couldn't compete with that, the 16 pound, it's too much.'

They went to 14, you see? Buggers. I worked for 9 pound and now was quite all right to jump to 14! Anyway, Forbes say, 'If you not get on there, come back. Job's here for you, just come back.' So I went and took charge of the work there in Inverness and what a mess that shop was! You wouldn't believe it! They had a cutter there who was not much of a cutter at all. He made a messes no end. So I straightened that out quite well and somehow it become a lull in the trade, and the bosses begin to cringe, this a big wages, and mother was still in Glasgow now with Catherine as well.

And in between the time I met a tailor that I used to work with. And he work in C & A. He was in charge of the coats section, makin' coats in the factory, you see? Met him in the Bay Horse, that's in Renfield Street. Still there to this day. James Easdale his name.

And he says 'How you doin'?'

I say, 'I'm in Inverness but thinkin' of comin' back.'

'Come to C&A! I'm sure you'll get the job! I'll see the manager for you!'

So Monday, I went there and manager start explainin' to me how tings workin' there and it's a very progressive firm.

'I used to be a machine mechanic and now I'm general manager. See it's progressive as that, if you have head screwed on your shoulder.'

I say, 'Here, I never worked in the factory, I don't know the way of factory workin'.'

He say, 'It's easy picked up, it's just like a riding the bicycle.'

I still remember him say that! You never forget that!

'We just been in the process to start a costume section. Would you take charge of the costume section and you do what you like with it, but production must be 200 costumes a day.' 200 costumes! 'First week, you come here , you doin' nothing, just to walk about the factory and pick up the machinists. You would need about 60 of a staff. Machinists, pressers, finishers, passers. You need 10 to 15 pressers and a rest machinists of various types, 'cos is various types of machines there. And you need about 10 to 15 finishers, to do the handwork.'

My pay was, by Jove, £25, was a lot of money that time, you know. After two weeks whole factory was shifted for me, bit by bit, to make a room for my band. It was circular affair. The whole costume came cut, ready, cut in London. Various

95

people were placed to distribute, the sleeves, the back, the fronts, the linings and all went to different machines. Every machinist done so much and a put it down and a chute went to another machine, to done the other thing and on and on and so far and went to the row of pressers, opening seams, stretching where is necessary, pressin' the canvas, and goes back to the machines again. The sleeves together, the fronts together, the collars there, back to the pressers and go back to the finishers. Buttons and a maybe the lining's to be filled. And a pressers again and on the hanger! Oh what a kalabazoo it was first week, my head was twirlin' like mad!

Now, production was 200 a day. I not come near the mark, first day. I tink I was short about 50 or so. But before the week was finished, I reached the 200. I was amazed. How on earth we could produce a costume in 8 minutes! 'Cos that's what's amount to! Between 8 and 10 minutes, costume been hanging up, you see? It went so fast.

After near a year, I was called to the office and he says you know, your section is runnin' very well, I tink we'll put somebody else to it. And you take the despatch. You see? That was, tremendous promotion. I have 8 models, and a secretary. And you know I was on that section two weeks and the blasted ting went on fire! Two weeks! Was such a job, you know! Pay was, och, double practically!

Went on fire on a Sunday. In the despatch department. Some basket left the fire on! And the dress silk caught, went up like a, bloomin' torch! So, Monday going to work, there's no work. And they offer me job in factory in Birmingham but mother didn't want to go.

So I say, 'What ta hell to do next? Hm, I tink I'll go back to Inverness.'

Just like that! I'll see my old place. So I went, to R.S. MacDonald there.

'You back?! You want a job?'

I say, 'Well, is job going?'

'Yes.'

I say, 'Right, I'll take a job.'

So I took back job in the R.S. MacDonald, which didn't last long. I have a bit of a fight with Colonel Campbell, he was the owner.

I just been back about three months and girl went to the bank for the wages and there was no money for the wages. So I went to the manager of the bank myself. He says Colonel Campbell took all the money out.

'How do you mean took all the money out? We have business to run.'

Campbell also have the frozen food place in Bunchrew and apparently that wasn't doin' well and he took all the money and put into that bloomin' frozen food. I went hotfoot to Bunchrew.

I say 'Here! What happened to the money? We doin' very well, we busy! And no money for the wages!'

'You not going to tell me how to run my business, I know how to run my business!' I say, 'Well, I'm not runnin' your business, I just want the money to pay the wages! And you run your business how you want and if you want to run it that way, just bloody well run it!'

And I just slammed the door and I went out. And that was that, I never went back.

And mother say, 'Now what we going to do, we going back to Glasgow?' She was in Inverness then, 'cos I got a house, that electric flats up there in Dalneigh. Oh mother start greetin'. 'We just got here and then you no job!'

I say, 'Well, we'll go back to Glasgow again. On the other hand, I might start on my own.'

So I went to look for a place. I was unemployed for, 2, 3 weeks. Found a place up in the gods, above Halifax Building Society. And I started.

From the day I started I never look back. I had the sewing machine, that's all I needed for a start. One of the furniture store give me a wooden bench for nothing. I bought another machine and started myself, for 2 or 3 weeks myself and then I got Jean Gordon. I bung a big advert, cost me a pound that time. Mathew Zajac, late of R.S. Macdonald, openin' his own business, you know? 25 Inglis Street, Ladies and Gents Tailor, your own cloth made up and all that, you know? From the very first week, I had such a pile of order, how ta hell I'm going to catch up with it?

So I took Jean and I took another girl and I took another girl so, work about 5 of us for a while, and then 3 and then 4 and then 2 and then 3. But Jean lasted with me all the time since I started. Aye, till she died, practically. Practically till she died, aye...We done reasonably well, you know, but I could have done better. I should have broke out, from bespoke tailoring and went to the ready-mades. 'Cos there was money in it. A lot of salesmen been advisin' me, take ready-made. Take a sale, because that time, it was possible to take sale or return, 3 months, they supply you for so many dozen of suits, and trousers so many this, so many that. If you not sell, 3 months they take it back. Sale or return, you know. Good mark and do the alteration myself, I would have made it definitely better, I know that now but, ach, too late now. Was somehow scared of the ready-mades. I don't know, you see, once you used to the top-notch work, good class o' work and then go to that, as I call it, rubbish, you somehow...and try to sell suit to a man...I would have lost good client that I had, you know. And they wouldn't come, you see.

That's the way I'm, more or less, carried on. The contracts, army contracts came in. Well I took that contract. Queen's Own Highlander were there at Fort George that time. They moved out, the Fort George was finished and I immediately got a proposal from RAF Kinloss, the contract with Kinloss, so I took that you see? I had that for about 15 years. I always put the prices up every two years. Up, up, up, I say, well if they not want to to to, they no want it that, I'm not er, you know. But oh, I always got it, you know? Till the last time and Joe Setts was quartermaster and I say well you want to renew again? He know my age, pension time, you know? He say maybe you want to retire? Well, I probably will retire. Well ok, just retire he says and we'll try to get somebody else. So they did, right enough, but that somebody else wasn't any good and they asked me few times could I take it back, you see? I say och, I no going to start again, you know?

I got a note, the letter from them, just about a 2 or 3 months ago. Would you renew the contract in February? But och, I didn't bother with it, no...so...

Mateusz, Easter Ross c.1988

I have the happy life in Inverness. Quiet life. Raised the family. Go to British Legion. Go to bingo. Good friends, aye. Every year in November to Invergordon to Polish War Memorial for the Service of Remembrance. So that's it. That's it. Aye.

PART THREE
Matthew

9: Semi-Detached

I went to university in Bristol, over 800 kilometres and a world away from my childhood in Inverness. I was naïve and eager to adapt and learn. My parents had invested a great deal of energy and hope in our education, but my decision to choose the theatre caused them some concern. This was assuaged by my agreement, and my desire, to attend university rather than a drama school. I knew I was entering a profession full of uncertainty, with no security and a great deal of competition. I was grateful to my parents for their forbearance. They may have been sceptical and worried about my future prospects, but they recognised that I had some talent and they respected my choice.

In the 1980s there were terrible periods of depressing unemployment, but I was relatively lucky, and I also worked a lot, creating new plays, acting in rep theatres around the UK, getting my first jobs in film and TV. Poland, and my connection with it, receded. I was preoccupied and, most importantly, I lacked the language. Occasionally it would gnaw away at me, but I didn't do anything about it. Most of the time, I simply forgot about it all. I did keep abreast of political developments, though, through newspapers and TV.

Like most people at the time, I watched the Gdansk dockers' strike of 1980 and the extraordinary rise of *Solidarnosc* (Solidarity), which became a massive oppositional movement in Poland with over 9 million members within months of its establishment. General Jaruzelski's government cracked down on *Solidarnosc* on December 13th 1981 by imposing a state of martial law throughout the country. Around 100 people were killed and thousands were interned. *Solidarnosc,* along with many other independent organisations, was outlawed.

In the spring of 1983, I was working with Bush Telegraph Theatre Company in Bristol. We devised a powerful theatre-in-education project set in Gdansk on the day martial law was declared. It was a site-specific production. We gained access to several buildings in the old docks of central Bristol, which were just beginning to be regenerated at the time. At the start of each performance, a busload of 12-13 year-olds arrived outside the newly opened Watershed Arts Centre and I'd jump on with a camera operator, posing as a journalist. I made a quick report to camera, explaining that we were on our way to Gdansk where we'd find out what life was really like in the Polish People's Republic. The bus drove into the dock area and we turned a corner into a street flanked by warehouses. We'd set up a road barrier there, the Polish border, where a soldier made a cursory search of the bus as the port director of Gdansk introduced himself to the children and explained that he was about to give them a guided tour of the port. During the next half hour or so, the children's 'official' tour was interrupted by Solidarity activists distributing leaflets and arguing with the port director. This culminated in the children working with the activists in a warehouse, printing leaflets and making banners.

During this sequence, a loudspeaker announced the declaration of martial law and the banning of public gatherings. This was followed a few minutes later by a raid on the warehouse by the ZOMO, the notorious Polish paramilitary police. Before the children were hurried out, they witnessed a riot policeman beating one of the activists. They returned to the bus where two activists were hiding, trying to escape across the border. They were discovered by soldiers and dragged off, despite the best efforts of the children to help them.

The bus returned to Britain and the children were taken to the reporter's TV news studio, to compensate for their early departure from Poland. A news bulletin was imminent. An assistant ran in with the first pictures from Poland. The pictures were broadcast. They depicted scenes which the children had witnessed, the beating, a leaflet, all doctored by the Polish state broadcaster to suggest that Solidarity members had instigated the violence.

As these pictures went out in our working mock-up of a news studio, the children invariably objected to the misleading images. The news production team realised their mistake and that they had missed the fact that they had journalistic gold in front of their noses, eye-witnesses to the events who were sitting in their studio. After a furious dressing down from their boss, the production team invited the children to rewrite the martial law item for the next bulletin. Just before their version was broadcast, the action stopped and one of the actors briefly cautioned the children to consider how TV news is constructed and how it can be manipulated.

That was the real thrust of the production. The Polish narrative served it well. It was its suitability for the theme which made us choose it rather than a burning desire to tell this particular Polish story, although I still elicited a kind of half-baked satisfaction at being able to engage with Poland on this limited level.

Aside from this production, I remained distant from Poland for most of my twenties. My parents continued to visit Adam and Aniela and, in 1986, took Uncle Kazik with them from

Glasgow. This was his first and only return to Poland although he had been reunited with Adam long before then. Adam visited Scotland several times from the early '60s, bringing with him, in turn, Aniela, Jan the Butcher and Ula.

My father became active in the Scottish-Polish Cultural Association, attending events at the Polish Consulate in Edinburgh and working with an Invergordon Pole, Andrzej Zamrej, and others, to organise the annual remembrance service which took place at the Invergordon Polish War Memorial on the Sunday after Armistice Day. Andrzej also managed to bring a Polish football team to Scotland, where they played the young Alex Ferguson's St. Mirren and visited Easter Ross.

My interest in Eastern Europe during the '80s was sustained by three friendships, two of which I made at Bristol University. Ted Braun was my tutor in third year, a fluent Russian speaker who ran courses on British political theatre and Marxist Aesthetics, among others. I also spent some time babysitting his sons, Felix and Joe. Ted had worked in intelligence during his national service. He was an expert on the great Russian theatre director Vsevolod Meyerhold, who was shot during Stalin's Great Terror of 1937-8. Ted had visited Moscow several times. We often discussed the history and current affairs of Eastern Europe and he took a great interest in my father's life. They met a couple of times, conversing a little in Russian and my father made him a coat, which Ted still wears.

I also befriended Misha Glenny. Misha was studying German and Drama a year ahead of me. His father was the brilliant translator of Russian, Michael Glenny. Michael's great love of Russia was reflected in his son's first name. Misha is an extraordinary and celebrated journalist and writer, a passionate, ebullient character and a wonderful linguist. When he finished his degree, he spent a year studying in Czechoslovakia, as it was then. Following the brutal clampdown which destroyed the Prague Spring, the Czechoslovak government had become perhaps the most oppressive in the Eastern Bloc. Ostensibly, Misha was studying the work of Karel Capek. He wouldn't have been allowed in if he'd proposed anything which the Czech authorities judged to be controversial or potentially subversive. But during his stay, Misha made contact with and befriended members of Charter 77, the underground Czech resistance movement whose figurehead was the great dramatist and subsequent first president of post-Communist Czechoslovakia, Vaclav Havel. As well as German, Misha learned to speak Czech, Serbo-Croat, Russian and Hungarian. In the mid-80s, he became a stringer for the *Guardian*, basing himself in Vienna, and within a few years, he was the BBC's Eastern Europe correspondent.

I occasionally met with Misha during his visits to London and Oxford, where his mother lived. He was, and is, always great company, full of energy and passionate commitment to his work. His understanding and analysis of the political developments and undercurrents in Eastern Europe were always perceptive and accurate. He was warning his superiors in London of the impending wars in the former Yugoslavia long before they took him seriously, long before they happened. I was somewhat in awe of Misha's achievements, which were to become even greater in the years after 1989, but I think he welcomed the relief of seeing old friends for the *craic*. I think he also appreciated the fact that I had some understanding of what he was talking about because of my Polish background. We'd chew the fat about what was going on in Poland, Czechoslovakia, Hungary and the rest over beer and whisky and usually move on to singing soul numbers. We even attended an Oxford United match once during their heyday with John Aldridge up front and the corpulent Czech-born media baron Robert Maxwell in the chair.

Tom Morrison was with me at Inverness High School. We

acted together in our school production of 'The Crucible' in 1976 and, as I've mentioned, spent our first independent summer holiday that year in Bavaria. By 1983, Tom was a graduate in German living in Berlin and working as a translator. I visited him there for a week in February 1984. The Wall was still there, of course. Most of my week was spent as a tourist in West Berlin, visiting art galleries and museums and drinking with Tom in his favourite pubs. I sampled West Berlin's counter-culture, dancing in nightclubs in Kreuzberg, with a mixed clientele of gays and straights, to Velvet Underground, Kraftwerk, Iggy Pop and post-punk German industrial noise and guitar bands such as Einsturzende Neubaten and DAF (Duetsche Amerikanische Freundschaft). Young men were exempt from National Service in West Berlin, I think as a way of maintaining the city's population, and there were several thousand from other parts of West Germany who lived there to avoid it too. Many of them lived in Kreuzberg, which was full of squats and anarchists. Often, it was these young people who were responsible for the vibrant graffiti which covered large sections of the western side of the Wall.

The East German authorities administered a system of one-day visas for visitors from the West, mainly as a concession to Berlin families which had been divided by the city's partition. The border crossing I used was underground, at a station in the Berlin metro.

Berlin had become the pre-eminent symbol of the Cold War. During the post-war rebuilding of the devastated city centre, the Communists and Capitalists of East and West competed with each other, constructing ostentatious buildings which attempted to show off the virtues of their regimes, taunting each other across the Wall. In the west, Mies van der Rohe's steel and glass Neue Nationalgalerie; in the East, Dieter and Franke's Fernsehturm (TV Tower); in the West, Scharoun and

Wisniewski's Staatsbibliothek and Kammersmusiksaal; in the East, Graffunder and Swora's Palast der Republik. Each of these buildings asserted cultural and political hegemony and superiority. Aside from the Palast der Republik, which housed the DDR Parliament and numerous cultural events, before being condemned for asbestos contamination and pulled down, they remain as essential parts of the reunited city.

In 1984, one couldn't escape the fact that they served two opposing ideologies, that they represented the architectural apogees of the two versions of contemporary German society. Alongside the buildings, the centre of East Berlin was decorated with socialist realist murals and slogans, West Berlin with the neon signs of multinational corporations, crowing from the top of its skyscrapers. It all seemed designed to make the individual feel small, insignificant in the face of such powerful organised forces. I certainly did, walking across the grey expanse of Marx Engels Platz and past the monolithic blocks of Karl Marx Allee. It all became more human for me in East Berlin when I visited a department store and bought some cute, kitsch kitchenware which caught my eye.

I watched goose-stepping East German soldiers change the guard at the Tomb of the Unknown Soldier and was careful to avoid photographing the Soviet Embassy on Unter Den Linden, not wanting to cause a diplomatic incident. There, I was only a few hundred metres from the Wall at the Brandenburg Gate. At one point during my stay, I took a train in the evening which ran alongside the Wall on a raised track for a minute or two. It was dark, and I caught glimpses through the windows of flats on the other side where people were living moments of their domestic lives, eating dinner, reading, watching TV. During these moments, where ordinary people on both sides of the wall were doing exactly the same things, the city's division seemed so absurd. I flew back to London and my own little flat in a tower block in Bethnal Green, depressed by the seemingly immovable *status quo* of the Cold War. I didn't know that the main architect of the Cold War's demise, Mikhail Gorbachev, would assume power in the Soviet Union within a year.

10: 1989

By 1989, I had been living with my partner, Virginia Radcliffe, for four years, sharing a flat in Dalston, East London. We decided to go on a tour of Eastern Europe that summer. My long absence from Poland – fifteen years – had been eating away at me for some time. During this period I exchanged annual Christmas cards with Adam, Aniela and Ula, but that was all. I was keen to see them again and regretted the fact that I had been too busy with my life in England to engage more fully in what had been happening in Poland. Martial Law had been lifted in July 1983. During Martial Law, thousands of Solidarity activists and other oppositionists had been interned. Some had been killed by Polish security forces. Thousands more, such as journalists and teachers, were banned from their professions. Public institutions and much of the country's industry and transport infrastructure were placed under military management. An economic crisis ensued which resulted in widespread rationing.

Around 700,000 people left Poland between 1981 and 1989. There are those who argue that General Jaruzelski's imposition of Martial Law prevented an invasion by the Soviet Union and its Warsaw Pact allies, as had happened during the Prague

Spring and the Hungarian Uprising of 1956. Jaruzelski himself has argued this. Whatever the case, this was the darkest period in post-war Poland.

Nationwide strikes in 1988 and continuing popular unrest forced the government to hold talks with Solidarity. These led to semi-free elections on June 4th 1989, the first democratic elections in the Warsaw Pact countries, less than three weeks before our departure. Solidarity candidates won all of the 33% of parliamentary seats they were allowed to contest, 99 of the 100 seats available in the second chamber, the Senate. The Communists were plunged into crisis. On September 12th, Tadeusz Mazowiecki became the first non-Communist Prime Minister in more than 40 years and the first anywhere in the Eastern Bloc.

Virginia and I drove away from Dalston in our red VW Golf on June 22nd 1989. Our planned route would take us to Misha's flat in Vienna, Budapest, Prague and finally Lesna before returning to the UK via Berlin. It would take 18 days. We had our visas for Hungary and Poland and the ferry was booked.

We caught the 2.00pm sailing from Dover to Ostend. It was quiet on the boat, which was furbished in ugly utilitarian browns and oranges, rigid laminated tables and moulded plastic chairs. There was an atmosphere of desertion and dinginess reminiscent of English seaside resorts in winter. The tannoy barked out the announcement of a film screening, a Belgian man gave us a half-used disposable lighter so we could light our fags and we tried to doze, mindful of the long drive ahead.

The sky was overcast as the Belgian coast came into view, great black-backed seagulls wheeling about the boat and soaring towards the grey housing blocks of Ostend. We climbed down to the car deck, thick with the noise and exhaust fumes of vehicles eager to disembark. 6.30pm became 7.30 on the continent and our long night's driving began. Through Ostend in 5 minutes, following signs for Brussels, we were soon on the long, straight Belgian motorway, passing through the typically flat terrain, with lines of poplar trees and narrow little houses. Friesian cows ruminated. We passed Brussels and then Luik/Liege, jumping from Flemish to Walloon to Flemish counties. In two hours, we reached the German border near Aachen and stopped for petrol and a coffee.

We travelled through Germany in the dark. Traffic was light. We took turns to drive in 3-hour stints, dozing in the passenger seat, smoking, listening to tapes, drinking coffee, enjoying the rhythm of the road. Koln, Frankfurt, Nurnberg, Regensburg and, as dawn broke, we reached Passau on the Austrian border by the Danube. We stopped by the river at 5.00am. Morning mist lay on the water which was oozing its great way into Austria, wide and thick. The sky was grey, the mist was grey, the road was grey and the water was a darker grey. Everywhere else: green. We were tired and alert, feeling a sense of magic at this spot which was so new and distant but which we'd arrived at so effortlessly. After the last of our coffee we resumed our journey.

After entering Austria, there was 40 kilometres of two-way road through picturesque countryside with rolling green fields, hilly little pine forests and grand square farmhouses with mighty roofs with wide overhangs to cope with heavy snow. These scenes continued most of the way to Vienna. We entered Vienna's suburbs at 7.00am, rush hour. Our efforts to find Misha's flat succeeded after an hour's experiment, thanks to a bank clerk giving us a map of the city and spending some time pointing the way. Thinking he'd be up by then we rang Misha, who was amused and surprised that we'd arrived so early. We were exhausted and exhilarated, but sleep wasn't on the immediate agenda.

Misha had a lonely life in Vienna at that time, with only one close friend living in the city, another journalist. Visitors didn't come often, so he wanted to make the most of our stay. Despite our need for sleep, we were whisked back into town, Misha promising a good breakfast and a brief visit to his office: he was taking the day off. Breakfast turned out to be brotschinken, ham rolls bought in a bakery, which were delicious, but disappointing as we'd expected to sit in a restaurant. We walked to the office, chewing our rolls and exchanging news. Misha didn't like Vienna and he emphasised the fact by referring to the 'anally retentive' Viennese bourgeoisie and the city's 'anally retentive' imperialist architecture.

His office was small, containing a little recording studio, two desks, a typewriter, tape recorders, books, a coffee machine and a constantly clicking telex machine. Misha's first task was to go through its overnight outpourings, selecting news items which were relevant. The machine received information from around the world, sent by various Eastern European news agencies, 95% of which was of no use to Misha. He whizzed through the yards of telex at an impressive rate, passing it to us to bin. Much of the information consisted of crop yields in Colombia, the arrival of a new consignment of tractor parts in a Bulgarian province, production targets being met ahead of schedule in a Yugoslavian shoe factory, and so on. Then it was time to make phone calls. When it became obvious that Misha would take some time we decided to go for a walk. It was a sunny morning and the Burgtheater was just round the corner. We passed it and strolled into a little park. In a few minutes, we were asleep on park benches.

A couple of hours later Misha took us for coffee and cake in an expensive café. We returned to his flat for a wash and then ate in town, a traditional dish of boiled beef, cabbage and dumplings. Afterwards, we visited a pub full of Vienna's affluent younger types, all looking quite conventional. The pub served draught Budweiser/Budvar, now common in the UK, but virtually unheard of then. The 100-year-old trademark dispute between this Czech beer's makers and the makers of American Budweiser, which had originally been settled by a gentleman's agreement not to market their product on the other's continental territory, was about to flare into a much more serious argument with the collapse of Communism, as Czech Budweiser expanded into new western markets and US Budweiser travelled in the opposite direction. On tasting the Czech beer in Vienna for the first time, it struck me that the Americans were about to have a real fight on their hands. Tired and merry after a couple of litres of the stuff, we returned to Misha's flat, drank whisky and vodka and sang songs until 2am before collapsing into bed.

We stayed with Misha for two days soaking in Vienna's history and culture, so informed by its unique geographical position, thrust into the midriff of the Eastern Bloc states, close to so many different countries: Italy and the states which then comprised Yugoslavia to the south, Hungary, Romania, Ukraine and the Black Sea to the East, Czechoslovakia and Poland to the north, Germany to the West. Once, before the First World War, it was the imperial capital of most of these countries and the flea market reflected this heritage to a degree, with Yugoslavian, Hungarian and Turkish stalls. The city housed small communities from a variety of nations but, of course, the overriding culture was Austrian.

The city centre is dominated by a series of opulent, ornate buildings, most of which are dedicated to church and state and designed to reflect the glory of the old Austro-Hungarian empire. Most were built during the 19th century in a variety of archaic styles: neo-classical, neo-gothic, neo-renaissance and neo-baroque. We walked through the manicured parkland of the Schonbrunn Palace, patrolled by an attendant on a bicycle who zealously admonished anyone who dared to walk on the grass, up to a folly of arches and columns, topped by a great stone eagle, which Empress Maria Theresa had built to add interest to her strolls.

As an antidote to all this overpowering grandiosity, we visited the beautiful art nouveau gallery which houses Klimt's friezes, erotic, luxurious, dream-like explorations of his own psyche which expose his obsession with women. Then we went to see the Hundertwasserhaus. An apartment block completed in 1986 by the Viennese artist and architect Friedrich Hundertwasser, its governing concept is irregularity. Verandahs poke out at different angles, windows are on different levels, straight lines are kept to a minimum. Trees grow through apartments and emerge through the roofs. Little statues and mosaics appear in surprising places, many of which have been used elsewhere before finding their way here. Pillars, many quite definitely not vertical, vary in thickness along their length, with brightly-coloured ceramic sections wrapping them.

We left Misha at the airport where he was to catch a flight to Belgrade and drove on to Budapest. The Hungarian border surprised me. It had a relaxed atmosphere unlike any of the crossings I remembered from my childhood. In May of the previous year, Janos Kadar, the 'benevolent' dictator who had been installed by hardliners with the blessing of Moscow after the 1956 Uprising and had been in office ever since, was deposed by a coalition of radical reformers and conservative technocrats. Kadar's Hungary mixed populism and nationalism with repression and has been described as 'the happiest barracks in the camp,' an eloquently ironic comparison with the other Eastern Bloc states. His deposition ushered in the end of one-party rule and the preparation of multi-party elections, which took place in spring 1990. On May 2 1989, Hungary's communist regime had begun removing its fortifications along the border with Austria. The new reformist government in Budapest undertook this move as a goodwill gesture towards the West and as a message to the world that it was unilaterally ending the Cold War and damn the consequences. At a ceremony held on June 27, two days after we arrived in

Budapest, the Austrian foreign minister Alois Mock and his Hungarian counterpart Gyula Horn formally cut the barbed wire in the presence of the international press.

We drove in the summer heat by vineyards and wheatfields, past the towns of Gyor and Tatabanya and into Budapest, Vienna's old imperial twin capital. Despite suffering much more wartime damage than Vienna, Budapest has preserved numerous historic buildings akin to those in its old sister city, but it had quite a different atmosphere. It was certainly poorer, grimy and surrounded by the gigantic housing blocks which are so prevalent in the ex-Communist cities, but it was also bustling and vibrant. One felt a sense of purpose there, an anticipation of things to come.

We were very fortunate in Budapest to have Endre and Veronica Kelemen as our hosts. Endre worked in educational broadcasting and was a friend and colleague of Virginia's father John, who ran the BBC's Open University Production Centre. They had become acquainted at a series of European educational broadcasting conferences. We found their flat and were given a warm welcome, and steaming plates of Veronica's goulash before Endre escorted us to our accommodation, a small flat in a block for visiting journalists. We felt a little fraudulent at being given this privilege, but blessed our good fortune and took it anyway.

The following day, we registered with the local police, which was a requirement for tourists at the time, and visited the Czech Embassy to obtain visas for our journey to Prague. We stayed in Budapest for four days, taking the funicular railway up Castle Hill to see the Royal Palace and climbing Gellert Hill for a great view of the city. The Citadel on this hill still bore the damage inflicted in January 1945, when the Germans dug in here and held on for a month before their surrender. We travelled on the elegant Line 1 of the Budapest Metro. Now a World Heritage Site, it was opened in 1896 by Emperor

Franz Josef, the year of the 1000th anniversary of the arrival of the Magyars. We visited the Opera House, the Museum of Labour History and the National Gallery.

We watched the extraordinary massed ranks of synchronised gymnasts at the Czech Spartakiada on TV and ate again at Endre and Veronica's house. We also visited the beautiful Great Synagogue, the largest functioning synagogue in Europe. It is situated on Dohany Street, which marked a boundary of the Nazis' Jewish Ghetto, established in 1944. Thousands of Jews took refuge in and around the synagogue. Around 7,000 died there during the winter of 1944-45. These victims are buried in the synagogue's courtyard. Adolf Eichmann, one of the principle architects of the *Shoah*, arrived in the city in March 1944. For a time, he used part of the synagogue as an office as he oversaw the deportation and murder of Hungary's Jewish population. In the space of not much more than six weeks, between mid-May and June 1944, 381,661 people, half of all the Jews in Hungary, had arrived at Auschwitz. Hardly any survived.

Endre introduced us to a young colleague, Gyorg, a good English speaker who spent a day with us as our guide. He was from Transylvania, a member of Romania's large Hungarian minority. He was glad to be in Budapest, free from the discrimination Hungarians suffered in education and employment in Romania. Gyorg took us to Szentendre *Skanzen* to the north of the city. *Skanzens* are open-air museums of rural life. The one at Szentendre is effectively a museum village. Thatched cottages and barns, in styles from the last 300 years have either been reproduced here or originals have been dismantled and transported in pieces from their original locations to Szentendre to be rebuilt there. They house farm implements and machinery, furniture, household goods and folk art. Szentendre gave me an idea of what my father's village might have looked like when he was a boy.

As we left Hungary, on June 29th, we knew that people had begun to take advantage of the newly-relaxed Hungarian-Austrian border, but we were unaware that up to 150,000 East Germans were beginning to flood into Hungary in order to escape to the West. The Hungarian authorities made no effort to stop them and actually set up refugee camps for them. Eventually, on September 11th, the Hungarians simply opened the remaining barriers and they were free to leave.

Our journey to Prague, via Bratislava, was uneventful. The Czech border was more akin to the ones I remembered from the '70s, threatening and unfriendly. I was struck by the thickness of the forest on either side of the motorway to Prague. Knowing about the grim oppressiveness of the Czech regime, I wondered if this was intended to hide the country from us. We stayed for only one night in Prague, camping at Branik by the River Vltava. The campsite staff were cold and brusque. It took a long time to check our passports, including a call to the local police to register our arrival. There were a lot of holidaying East Germans at the campsite. We pitched our tent next to a young East German family and got talking to them, sharing a beer.

News of the Hungarian relaxation had spread, but these people were sceptical about the idea of a better life in the West. They had jobs, a decent house, security. They were happy to stay at home and see how things developed. As it turned out, the Czech leaders couldn't tolerate the stream of East Germans moving through their country to Hungary. They eventually sealed their border with the treacherous Hungarians and Czechoslovakia became the only country that East Germans could travel to without a visa. By early September, over 4,000 were camping in the gardens of the West German Embassy in Prague and more were arriving every day. On the evening of September 30th, the West German Foreign Minister, Hans Dietrich Genscher, himself an escapee from the DDR in

1952, arrived at the Embassy after negotiating with his East German and Soviet counterparts Oskar Fischer and Eduard Shevardnadze. He announced to the muddy campers that their wait had come to an end and that they would all be taken in special trains to West Germany. On the following day, train after train carried around 17,000 East Germans to the West. This event marked the beginning of the end for the DDR. A clear demonstration of the will of ordinary people, it led directly to the collapse of the Wall.

Despite the brevity of our stay in Prague, it was easy to appreciate the city's beauty. It's a popular tourist and party destination today, but its atmosphere was very different then. We would have liked to have stayed longer, to have visited all its beautiful buildings and to have soaked up its history and culture, but its sobriety then and our awareness of its hardline, suffocating government made us happy to leave it behind.

Besides, I was eager for my home from home, for Adam and Aniela and the bucolic charms of Lesna.

11: Return

The journey from Prague was a distance of only 183 kilometres, driving north-east to the border in the Karkonosze Mountains at Jakuszyca and on via Szklarska Poreba and Swieradow Zdroj to Lesna. Having travelled the route from Szklarska Poreba several times in my childhood its familiarity returned to me as we approached Lesna. I recognised the wooden houses of Swieradow and the stretch of open road through farmland where we had encountered Soviet military vehicles in 1967. We slowed down for a few kilometres, keeping our distance from a drunken moped rider, who swayed and wobbled from one side of the road to the other. It looked like he'd been to a market in Szklarska Poreba, his handlebars were weighed down with plastic bags full of vegetables and cooking oil, which made him even more unstable. Maybe the same thing happened every week.

Lesna hadn't changed much. The little pink-painted pub was still there, next to the driveway. We turned into it and trundled up to the house. A little boy saw us and ran in to call his grandparents. This was Wojtek, Ula's five-year-old son, who was spending his summer holidays in Lesna while Ula worked at her new home in Gdansk. Adam and Aniela were older and greyer, not quite so sprightly but full of warmth and happiness at our arrival. They hugged and kissed us and exclaimed that Virginia was very beautiful.

'Shall I say wife?' asked Adam, with a twinkle in his eye, knowing that we weren't married. Adam hadn't lost his sense of humour, but he had developed gout. He still put thick slabs of butter on his bread when Aniela wasn't looking and she'd banned him from smoking in the house, but he still puffed away in the garden. We sat out there and drank some of the whisky we'd brought. Mr. and Mrs. Wraga, the vet and his wife, came over to greet us, delighted to see that I had grown into 'a fine young man'. A man turned up to deliver a couple of huge cabbages and a woman appeared through the trees at the end of the garden carrying a shopping bag full of meat. Adam no longer received his meat from the abbatoir. The drink had taken over Jan the Butcher's life. It had killed him a few years earlier.

We stayed in Lesna for a week. I revelled in the nostalgia of recognising childhood haunts. Ula made the long journey from Gdansk to see us. We swam in Lake Czocha, picked cherries in the garden and I met friends who had now grown up. Ella Wraga was a teacher at what she sternly called 'The House of Correction' in Szklarska Poreba, a residential school for young offenders. Wladek Limont was visiting his parents, the Argentinian Communist and his wife. Wladek was an electrician in the tank factory in Gliwice. With the end of the Cold War imminent, and the prospect of free-market reforms, Wladek feared for his job. His factory was out of date and overmanned.

We spent most of our time sitting in the garden, eating tomatoes and drinking vodka, sometimes Adam's *bimber*, his home-made hooch. As in the past, friends and neighbours would turn up for a chat and a drink. Aniela and Mrs. Wraga sang us songs and showed us photographs of their youth.

Adam recounted his education in speaking English through Radio Free Europe and how amused he was to learn about the royal 'we'. 'We want a wee wee (a piss)' had become one of his English catchphrases. I quizzed him about his visits to Gnilowody but he wasn't very forthcoming, describing it as a backward place. It wasn't the same, there was no one there he knew. It wasn't worth seeing. He was reluctant to say any more. It seemed to me that there was a lot more to say about it all. I had made the recordings which form part two of this book during the previous year and they had stimulated my curiosity about Gnilowody and Podhajce, but Adam was wary and reticent, albeit with a smile on his face. For him, it was best to leave all that in the past. I didn't press him. I reasoned that he was only sixteen or seventeen when he was taken away by the Germans and his memories might have been too painful. I refrained from probing him about his experiences as a forced labourer. I could see that, like so many war survivors, Adam was happier to enjoy the moment without looking back.

Our visit to Lesna enabled me to reconnect with my Polish family, to introduce Virginia to them and to revisit an important part of my childhood. For reasons which still aren't clear to me, – immaturity? – naivety? – respect for the words and opinions of my father and Adam? – the still-existing blanket of oppression in Eastern Europe? – I hadn't felt a pressing need to investigate my family's past more deeply. I was simply happy to have returned. What was clear was that fundamentally important reforms had been taking place in Eastern Europe, even during the 18 days of our trip. We had been lucky enough to have spent time with Misha, whose analysis of the political situations in the Eastern Bloc countries would prove to be so thorough and perceptive, articulated brilliantly in his 1990 book *The Rebirth of History*. His enthusiasm for, and anticipation of what was unfolding were infectious. However, enthusiasm and anticipation weren't reflected in the moods and attitudes of Adam and Aniela and the other older Poles, Hungarians and Czechs we encountered. The tragedy and upheaval of the war, followed by over 40 years of Communist rule, had engendered scepticism and caution. Sure, they were happy to see the beginnings of liberalisation and freedom of movement, but they weren't sure yet that it would last. The Communists were still in power, and who was to say that new, non-Communist politicians would be any better?

Leaving Adam and Aniela and Lesna had always been an emotional experience in my childhood and it was no different this time. In fact, it was even more moving. We all found it difficult to speak as we made our farewells. We just hugged and wished each other well. I promised to return soon, and had to take deep breaths as we drove along the tree-lined road out of town, reliving all the farewells of my past: my father gripping the steering wheel, wiping away tears as he used the mechanical necessities of driving to control himself.

As I left Lesna on that day in 1989, I knew that I had reconnected, but I was also painfully conscious of the inadequacy of my reconnection. So much of my life had nothing to do with Poland and yet here I was, weeping for my distant family and a home I had never seen, Gnilowody, that place from another time which had taken on a kind of mythical status. I wept for our parting from Adam and Aniela, but I wept even more for selfish reasons, for my own sense of incompleteness. I don't think I understood this fully at the time. I simply felt it: a hole in the pit of my stomach, a longing, an ungraspable desire.

We stopped for a night in Berlin on our trek west. It was a relief to be with Tom, free from the stresses of communicating in my limited Polish, able to recount our journey to a sympathetic ear. We drank in a Bohemian bar. The barman wore nothing but a diaphanous black shirt, a pair of tackety boots and a jockstrap. We walked to the Brandenburg Gate and stood on an observation platform which gave us a view over the Wall. Virginia had never seen it before and it upset her. We speculated about the changes that were taking place and wondered how many more years it would remain. We didn't imagine that it would come down in a matter of months. We set off early the following morning and chugged all the way to Ostend. One of the car's engine cylinders had given out, reducing its power so that instead of sailing past the little Trabants on the East German autobahn, we kept them company. We made it to the ferry and kept going all the way to Dalston, arriving home at midnight, elated and exhausted. I had finally made my return.

12: The Promised Land

During the previous year, my father had been admitted to hospital for tests due to low blood pressure. The doctors identified a thickening of his blood and high cholesterol levels and prescribed a regime of anti-coagulant drugs. Unfortunately, he left the hospital more ill than he was when he was admitted having contracted a streptococcal infection of his blood there, the result of inadequate hygiene, and it knocked him for six. He was in and out of hospital for the following year, receiving heavy intravenous doses of antibiotics to fight the infection. He was considerably weakened and lost a lot of weight. By the summer of 1990, he had made a reasonable recovery, though he was diminished. Always a big, hearty fellow he was thinner now, and weaker. He wanted to return to Poland, and Virginia and I were happy to drive him and my mother for our second visit in a year.

The Wall had collapsed in November '89, the Velvet Revolution had taken place in Czechoslovakia, the Ceausescu regime had been violently overthrown in Romania and Bulgaria and East Germany had held their first free elections. Eastern Europe was seething with new energy which we wanted to witness for ourselves. I drove Mum and Dad to London from

Inverness and we set off for Poland the following day. We stopped for the night at Herleshausen.

Even though we knew what had happened in Germany, we could hardly believe the new reality of the border between East and West when we saw it the next morning. It was deserted. The gun turrets had been dismantled, the barriers removed. The buildings where we'd sweated and fretted with our forms and passports were empty and boarded up. We had to slow down, to see that this had really happened, to mark the occasion and savour the freedom of the border which had disappeared. For those euphoric, surreal moments, I felt as if we were floating in a happy dream, that a dead weight was being lifted from our shoulders. It all happened so quickly. All we did was drive past a few empty buildings, but it really felt like we were entering the Promised Land, a new world.

Money was already being pumped from West to East and we passed large-scale road works and drove on newly-surfaced stretches of the old autobahn, alternating with the clunka-clunka stretches of old concrete blocks which we were so familiar with. Without the strictures of the old transit visa, we took the wonderful liberty of turning off the autobahn and spending a few hours in the centre of Dresden. It was dominated by the ruins of its magnificent old Baroque cathedral, a monument to the city's near-total destruction during the fire-storms caused by Allied carpet-bombing in 1945. (It was restored to its former glory and reopened in 1995.) As we strolled around the ruins, I could never have imagined that 21 years later I'd be performing my play about my father in this city. We bought ice cream and set off for the final 100 kilometres of our journey and the open arms of Adam and Aniela.

That August, Western Poland seemed like one big car boot sale. Thousands of Poles were scurrying back and forth across the German border to buy goods, any goods: chocolate, disinfectant, power tools, cuddly toys, Coca Cola. They would return to Poland with overloaded cars to their chosen town and set up shop. Sometimes, the Poles would trade in Germany, carrying honey and vodka for the Germans. Suddenly, the free market was everywhere. State-run industries were being dismantled and sold off. Factories were closing or being stream-lined, shedding thousands of workers in the process. The car boot sale had become a vital necessity for many Poles.

We enjoyed another happy reunion with Adam and Aniela. Being there with my parents for the first time since 1974 gave the occasion an added poignancy, especially after my father's illness. As in the past, friends and neighbours visited and the vodka glasses were filled round the garden table, but the celebrations of the ageing generation were more sedate and measured.

During our stay in Lesna, we were surprised to discover a street theatre performance in the town square by the Krakow-based Teatr KTO. It was part of a festival whose centre was the small city of Jelenia Gora, some 60 kilometres away. We

Adam, Mateusz and me, Lesna 1990

introduced ourselves to members of KTO, including its artistic director, Jerzy Zon. Jerzy invited us to visit them in Krakow. A couple of days later, we went to Jelenia Gora for more of the festival and watched a spectacular, sculptural street performance by a visiting French company. The performers were completely white, white clothes, white painted faces, legs and hands. They performed individually and in twos and threes like moving statues, operating a series of strange mechanical contraptions of wheels, cogs, poles and metal cages which moved slowly and gracefully, imprisoning them, liberating them and elevating them. This was accompanied by industrial rock music, played by the company's musicians sitting on a black metal truck which had been fitted out with pipes, horns and drums.

We were in Poland for seventeen days. In the middle of our stay, Virginia and I left my parents for a few days and took the car to Krakow, stopping at Gliwice on the way to visit Wladek Limont and his young family. They were living in a flat in a standard post-war suburban housing scheme, an ordinary Polish working family. In true Polish style, they greeted us with generous hospitality and gifts of vodka and a crystal butter dish. The tank factory was still going, but the outlook for Wladek's job remained uncertain. He wanted to come to England to work he told me. He hoped I could help him. I was pessimistic about this proposition, having no connections whatsoever with his trade back in Britain, and knowing that he would have to work illegally, but I said I'd see what I could do. As it turned out, I didn't succeed in finding Wladek work and we eventually lost touch.

In Krakow we hooked up with our new friends at Teatr KTO, seeing a couple of performances and talking with them about possible co-productions. We pursued this idea for over a year and fixed on the suggestion of the company's dramaturg and writer, Bogdan Pobiedzinski for an adaptation of William

Golding's novel *The Spire*. This tells the story of an ambitious medieval bishop and his relationship with a group of stone-masons who have been commissioned by him to build the tallest spire in England. Bogdan proposed this story as a starting point for an allegorical play about the reconstruction of Poland and Eastern Europe and the fundamental influence western free-market capitalism would have on it. It was a good idea, which sadly never came to fruition. Our company at the time, Plain Clothes Productions, was new and though we had several notable successes during the '90s, we never gained sufficient stability or capital to exploit all our opportunities. Teatr KTO still exists, retaining several of its original members. The principle of ensemble theatre has been central to the develop-ment of Polish theatre, unlike the UK where theatre has depended far more on the initiative of individuals.

I was old enough to be admitted into Auschwitz this time. We spent most of a day there, walking through the exhibitions. Each country which had citizens who were victims had its own exhibition and I was struck by the contrast between the Dutch and Polish exhibitions. The Dutch explained the history of the Jewish community in Holland, describing its many impressive achievements and telling the story of the Nazi persecution of Dutch Jews. The Polish exhibition did not mention Jews. It referred to its victims only as Poles. Of course, there were many thousands of non-Jewish Polish victims, but the great majority was Jewish. The Polish authorities had chosen to ignore this fact. In one room of the Polish exhibi-tion, there were lists of victims in alphabetical order. I found a group of Zajacs, about ten of them. Perhaps one or two were distant relatives.

The exhibitions were situated at Auschwitz I, the original concentration camp. They provided more detail to facts which I was familiar with: transports, routes, dates, camp conditions, methods of extermination, 'medical experiments.' There were many photographs and the well-known heaps of personal possessions, spectacles, suitcases and shoes.

Most of Auschwitz I had been given the form of a conventional museum which mediated the experience, enabling the visitor to receive its horrific evidence with a degree of objectivity. This didn't prevent the obvious distress of some young visitors on the day we were there and there were many visitors who ventured no further. But it was at Auschwitz II, Birkenau, where I found myself more deeply moved.

There are no exhibitions here, just the desolate wide expanse of the huge barracks with the stone chimneys of each barrack standing alone in rows like gravestones and the infamous archway with its railway line running the length of the camp to end close to the ruined gas chambers and crematoria. There's a stone memorial here. The whole place was silent. The absence of birdsong at Birkenau has become something of a cliché, but we heard none, and saw only one bird, a hawk, drifting in the still air. In the woods behind the memorial, where improvised cremation pits had been used when the volume of corpses exceeded capacity, we tried to absorb the scale of this industrial factory of murder and wrestled with the reality of it, that human beings had planned and constructed it. We knew all this objectively, of course, but there was something visceral about standing in this place where it had actually happened. We felt compelled to see everything and by the end of the day, I was in a state of outrage.

Members of my own species had done this and because of this stark fact, I was tainted, responsible. Every living, mature human being is responsible. Perhaps this is the real meaning of what I have always considered to be the most evil, objectionable Christian concept, that of original sin. Maybe this really refers simply to the fact that we humans are capable of terrible acts and this has been distorted into the idea that we are guilty from birth.

We returned to Lesna and our anxious relatives, a few hours late. Ula had already arrived with Wojtek. She was in the process of building a large new house with her husband Janusz in Gdansk, not an easy task at the time as materials were often expensive and hard to come by. They needed to finish their roof. Adopting the new spirit of enterprise and freedom of movement, Ula reckoned she could buy what she needed more cheaply in Ukraine. She wasn't allowed to exchange zloty or any other currency for Soviet roubles in Poland or Ukraine, so she purchased a sack of American chewing gum with the equivalent of two days wages. She then travelled the 900 kilometres to Netishyn in Western Ukraine, where her Polish mother-in-law was working as a cook with a group of Polish building workers who were assisting the Ukrainians in the construction of a new nuclear power plant. I guess chewing gum was a luxury item in the Ukrainian market at the time. She sold her sackful and purchased enough tinplate roofing for the entire house, including delivery. The tinplate arrived in Gdansk with the building workers. The workers travelled in a bus and they were followed by two trucks, full of the Ukrainian goods they had bought, including the tinplate.

The remainder of our holiday was spent quietly in Lesna, socialising in the garden, taking my parents to Czocha and Swieradow, walking in the forests and hills around Szklarska Poreba and visiting Ella Wraga at her apartment there. As always, our parting from Adam and Aniala was tearful. My Dad hugged his younger brother and kissed him on the cheek, telling him to take care of himself and to heed Aniela's exhortations about his diet, his smoking, his heart. As we drove away from the house, we didn't know that this was their final parting.

Dad died at around 7.15am on March 11th 1992. He'd just cleared the car windows of snow, ready to take mum to the railway station. She was going to Leeds to see my sister Angela.

Just before they set off, Dad remembered a sample of material he wanted Angela to look at. He was planning to make her a coat from the material. He was often a man in a hurry and he rushed upstairs to fetch the sample. In his workroom, he suffered a massive heart attack. Mum heard the crash as he fell and found him lying there. She hurried to the phone and called the doctor. She received an answerphone message. In a panic, she fetched Flora, our next door neighbour and she called 999. The paramedics were quick to arrive. They tried to restart Dad's heart for over an hour, but it was no use. Myocardial infarction. Rheumatic heart disease.

I got the call from my sister Casia. It felled me.

Casia and I took the plane from London that afternoon and arrived home in time to see Dad before the undertakers took him away. He looked at peace on his bed, the big man, pale and cold. Left alone with him for a few minutes, I stroked his face. I was full of grief and so proud to be his son. He was such a kind, generous man, unassuming and open. I told him he would always be with me. I told him I was sorry that he wouldn't meet my children, but promised that they would know of him.

At a funeral of an old Pole during the previous week, he had told a grieving compatriot 'We've got to keep going as long as we can.'

I tried to get through to Adam all day on the phone, but in the end had to write instead.

My last conversation with Dad had been two weeks before. He wanted to make new suits for Virginia and me. I told him we couldn't afford it at the moment. We talked about them coming down in May perhaps. It was a short conversation. He always worried about spending too much money on the phone.

About 400 people attended the funeral. His Masonic friends carried him out of the church. He had been made Master of his lodge that year, the crowning achievement of his integration into the life of Inverness. He had told his friends that he fully intended to enjoy his year. There was a short blizzard at his graveside, snow and sunshine. We had drinks and sandwiches at the Haughdale Hotel by the river where I struggled through a speech of thanks.

Angela, Casia and I sorted through all his tailoring gear, dividing it up and throwing out old bits of cloth he'd kept for patches. Angela took the bulk of the thread, catches, buttons and pieces of lining: she does the most sewing. We had a pair of scissors each and distributed parallel bars, rulers, his irons, zips, cords, piping, elastic, fasteners and his stationery. We went through his clothes. Beautiful suits which could fit me with alteration or if I fill out, jumpers and shirts, bow ties, socks, long johns and vests and two lovely coats. Mum found his maroon polo neck jumper. We were in a jolly mood. This is in good condition she said, offering it to me. I found a large tear in the arm. I don't think so, mum. Angela laughed. Catherine and I followed suit. Mum's face crumpled. They had to tear it, she said, he was wearing it.

I feel a responsibility, now you're gone. There are certain parts of the living you which only exist now in me.

13: The Tapes

The months following my father's death were filled with a sense of loss. I stayed with my mother for three weeks and then took her down to London with me for another week. I worked on my company's next production and in the autumn, I toured the Highlands in George Gunn's play *Songs of the Grey Coast*. The play was a family drama which took place immediately after the death of the patriarch. I played his son. Art was imitating life. I don't know whether my loss made my role easier or more difficult. What I do know is that I drank heavily while I was performing the play and was more prone to emotional outbursts.

I didn't return to Poland for ten years after his death. I made a couple of attempts to learn Polish by attending adult education classes in Islington, but each time, the course was curtailed by new acting jobs which clashed with class times or took me away from London. I gave up. The wars in former Yugoslavia had broken out during this period and, in August 1994, my theatre company, Plain Clothes Productions, mounted a new production in response, 'Wolf' by Michael Bosworth, a dream-like play which attempted to examine the causes and effects of these wars through its characters: a general and his brutalised daughter; a prisoner from an opposing ethnic group who had been spared for his supposed storytelling powers, charged by the general with reawakening the innocent child in his daughter through his stories; the storyteller's dead companions, doomed refugees from the war. Bleak, poetic and challenging, it was a fairytale set in a war we were witnessing through our TV screens.

A few months before the production went into rehearsal, I invited Misha round to my house to listen to a reading of the play. He was back on a brief visit, some work and some rest. His life at the time was completely dominated by Yugoslavia's bloody demise. He had been continually travelling throughout the region, researching, reporting, utilising his extensive network of contacts, cataloguing the atrocities and the folly and beginning to prepare his mighty history of the region, *The Balkans: Nationalism, War and the Great Powers 1804-1999*. He had also married a Serbian woman. His book, *The Fall of Yugoslavia*, essential reading for an understanding of the wars in Bosnia, Serbia and Croatia, was first published in 1992 and he had received a Sony Gold Award for his contribution to broadcasting in 1993.

As we read the play, Misha became restless. He seemed tired and jaded, harder, and burdened by his grim experience. He expressed happiness at seeing us, but he hardly said a thing about the play. He made his excuses and left. I think he found our enterprise an indulgence, perceiving us then as a group of comfortable middle-class Brits pontificating about a war we knew little about, wringing our hands from a safe distance and the comfort of our kitchens. I was disappointed and angry with him. I believed that Michael's play handled the subject with perception and honesty. I knew that although Misha's knowledge and grasp of the history and politics of what was going on were far greater than mine, I had some understanding of the subjective experience we were trying to deal with through my own experience and that of my father. But Misha was elsewhere, preoccupied with unfolding events. I felt great sympathy for the huge responsibilities he was undertaking and for the pain he undoubtedly felt for a region he loved, but didn't see him again for several years.

During those years, I remained distant from Poland. My daughters were born and my life was taken up with caring for them and making a living. My mother adjusted to living on her own after a long grieving process and made the journey from Inverness to London a couple of times a year. I worked regularly in Scotland and had a growing desire to live there again. I often thought of my father. Finally, some time in the late 90s, I can't remember exactly when, I decided to transcribe the conversations I had recorded with him.

I hadn't touched the tapes since the recordings. I think there were two reasons for this. When he died, I immediately regretted my negligence in failing to record more. I knew, even when I made the recordings, that there was much more behind what he had told me and that I wanted to try to dig deeper, but I hadn't. I felt that it was a job half-done and that was painful and frustrating. Listening to the tapes would simply exacerbate these feelings. Also, in the year or two after his death, I was afraid that listening to his voice would have been too upsetting, that it would have hindered my recovery from grief.

As I dug out the tapes, I remembered those hours we'd spent recording them in his workroom in our house in Dalneigh. He'd set it up in my old bedroom after selling his shop in the town centre a couple of years previously. He only took on work from his long-standing customers then, semi-retired. By then, Dalneigh had become a quieter place. The roll at the primary school had fallen to under 200 as the children of my generation had grown up and moved out, leaving their ageing parents at home. Many of those parents had taken advantage of Margaret Thatcher's right-to-buy legislation and had bought their houses, adding new coats of masonry paint, porches and extensions in the process. As a consequence, the aesthetic unity of the estate had been replaced with a patchwork quality. This disunity seemed to me an expression of Thatcher's individualistic creed. A few years later, the council spent hundreds of thousands of pounds renovating all the houses on the estate, except the ones which had become owner-occupied, so my disgruntled parents missed out on that particular benefit of public ownership.

I switched on the first tape and was immediately with him. The deep timbre of his voice filled the room in my flat in Dalston, but I was back in my old bedroom, his workroom, with its muted, pale floral patterned wallpaper and white painted woodwork and its window looking down on gardens and sheds, a telegraph pole with a fan of wires reaching out to the surrounding houses and Craig Phadrig on the skyline, forested and ancient, indifferent to the new housing estates at its feet which would eventually go the way of the Pictish vitrified fort at its summit. The tape preserved those moments, then ten years old. I saw him sitting on his workbench with his feet on a chair, in that elevated position he liked as he worked.

I didn't write anything down for more than an hour, I just listened, thrilled and moved to hear his voice again, deep, animated, warm. The voice I loved so much and hadn't heard for ten years. I was lost in it until the rude interruptions of my mother on the tape jolted me out of this reverie. What are you telling him your business for? Haven't you got better things to do? When are you going to chop the wood? She clearly didn't like what we were doing. She resented being left out or was perhaps afraid that Dad would reveal something she would prefer I didn't know. I couldn't tell which. My father just brushed it off. At the time, her behaviour didn't seem out of character, she often expressed disapproval of my schemes, so I thought little of it. I was to discover later that there were very strong motives for her agitation.

I set to work, pressing the stop and start buttons, typing in his words and mine, the questions and answers. The laborious detail of this process gave me time to think about what was being said and I chafed at the inadequacy of my probing: the lines of inquiry which I didn't pursue or which were limited by his loss of memory or his unwillingness to go into detail. New questions kept forming in my mind as I listened and typed. One dominated all the others.

There were nearly four years between these recordings and his death. Why hadn't I listened to the tapes, thought of these new questions and conducted a second series of recordings? There were a number of answers: living so far apart, we didn't see each other often; the time we had together was usually filled with family obligations and routines; his illness during this period made me hesitate. Above all, I think I had an understanding that there was a limit to what he would or could tell me. My questioning on some subjects had been quite persistent, I had often pressed him for more detail and he had appeared to try to give me what he could. Repeatedly, I had found myself at a dead end, with little more than general facts, commonly-held attitudes or well-known history. The fact was that after I made these recordings, I didn't believe he would tell me any more. He had given me as much as I was going to get.

As I typed, it was a relief to find passages which were personal, which revealed something of what happened directly *to him*. There was more of this in the first tape, which covered his childhood and the years leading up to the war. His descriptions of Gnilowody and life in the village were vivid: the harvest, his school, his sister's wedding, characters in the village like Wawolka and the Kuszpisz brothers. There were the dramatic episodes: being chased by wolves on the sleigh, his experiments with his brothers with the explosive ordnance from World War One battles they had found in nearby fields. All of these elements drew a rich picture of his lost world and, as I transcribed his words, they made me want to see the place for myself. I knew that sooner or later I would have to travel to Ukraine.

His account of the war years was more problematic for me. There were fewer personal recollections, much more in the way of general descriptions of the historical events which swept him from Poland to Russia to North Africa, Italy and finally to Britain. He struggled to remember place names, dates and people. I doubted the accuracy of his geography. It was curious that the name of the Uzbek village, Halenka, was almost the same as the name of the Russian doctor who told him about Stalin's amnesty for the Poles, Halinka. I remembered that I had asked him to point on a map of Russia to the region where he had searched for a Polish officer. He was full of uncertainty until, after dithering for some time, he settled on a region immediately to the south-west of the Ural mountains, over 1500 kilometres from Uzbekistan. I'd let it pass at the time, knowing the vastness of Russia and the huge distances many people had travelled in transports to the gulag or individually as escapees, searching for reconciliation with loved ones or simply in attempts to free themselves from the Soviet authorities. There were no detailed descriptions of combat. I attributed this to the pain such memories can renew, knowing that it was rare for ex-combatants to talk about these things.

I completed my task of transcribing the tapes with his energetic post-war life in Scotland, moved by his reunion with Kazik and the loss of contact with his parents, full of admiration for the zest with which he embraced his new life. It was natural that he could describe the post-war period in a happier tone. These memories weren't difficult. They weren't about loss and displacement; they were about renewal and hope. In spite of my frustration with the brevity of my recordings, I felt grateful for the generosity he had shown. His life had been both ordinary and extraordinary. In its own small way, it was a testament to survival, a defiance of war, but I was left with an incomplete story and knew that I would never be able to fill in all the gaps or answer all the questions which remained. I needed to know more, as much as possible, but didn't know how to begin. I felt weighed down by the seeming enormity of this task, which engendered a demoralised inertia. Having explored some of the rooms of my father's house I had reached one with a locked door. I combated this feeling with the demands and delights of work and parenthood. I allowed life to take its course and as it did so, a few years later, I found the key to that door.

PART FOUR
Aniela

14: A New Road

In summer 2002, I returned to Poland with my family, taking my daughters Ruby (8) and Iona (6) for their first visit. We opted to drive. I was excited at the prospect of retracing the journeys of my childhood and opening up my Polish heritage to my daughters, but we weren't going to Lesna. Uncle Adam and Aunt Aniela had sold their house in the early 1990s to enable Ula and her husband Janusz to finish building their new house in a suburb of Gdansk, more than 700 kilometres north-east. In return, Adam and Aniela moved in with them. This arrangement lasted only a couple of years before they moved again, to Aniela's birthplace of Augustow, a town in Mazuria, the beautiful lake district in the north-east corner of the country on Poland's borders with Belarus, Lithuania and the Russian enclave of Kaliningrad. So we took a new road.

By then, we had moved to Edinburgh. We drove to catch an overnight ferry from Harwich to Cuxhaven, near Hamburg. Arriving early in Harwich we whiled away the time with lunch in a quiet pub near the docks, watching the dull 2002 World Cup Final between Germany and Brazil, held in the reunited Berlin. We'd be there the next day. On the ferry, I joined with the children's excitement, remembering my own from all those years ago as they delighted in exploring the decks and discovering the compact features of our cabin.

Arriving in Cuxhaven at lunchtime the next day, we drove to Berlin and its World Cup hangover, where we were reunited with Tom and his friends Klaus and Johannes. Twelve years after reunification, the new Berlin was taking shape. The old centre around Potsdamer Platz and Unter den Linden, formerly bisected by the Wall, had been reclaimed. The machine-gun-turreted, barbed wire wasteland that was Potsdamer Platz had been transformed into a towering steel and glass symbol of the triumph of the West, the Sony Centre conspiring in a giant huddle with the Bahn Tower under a huge glass umbrella. Shoppers, office workers and cinemagoers milled through its plaza or sat at its terraced cafes, gazing at the geometry and light, and at the enormous inflatable Spiderman which pretended to climb a wall of this capitalist cathedral, there to herald the latest Hollywood blockbuster.

We drove past all this on our way out of Berlin. The other new glass umbrella, the transparent dome of the reborn Reichstag, with its spiral walkway, was off in the distance. The sight of the tourists, as they made their way up the spiral, suggested something extra-terrestrial, souls journeying up to heaven, aspiring to a higher plane, dazzled by the light of hope or delusion. Beside the Reichstag, the Brandenburg Gate was open, no longer a border, and Unter den Linden was complete once more. The old Mexican stand-off between buildings, the great architectural projects of East and West which symbolised the political power game that was the Cold War had faded into absurdity. I remembered how impressive and disturbing it had been to walk through the two half-cities as they desperately masqueraded as separate entities. Now, that was all over and the unified, single Berlin was striving to define and assert its new identity, eager to achieve a new cohesion.

Diversity was the buzzword in Berlin in 2002. Still painfully conscious of the crimes of fascism (though less so of the crimes of communism: the communist period, though full of iniquity, was like a 40-year sleepwalk as a stunned, defeated East German population tried slowly to understand what had happened to them), the city was promoting multi-cultutralism. The huge Neue Synagogue at Oranienburgerstrasse had been restored and a small new Jewish population, mainly emigrants from Russia, had settled in the city.

During this summer of 2002, the centre of Berlin was peppered with around 350 two-metre tall multi-coloured fibre glass bears, the bear being the symbol of the city. The United Buddy Bears of Berlin, you either loved them or hated them. They were psychedelic, two-tone, uniformed, chequered, striped, landscaped, stellar and everywhere. A grassy area between the Reichstag and the Brandenburg Gate was designated as the exhibition space for the International Bears. Each of the world's countries was represented by a bear. An artist from each country, or a German artist associated with a country if no native artist was available, was commissioned to paint a bear in a way which represented his or her nation.

The International Bears stood side by side in an 80-metre wide circle, facing inwards, having a pow-wow. The British bear held a cup of tea, wore Union Jack knickers and was adorned with several gilt-framed pictures of, amongst others, the royal family, Wallace & Gromit and a London bus. The Yugoslavian bear was riddled with bulletholes. Other bears depicted Caribbean scenes (Jamaica), national costume (Belarus) and national symbols (India). But underneath all this variety, the bears were identical, all cast in the same mould. I think the concept was that we're all the same under the skin. My children loved the bears and I liked them too. A couple of young women from London of Cameroonian descent jumped for joy when they found the bear from Cameroon.

We headed out along one of the spokes which connects the city centre to the Berliner Ring, out through the city's north-east. This was part of the old East Berlin and it showed. With the affluence of the centre behind us, we drove through neighbourhoods which were more down-at-heel, not poverty-stricken, but all part of a quite featureless urban sprawl. We paused at a set of traffic lights beside a tram stop. People were waiting there: a woman in her sixties, a picture of fatigue in a worn brown skirt and cardigan and a look to match, she seemed to be held upright by the heavy shopping bags which surrounded her feet; a group of teenagers in denims, trainers and T-shirts, one with a mullet, Germany being the last bastion of that hairstyle; an harassed mother coping with a baby, two toddlers and her shopping; a man bursting out of his cheap suit, thick-necked and earphoned, carrying a fake leather wallet briefcase. It could have been Newcastle-upon-Tyne or Warsaw. From our passing car, I couldn't tell whether these people were happy or not, just living their lives, getting on with things, working, striving, hopeful, resigned.

We joined the autobahn which would take us to the Polish border and after about 20 kilometres, I was surprised and dismayed to find that it appeared to be the only stretch of motorway which the united Germans had failed to improve. Suddenly we were back in the holidays of my youth, ker-thunk, ker-thunk, ker-thunk, as we, ker-thunk, drove over, ker-thunk, the gaps between, ker-thunk, each of the old, ker-thunk, concrete slabs which made up the original autobahn. Potholes, cracks, low speed limits, roadworks, I wondered if the appalling surface remained to deter Germans from visiting Poland and vice versa. It began to rain heavily. The catch on our jam-packed boot snapped and the boot swung open. I repaired it in the rain with a piece of rope and we carried on to the border at Kolbaskowo, where we queued for a mere ten minutes before showing our passports and driving on over the Oder south of Szczecin into Pomerania.

As soon as we entered Poland, it was clear that substantial changes had taken place. The first and most obvious signs were on the road: cars, lots of them. The Poles had rapidly made up for all those years without them, and the road surface was smooth! The cars filled up the smooth road, racing along, overtaking at every opportunity, vying for space. Often the road was a kind of three-lane highway with the middle lane for overtaking, in either direction, and the Polish drivers seemed to revel in its risk. In the towns we passed, there were still plenty of crumbling facades, but there were also lots of new buildings, complete or under construction, especially new houses, and signs everywhere, advertising hoardings, white boards proclaiming the existence of every conceivable private enterprise apart from prostitution and drug dealing. They seemed to multiply before our eyes in the larger towns and cities. It was difficult to spot the road signs.

Having left Berlin later than planned due to a celebratory evening with Tom and co., we realised that we weren't going to make it to Gdansk, so we turned off the main road and made our way north to Kolobrzeg, one of several seaside resorts dotted along Poland's Baltic coast. We spent the night there in a Soviet-era hotel block. In the morning, we briefly paddled on the sandy beach, which stretches along nearly all of the 300 kilometres of coastline between Szczecin and Gdansk. Szczecin was once Stettin, Gdansk Danzig, Kolobrzeg Kolberg.

Most of Pomerania has been outside Polish borders for longer than it has been inside them during the last thousand years, only returning to Poland after a 425-year absence in 1945. During those 1000 years, its population was a mixture of mainly Poles and Germans with some Scandinavians thrown in due to Sweden's 100-year rule of most of the region from 1620. The Red Army rampaged across Pomerania in early 1945, taking a terrible revenge on the German population, whom Hitler had refused to evacuate. The remaining Germans were subsequently expelled from Pomerania across the new German borders and, as in Silesia, the region was repopulated with Poles, most of whom were refugees from the eastern Polish lands annexed by Stalin's regime. It was hard to imagine such upheaval as we travelled through Pomerania's peaceful, sparsely-populated farmland, even though we were accompanied by an army of racing drivers.

We drove on through Koszalin and Slupsk to the Gulf of Gdansk, through the sister towns of Gdynia and Sopot to the city itself, finding our way to Ula's suburb of Jasien. The building trade was booming here, with smart new blocks of flats going up. It was booming everywhere. We saw hundreds of individual houses being built on their own plots of land and many startling modernist churches, full of sharp angles, smooth pale surfaces and colourful stained glass, thrusting upwards, spearing the sky. At the turn of the century, Poland was surely the world's church-building capital. It must also have been, and still is, one of the most religiously observant countries in Christendom.

Homogenised into an almost exclusively Roman Catholic population after the genocide of the Jews and the expulsion of most Germans and Ukrainians, and suppressed by the anti-religious atheism of the Communists, many Poles turned more and more to the Church during the Communist decades, for succour and as a focus for opposition. This grew to a spectacular climax during the 1980s with the accession of the Polish pope, Karol Woytla (John Paul II) and his support of Solidarity. Now, the devout Polish people were repaying the church's solidarity and resistance and its endorsement of Poland through Karol Woytla's papacy, reasserting its impressively successful association with the spirit of the nation. Through history, particularly during the 19th century partitions, some Polish artists, theologians and philosophers have equated

Poland's suffering with Christ's, propagating the idea that Poland *is* Christ. The crucifixion has become a national symbol. Poland has been crucified, and has risen from the dead, though this new land of cars, building sites and advertising hoardings can hardly be described as heaven.

Ula's spacious house, protected by the tinplate roofing she had acquired in Ukraine, lay in a neighbourhood of independently-built houses which all pre-dated the building boom we were witnessing. These were all built during the 1990s by those old enough, sharp enough, rich enough to be quick off the mark, to take advantage of the new freedom, one might even say anarchy, of that time. Ula's drive for a better life for her family and the material gains which she saw as central to that had taken her to Australia for six months, where her brother Jurek had found her work. She also worked for another six-month stint in Chicago, a city which is second only to Warsaw for the size of its Polish population, getting work through friends who had established themselves already. She welcomed us with open arms, delighted with the girls, who immediately started playing basketball with 17-year-old Wojtek, and introduced us to Janusz, a telecoms engineer. He'd been working for his company in Belarus, erecting new mobile phone masts. We spent the evening eating and drinking in Ula's garden, reminiscing about Lesna and our dead fathers, renewing our shared history. My mother flew in to join us the following day.

Our days in Gdansk were spent sightseeing and going to the beach at Sopot, the home of Polish pop and rock festivals. We visited the lovingly-restored Old Town and the Solidarity Monument at the entrance to the Gdansk Shipyard, the scene of the movement's birth. Three tapering, tree-like granite crosses inlaid with anchors stand in a triangle. Beside the monument lie rows of plaques commemorating each of 28 people who were killed by Polish security police during the dockers' strike of 1970. Fresh flowers had been placed here. We drove to the huge medieval fortress of Malbork, founded in 1274 by the Teutonic Order. The largest fortified Gothic building in Europe, Malbork is a testament to the power of the Order. I remembered the epic film I'd seen as a child, *Krzyzacy*, and its depiction of the mighty Battle of Grunwald between the Poles and the Order, only 70 kilometres from Malbork. Like Gdansk's Old Town, Malbork was virtually destroyed during the Second World War, but now stands restored, glorious and solid. Looking at a photograph of the fortress from 1945, its hard to reconcile the burned out ruin it was then with the seemingly impregnable structure it is today. I'm struck by the mockery modern explosives can make of so much human effort, by the irony of so much enquiry and invention resulting in so much destruction.

15: Augustow

A few days after our arrival, we set off for Augustow and old Aunt Aniela. Our 370km journey took us across the watery flatlands of the Vistula delta and into Warmia and Mazuria. Most of the ground we covered lay in the German territory of East Prussia in 1939. We skirted the small cities of Elblag (once Elbing) and Olsztyn (Allenstein). We stopped for lunch by one of the many hundreds of lakes in this region. Not far to our north, near the town of Ketrzyn, was the site of the Wolf's Lair, the name given to the heavily bomb-proofed concrete complex which was Hitler's home and headquarters for the best part of three years as his armies swarmed and swaggered into Russia, ground to a halt and defeat at Stalingrad, then retreated to their ultimate destruction.

During the afternoon, we passed swathes of forest where a storm had swept through a few days earlier with gusts of hurricane-force wind. The power and paths of these gusts was clearly marked by the jagged stumps of tall trees and their slaughtered bodies. Some lay next to the roadside, only recently cleared from the road itself. For 20 or 30 kilometres, we drove behind a large black Mercedes with smoked glass windows and Belarussian number plates. It was heavily loaded with goods or people or both, we couldn't tell. Its chassis sank towards the road as it beetled along bumpy tree-lined roads. It seemed sinister and mysterious, like the country it was returning to, still in thrall to a militaristic, Soviet-style dictator, a strange surviving remnant of the old regime.

Augustow is a pretty little market town surrounded by lakes and forest, a tourist resort full of smiling holidaymakers in summer. We found Aniela's smart, modern three-storeyed house quite easily. It was an emotional reunion. We hadn't seen each other for 12 years and during that time, both Adam and my father had died. Aniela lived on the top floor of the house where she had her own bathroom and kitchen. Below was her older sister Helena and her husband Julian. They greeted us warmly, Helena excited and voluble, though I understood only a little of her Polish, while Julian beamed.

Aniela had to make some final preparations for the dinner she was cooking and I needed to stretch my legs after the long drive, so Julian offered to take me for a walk along the nearby canal. The girls came with us. Julian was sprightly and neat, no doubt much slower and more careful now he was approaching eighty, but still light on his feet. We weren't in a hurry. It had been a hot day, which was only just beginning to cool as dusk arrived. I was in the slightly dazed state of a man who has been driving for five hours. I was also beguiled by this new place, which was so close to places I'd often gazed at on maps: Belarus, Russia, Lithuania and Ukraine. As we sauntered along the canal bank, I noticed a figure slowly cross into our path. She walked about 50 metres ahead, matching our pace, a tall, statuesque woman with black hair and a long black skirt which hugged her hips. They swayed slowly as she walked. The sight of this woman attracted and disturbed me. She reminded me of the black Mercedes, sleek, forbidding, tantalising. She stayed ahead of us, maintaining the same distance for perhaps ten minutes until Julian announced it was time to turn back for dinner. She kept on walking, my romantic embodiment of the East.

Her image swayed around in my head as we returned to the house for *pierogi, bigos*, vodka and an animated dialogue of reunion and family in Polish and sign language. Aniela urged me to eat and eat, piling seconds and thirds on to my plate until I had to almost physically restrain her from giving me any more. Virginia and the girls entered into the boisterous spirit of the occasion as we took our coffee and cake down to the garden and showed old and new family photographs to each other: party nights in Lesna during the '70s and '80s led by Adam the mischevious rogue, always with a twinkle in his eye, my father fully engaged, laughing and smiling, my mother in various attitudes of amusement, bemusement and quiet intoxication, her fun always tempered by her lack of Polish, and Aniela, who was always sober, watchful and reliable; our mountain walks in the Highlands and the girls with their grandparents in Islington and Inverness. Julian produced his harmonica and played old tunes which we hummed along to. We sang a few Scottish and Irish songs in return. Ruby and Iona picked ripe cherries from a tree in the garden as the low sun dazzled us then sank out of sight.

We stayed in Augustow for five days, swimming, sunbathing, boating and eating Aniela's enormous meals. Helena would pant and wheeze her way up to Aniela's floor carrying bowls full of yet more food, eager to contribute to the overwhelming hospitality. I was expected to eat the most, being the man, which was a relief for Virginia as she groaned at the thought of yet another *golabki*. Downstairs, Helena and Julian lived to the soundtrack of Radio Maria, the ultra-conservative Catholic radio station which poured out its daily diet of church services, hymn-singing, homilies, diatribes and phone-ins, at once serene and savage, where the sweet voices of newly-confirmed children would mix with those of ranting homophobes, anti-semites and anti-abortionists.

We paid a visit to Augustow's cemetery and Uncle Adam's grave, a great slab of polished black marble. Aniela had already paid for her space beside him. We laid our flowers down, and a little metal lamp with orange glass, lit by a tealight, which we'd bought at the shop by the cemetery entrance. It was strange to me that Adam should be here, when I associated him with nowhere but Lesna. It seems that memory can have a permanence which the business of everyday life can never have.

On the only Saturday during our stay, we visited the weekly market in a square in the town centre. Here, there were stalls with fruit and vegetables, clothing, household goods and tools. There were rows of old men and women in scarves sitting on stools and wooden boxes with their produce laid on the ground or on little tables in front of them: jars of honey and blueberries; eggs, cheese and cakes; knitted socks and mittens; tomatoes, courgettes and cabbages; straw dollies and carved wooden boxes and horses. Some of these traders had come bearing the fruits of their farms and gardens from the nearby borderlands, from Belarus, Lithuania and the Russian enclave.

In one section of the market, there were a few traders sitting behind large tables which were covered in a chaotic multitude of bric-a-brac and antique items, large and small: watches, jewellery, carved animals, mirrors, candlesticks, coal scuttles, dolls. There was some post-war communist memorabilia: a toy Soyuz rocket, a framed picture of Stalin, Lenin lapel badges. My eyes widened as I noticed that on each table there were numerous items of militaria from the last war. They were from all sides, from the armies of Poland, the Soviet Union and Germany, but mainly Germany. Perhaps the Nazi stuff sold best. Little busts of Hitler, Nazi ashtrays, Iron Crosses, SS breastplates, flags, medals, caps, helmets, uniform jackets, bayonets, badges, mess tins, even the odd Luger. One of the helmets had a hole shot through it. Paperwork from the Nazi occupation: identity cards, anti-partisan posters, *arbeitsbuchen* (workbooks).

There were faded armbands of the racially-defined forced labourers and prisoners, the *ostarbeiter*, the *untermenschen*: the red and white of the Poles, the blue and yellow of the Ukrainians, the blue and white of the Russians, the yellow armbands and stars of the Jews. Among all this ghoulish commerce, the most shocking items of all were *mezuzah* cases, the long decorative boxes containing the prayer *Shema Yisrael*, which are nailed to the doorposts of observant Jewish houses; *menorahs*, the seven- and nine-branched ceremonial candleabra for *Hannukah* and the Temple; and *tallitot*, the fringed, black and white Jewish prayer shawls.

The looted possessions of the murdered. What journeys had this plunder taken, how many hands had it passed through to arrive here? How many lives and stories were represented on these tables? Whose hands had torn these medals from the corpses of the soldiers who had owned them and had they bought the bread which meant life for the looter? Where was the house in whose window that *menorah* had been lit on a dark December evening as the family prepared the meal to celebrate the *Hannukah* holiday? Was it still standing? Who lived there now?

The tables themselves were an echo of the aftermath, a silenced battlefield of plunder from each constituency of its victims. Seeing it all laid out for us to buy seemed offensive to me, but was clearly quite normal to its sellers. This wasn't a museum, these items weren't mediated by the interpretation of historians and curators and glass cases. They were there to be bought and sold by profiteers, by those who wanted to rescue memory or by those who wanted to perpetuate myths, neo-fascists, anti-fascists, or just the mildly curious.

One day, I explained to Aniela, Helena and Julian that I

wanted to visit Podhajce and Gnilowody. Julian fetched a map of the region. We spread it out on the kitchen table and he drew the old Polish border to the east with his finger, the one which existed when he and my father were boys. 'To jest Polska' he declared. 'That is Poland.' He pointed to a village near Lviv. 'That is my home. Poland should have it all back.' This playful, impish old man was suddenly fierce, angry. I recalled our visit to Lesna in 1990, eight months after the collapse of the DDR when, just 40 kilometres away at the Gorlitz/Zgorzelec border crossing, a group of Germans had staged a demonstration, demanding the return of Silesia.

Aniela had gone to her bedroom. She returned with an old envelope and a small black and white photograph. She handed me the photograph. 'There is your father.' I was surprised. I stared at the photograph, at first uncomprehending, trying to take in what it was telling me. Here was a picture of my father from 1940 or '41, younger than I'd ever seen him, in an army uniform. There were seven soldiers in the picture, arranged in two small rows for the photographer. The photo appeared to have been taken in a rather run down, functional building, a barrack room or classroom perhaps, possibly a tent. The floor was sandy and a curtain covered the wall behind the group, probably put up as a temporary background for a morning of soldiers' photos.

The group in the photograph is solemn. Seven young men, three seated on wooden chairs at the front with crossed legs all at the same angles. These three seem more assured than the four behind them. The one in the centre of the front row has stars on his lapels. He must be the senior one in this group. His right cheek is swollen. He must have had a tooth problem at the time. All seven of the young men are fair skinned, but tanned. They look like they've spent a lot of time outdoors. My father is at the back, on the right, taller than the others. Handsome and erect, he is staring at the camera. His look is

155

serious, possibly defiant, perhaps betraying a hint of fear. Like the others, save for the one seated at the centre, his uniform bears no insignia. As I studied the photograph, I could just make out a star on each of their caps.

A communist star. A communist star.

Soviet Army 1940, Mateusz is standing, far right

I didn't understand. I turned to Aniela. '*Armia Sovietski?*' 'Soviet Army?' She shrugged and nodded her head. I frowned and silently cursed my poor Polish once more, which prevented me from probing. I tried to make sense of this. How could he have come to wear a Soviet uniform? There seemed to be only two possible explanations: perhaps the Soviets had issued the Poles with these uniforms as a stopgap, as they re-formed in Kazakhstan after Stalin's amnesty for Polish prisoners-of-war

156

was declared; or he had been in the Soviet Army. It had to be the former. He'd never been in the Soviet Army, he'd been a prisoner of the Soviets. It was all there, on the tapes.

Disturbed and confused, I took my eyes away from the photograph to look at the envelope Aniela had given me. It had come from the former Soviet Union, from newly-independent Ukraine. She pointed to the details of the sender. *'Twoj tato kuzyn.'* 'Your father's cousin.' I couldn't read it as it was written in what I thought was Russian, in Cyrillic script. She wrote it out for me in Roman. *Bogdan Baldys, from Podhajce.*

'Is he still alive?'

'Yes. He's still in Podhajce with his wife. That's his address.'

On the day before we left, we hired two kayaks, put one daughter in the front of each and paddled along the meandering Czarna Hancza River for 25 kilometres. We had been driven to our departure point by the hire company and arranged a rendezvous time of 6pm that evening. It was a warm, muggy day. Hundreds of electric blue dragonflies hovered over the water and around our boats, the occasional one pausing to rest on Ruby's hat or Iona's knee as the girls sketched their surroundings, the fallen trees, fields and reedbeds we passed. On a little jetty among the reeds, an old lady appeared, calling to us to buy as we approached and extending a plateful of cakes over the water. We veered towards her, but overshot, the current carrying us away, our kayaking not expert enough to time our liaison with the tempting cakes. We craned our necks backwards to make our apology and she laughed and waved.

At lunchtime, we did manage to stop at a little hut where another woman was cooking *placki* and selling bottles of beer and lemonade. We sat next to a group of students, all learning English and anticipating the job opportunities Poland's imminent accession to the European Union would bring. We paddled on. 25K is quite a long way in a kayak, even with the current, and as 5 o'clock passed, we realised that we had a race on our hands to make the rendezvous in time. What had started in an idyllic, languid fashion became punishing and sweaty.

The final stretch of the journey was along the Augustow canal. As the river joined the canal, we had a choice, west or east. Our destination was a couple of kilometres to the west. Not far to the east lay Belarus and to its south, Ukraine. I felt its pull, the pull of the unknown, of the low black Mercedes, of the tall, dark, swaying woman by the canal, of the new image of my young father in his Soviet uniform, of the creased and worn envelope from his old cousin Bogdan, of the mysterious birthplace of my father which was now so tantalisingly close. It was as if this whole trip had been a staging post, an inevitable part of my longer journey. It struck me that, without fully realising it, I had been engaged for most of my life in an investigation, to know my father and, by doing so, to know myself. As Virginia and I ploughed westward through the water against the current of my thoughts, to meet the driver who would return us to Augustow, I knew that I now had no choice. I had to go to Ukraine.

16: Letter from Ukraine

Pidhaitsi, Ukraine 29th May 2003

Dear Matthew,

Many thanks for the letter you have written. We are greatly satisfied that you have found us. We heard about you from our relatives. And we are ready to help you. We are waiting for you any time you like at the end of September or at the beginning of October.

I was a child before World War 2. I remember your father but slightly but I can tell more about Adam and Kazik. But I have a brother, Nick by name. He is 82 and he can tell you more. He remembers your grandparents very well. He was a cousin and a friend of your father. He remembers these terrible events that were taking place here before the war, during it and in the postwar period. He was a member of it.

We have made some plans of where to go, what places to visit. Of course, we'll go to the cemetery in the village of your ancestors, to the grave of your grandparents, your father's sister and her husband.

*I'll be 70 in August and my wife will be 65. We're going
to mark our Jubilee with a visit to the Black Sea Coast.*

*I want to tell you that our best friends have a daughter
who is a teacher of English at our local college and she
agrees to be an interpreter for us. That's why I think
there is no need to take someone from England. But its
up to your thinking.*

*We'll try to do our best for your visit to be successful
and pleasant.*

*Best wishes from all of us here to all of you there.
Looking forward to seeing you.*
Bogdan and Halyna Baldys

On the 29th of May 2003, the day that Bogdan and Halyna
sent their letter to me, the sun was shining in Edinburgh and
the temperature was high. I spent most of the day getting
cars fixed on the council housing estate of Lochend with
Nureddin from Sudan. I had skidded my car into his, coming
down steep, narrow and wet Lilyhill Terrace the night before.
There was an old man cutting grass with a pair of shears in
a garden beside us. He straightened up, holding his back,
and groaned.

'Keeps you fit, but gives you a sore back,' I said. 'It has to
be done, see how long it gets? You leave it too long and then
look at it.'

Was that a Polish accent?

'Are you Polish?' He registered the question, wary. 'My
father was Polish and you sound a bit like him.'

'I'm from Ukraine.'

'Which part?'

He paused, still wary. 'Western Ukraine.'

'Whereabouts?' This was getting too intimate, it seemed, so

I tried to reassure him. 'My father was from Podhajce, near Tarnopol.'

'Pidhaitsi, yes. It's quite flat there. I'm from the Carpathians.'

'My father was in a Carpathian regiment.'

'It's flat in Pidhaitsi. I'm a Highlander.'

'So am I, I'm from Inverness.'

He smiled. He was a Ukrainian nationalist, joined the Germans when Hitler, running short of Aryans to send to their deaths, finally agreed to the formal recruitment of Slavic *untermenschen*. He fought the Russians. He was anti-semitic too. 'The Jews took a lot of Poland's gold when they fled before the war. If you were rich, you could escape. Some of them are still living off it in London.'

'But the great majority suffered a lot in the war.'

'Not as much as the Poles and Ukrainians. Many Ukrainians were betrayed to the Russians by the Jews. When the Germans took over, Jewish women were made to wash the clothes of victims of the Russians, so that we could identify them. They were found in mass graves, they usually weren't recognisable, although some of the graves were only a few weeks old.'

I didn't want to challenge his anti-semitism. I wanted him to tell me more. Nureddin was examining the second-hand Toyota bumper we'd just taken from the auto salvage dump at Loanhead.

When the Germans capitulated, he and his comrades were stranded on the Austrian front and taken prisoner, fortunately for him by the British. He was a POW in Italy for two years, then a forced labourer in Britain for 18 months, receiving one shilling a day. 'Enslaved, like you people were once' he tells Nureddin.

Then he was a miner in Fife for nine months. He hated it and left. No one would give him a job, so back down the mines he went, for 33 years. Now he was living on his own, nearly 80, in reasonable health. Two months ago, he blacked out, fell over and dislocated his shoulder. He's not so strong. Nureddin told him he should get the council to cut his grass, the doctor could certify that he's not fit enough. Nureddin has a neighbour across the road who works for the council and has fixed up grass-cutting for other elderly neighbours. Paul Batyr, the Ukrainian, was grateful for the offer. 'Look at us. We're all international now!' I said. We all laughed.

I'll carry detritus and stories from the streets of Edinburgh to Ukraine.

PART FIVE
Hnilowody

17: The Journey Home

Slivers of stretched candy floss clouds, pink in the dawn, float by as we pass above the Humber Estuary and over the North Sea. It's a clear, sunny morning at Warsaw Airport. The smell of aircraft fuel and exhaust fumes mix in the sunny breeze as we board the flight for Lwow: Lvov, Lemberg, now Lviv. I'm again struck by the speed with which the Poles have absorbed the free market economy. How will Ukraine compare? What is emerging from the economic chaos, the free-for-all which followed the collapse of communism? There are a few signs among my fellow passengers. Most of the Ukrainians appear to be businessmen, though few are wearing suits. They wear belted slacks, slip on shoes, black leather jackets and open shirts. They carry small, soft briefcases. There are a couple of heavily made up peroxide glamour grannies wearing completely crease-free crimplene trouser suits. These people aren't poor. They are, after all, travelling by air, but their clothes are cheaper than those of the Poles and the sizeable minority of Americans on the flight, and they have a different style, reminiscent of the '70s in the UK.

Material poverty is one thing. Cultural poverty is another. In Britain, we have a surfeit of culture, we can be smothered by it, it's hard to see the wood for the trees. And so much of it is managed forest, Sitka spruce, commercial, homogenous. Pop culture, pop videos, fame academies, celebrity. A Sitka spruce is, in itself, a beautiful tree, but standing among a hundred thousand? I wonder how far down the road of Western homogenisation Ukraine has travelled, how much the indigenous, the particular, the local, the regional, the national has been preserved or adapted through the extraordinary changes since independence was gained in 1991. What a very young country. Independence came on a wave of nationalism and an irresistible urge to break fully free from the crushing grip of the Soviet imperium.

August 1939. September 2003. 64 years since Mateusz left his homeland forever. And here I am, his representative, returning, for him and for me. A new relationship is beginning.

Beneath the brilliant blue and the engine with its propellor, a massive field of towering, bulbous, cumulus clouds, and beneath them, through generous sunny gaps, thin-striped field systems which suggest smallholdings, still the stronghold of the peasant farmer. South-east Poland, or are we now over Ukraine?

A smartly-dressed woman, late 40s, sits next to me. She reads printouts in Russian. I'm curious, but initially, she's intent on her work. She relaxes after a while and we get talking. She's a New York banker, making the trip to Lviv to meet Ukrainian financiers and government representatives to discuss her bank's investments in Ukraine. She has her own ancestry from the region, Polish Jewish, from a town where she told me the Jews were rounded up and murdered not by the Germans, but by their Polish neighbours. This could be Jedwabne, in the Bialystok *voivod*, where the facts of the murder only came to light fully in 2000. Now her mastery of Russian and money brings her back to lubricate the new settlement.

The plane lands and we disembark. Before us is the airport terminal, a fine example of Austro-Hungarian neo-classical architecture. I've no idea what this building's function was before it became an airport terminal, but how refreshing to have avoided a glass and steel consumer cage for once. Once more, the American banker is back to her brisk, business mode. She's separated from the crowd of travellers and joins a couple of other VIPs who'll be whisked through passport control ahead of us.

Into the terminal and I'm immediately reminded of Poland in the 1970s: a formless crowd rather than a queue pressing towards an under-manned passport control; dark formica and wood veneer; you learn that the thin grey forms lying loosely on a coffee table are to be filled in and there are none in English. The hall is filled with the smell of cheap tobacco, and two officials who look like a sado-masochist's dream, pretty young women, one peroxide blonde, the other auburn-haired, both heavily made-up with dark, plum-coloured lipstick and tons of mascara and eyeliner, both in dark green uniform and knee-length high-heeled boots.

After a few minutes, I learn about the form-filling with assistance from a couple of Ukrainian English speakers. Ten minutes later I gather that passengers from Warsaw are allowed through to passport control first, before the throng of internal travellers in front of me, so I'm ushered to the head of the queue by the peroxide official, who's friendly and smiling. She checks that my papers are in order and then the same happens at the desk. It's so noisy in the hall I have to bend my ear and mouth to the narrow gap between the window and the counter to communicate with the passport inspector. The male customs officers, dull in appearance in comparison with the young women, wave me through and there, in the reception hall stands a woman holding a piece of paper with MATTHEW ZAJAC printed on it.

This is Lesia Kalba, the English teacher who has been translating for Bogdan and me. She's in her mid-forties, smartly dressed with piercing eyes and a firm set to her mouth, a determined looking woman. We greet each other. She speaks clear, measured English, imperfect but impressive nonetheless. Her role today is to look after me for the few hours I have before I catch my train to Ternopil. She leads me out of the terminal to her brawny, moustachioed and smiling husband, Vasyl, and their little van. Lesia insists on sitting on a box in the back and we drive through Lviv to one of the university buildings, where Lesia's sister is going through a viva for her doctorate.

As we drive through the city streets, I'm struck by the similarity of the architecture to that of Silesia, and by the condition of the place. Aside from the fact that there are now capitalist advertising hoardings and some modern cars, it looks like Poland did 20 years ago. The buildings, many of them fine pieces of architecture, are shabby, in need of cleaning and renovation. Stonework is broken and crumbling in places. The roads, too, are full of patches and bumps. Tramlines snake and undulate amid rippling waves of tarmac and cobbles. It seems miraculous that they actually manage to function. There's a fair amount of traffic, but not nearly as much as a city to the west. Most of the cars are pre-capitalist, old Moskvitches and Ladas kept going by owners who can't afford newer models.

Lesia waits in the university for her sister and I hang about outside with Vasyl, who is a PE teacher, and his brother Volodomyr, who owns a supermarket in Ternopil. We manage a conversation about our jobs, football and families. Vasyl's sporting specialism is wrestling, which I gather is popular in Ukraine. Lesia returns. The viva has gone well and we drive to the railway station, another impressive edifice, Art Nouveau, which opened in 1904.

At the station, Lesia and I have a good meal of borscht, pork cutlets and salad. Lesia tells me that she also studied at Lviv University, in the '70s, reading English. 'There were twenty students in my class, only four Ukrainians, and the rest were Russians and Jews. It was more difficult to get into university if you were Ukrainian and it hasn't changed much since.' I frown and pause before I respond. 'Really?'

'Of course! The government in Kyiv is still dominated by Russians and Jews, just like it was with the Communists.' I'm taken aback by this open hostility, especially the anti-semitism. I've only known this woman for a few hours and she's volunteering an opinion which shocks me, in a calm, matter-of-fact way, but I remind myself that I've heard this before. Throughout the former Soviet Bloc, there was, and remains a common perception that the whole Communist project was a Jewish conspiracy and that, one way or the other, the conspiracy carries on. So among millions of people, the revulsion felt at the murder of their Jewish neighbours, the mass executions into pits dug just outside their little towns, the industrial slaughter of the concentration camps, was tempered or even cancelled out by an absurd belief in this fantastical, furtive Jewish hegemony. Old prejudices die hard.

I bite my lip and accept that I am a foreigner here, and that I need to listen and learn about this new country and its culture. I have nothing to fear, Lesia is here to welcome and guide me. And I'm not Jewish. Maybe I should have told her that I was. I may not like the attitude she has just revealed, but it is clearly deeply felt and based on some kind of experience and the rigid social divisions of a past which remains in living memory. She is showing me kindness and consideration, here to see me safely on my way to Ternopil, and I must respect that.

I have my train ticket, supplied by Bob Sopel, the avuncular travel agent in Manchester who has specialised in travel to

Ukraine for years. Lesia sees me on to the train. Each carriage is a sleeper with its own attendant. It's the train to Donetsk, far to the east, a day's journey. There's one other person in my compartment, an officer in the Ukrainian army. Having been warned of high levels of crime by Lesia, I can't help feeling a little reassured by the officer's presence. He appears upright and friendly, and so it proves to be. We set off.

Roman is 40, a healthy-looking man with the fair complexion and blue eyes of so many Ukrainians. He's a *nipolkovnik*, one down from a major, with 2 stars on his epaulettes (my knowledge of army ranks is limited, I guess that's something like a captain). He has a 38-year-old wife, Ola and a 15-year-old daughter, Natalia. They live in Ternopil. I get the video camera out and shoot the countryside and villages as we pass. Roman is fascinated and amused by all this. He holds the camera as I talk to it. I show him my family photos. In addition to army ranks and family information, we manage to describe our respective houses, discuss our ages and the populations of Ukraine and Scotland, Ternopil and Edinburgh, our careers in the army and the theatre, the castles of Ukraine and Scotland and the Loch Ness Monster, aided by drawing pictures and writing numbers. We travel through continuing expanses of farmland, past houses, geese, hayricks, silver birch, beech and chestnut trees yellowing into autumn.

Night falls and the train slows as we enter Ternopil. I keep the camera out and Roman kindly takes my holdall. I climb down to the platform. Weak, yellow lights and the grimy green trains on either side form a kind of corridor and, as I'm focussing on this, a small man, bald with white hair above his ears, dapper and intent, catches my attention. He has a penetrating stare, blue eyes set deep under dark brows. His face shows little expression. It's Bogdan. And then I'm surrounded by people. As he takes this in, Roman says a swift and discreet goodbye.

To my right stands a tall old man in a baseball cap and tweed jacket, full of good humour and more gold teeth than I've ever seen in one mouth. He clutches my hand with a strong grip. This is Mykola, the 'Nick' mentioned in Bogdan's first letter to me, his 82-year-old brother. Next to him, Xenia, his rotund, rosy-cheeked wife, who kisses me and holds both my hands in hers, felicitous and warm, exclaiming how much I look like my father. A great wave courses through me and I catch my breath as it almost overcomes me, steeling myself against it to maintain my self-control. The three old folk are accompanied by three grandchildren in their late teens or early twenties, smiling and watching. None of them speak English and I do my best and we stand on the busy platform as people go by, smiling at each other, pressing each other's hands, exclaiming, laughing and nodding.

And then there are two others. *'Bon soir monsieur, je suis Vlada, bienvenue a Ternopil. Notre directeur attend au theatre et nous devons aller maintenant.'* 'Good evening sir, I am Vlada. Welcome to Ternopil. Our director is waiting at the theatre and we must go now.'

Vlada is a sophisticated middle-aged woman, an assistant to Mykhaylo Forgel, the Artistic Director of the Schevchenko Theatre. She is accompanied by a younger man who wears a suit, Yuri, an actor who speaks some English. They are rather impatient and now I feel deep regret and frustration that the Ternopil Theatre Festival is getting in the way of this family reunion. How much better for it to be at the end of my stay, not at the beginning! But I must go with them. I explain all this, although they already know it, and I assure Xenia and Mykola that I will be in touch in the morning. *'Jutro! Jutro!'* We part amid much hand-clasping, hugging and kissing. Bogdan sticks by me stoically as we are led away. Yuri carries my bag. 'Welcome to Ternopil. You must be very tired! I have heard of the Loch Ness Monster!'

We cross a square towards the theatre, its façade a row of Roman columns topped by a relief depicting a group of players or Muses around a central figure, Taras Shevchenko, one of Ukraine's national poets. A performance has recently finished and the last audience members are leaving the theatre. Bogdan and I are led round to the stage door, up stairs and through unlit corridors to the auditorium, where we're asked to wait. After a few minutes, Yuri and Vlada reappear with Mykhaylo, another dapper, small man. He greets us in a business-like manner and assures Bogdan that I will be taken care of. Bogdan takes my hand, kisses me on both cheeks and goes. He's done his duty.

18: At the Ternopil Theatre

I'm immediately led through the grand foyer, past rows of actors' headshots and a huge bust of Shevchenko, up to the circle, on to the upper circle and into a gallery at the side of a vast marbled and chandeliered hall. Everywhere is either unlit or only dimly lit, except this small gallery. I climb the steps up to it and I'm greeted by a long table, on it a lavish spread of food and drink and, crammed around it, the festival elite, around twenty five people, who all look up as we enter.

Mykhaylo introduces me. I feel a little daunted, a little like an interloper. Here are the festival judges, professors, actors, directors, critics, a high-ranking civil servant in the culture ministry, guests from Macedonia and, at the opposite end of the table, Robert Longthorne and Rebecca Ross from the Liverpool Everyman and Playhouse Theatres. Mykhaylo leads me down to sit near them and I greet them with some relief. Sitting beside them is Sasha Papusha, a debonair actor from the Shevchenko's ensemble and a fluent English speaker. I sit and join the proceedings. My arrival has briefly interrupted the toasting. I welcome the opportunity to eat, relax and drink but the overwhelming torrent of new people and places coupled with physical tiredness proves to be a dangerous combination.

I'm eager to bond with these people, to accept their hospitality, to join the party. The *horilka* (vodka) flows and I don't hold back.

I'm garrulous, excited and fascinated by the gallery of characters before me. One or two of them eye me with suspicion, most are smiling and welcoming. Within an hour, I'm tipsy, within two, I'm drunk and we go on toasting each other and talking, comparing working conditions and productions in our respective countries, explaining aspects of our histories, singing the odd song. The party breaks up at 2am and I'm staggering. I've been rash. I haven't even checked in to the hotel. My bags are – where? Ah, there they are! Yuri is looking after me. Rebecca, Robert and I are escorted through the streets to the hotel, a five-minute walk, though I can't really tell. Yuri carries my holdall and we make it to my room. Yuri dumps the bag and bids me good night. I trip over my bed and fall on my face, cracking my neck. And after all that, it takes me an hour or so to get to sleep, images and sounds of the day racing about in my head.

I wake at 10.30 with an appalling hangover. I lift my head towards the window and immediately let it fall back onto the pillow, a sharper pain shooting up from my neck. I remember the fall and lie there, prone, for an hour, dozing, groaning, staring at the ceiling and recalling the events of the previous day: Captain Roman, the welcoming party on the platform, the American banker, the line of carriage lights through my video lens, my silent escort Bogdan, the long, laden table, the ugly airport hotel I stayed at in Manchester, the toasting, the vodka, the drunkenness. The alphabet. I've got to get on top of that. Д = D, П = P, Ц = TS, Я = YA. I listen to the sound of chambermaids along the corridor, unlocking doors, calling to each other. So I'm here.

I rise and look out of the window. Before me is a lake, 2 or 3 kilometres long, kidney-shaped. It's surrounded by trees, a busy road on one side, a tall church with an onion dome and buildings in the distance. I'm parched. I have a water bottle. I take a shower and, afterwards, feel a little better, but I still feel like shit. Fortunately, it's the only hangover I'll have in Ukraine. My body adjusts quickly to the vodka intake and, for the remainder of my stay, I'll retain a certain manageable level of pickling.

I get dressed and wander out. It's a fine day, with a little autumn chill in the air. I cross the wide road in front of the hotel and walk through a well-kept square of rectangular lawns, flowerbeds, trees and paved walkways. There's a large bronze statue of a horseman, the Hetman Halitsky, who founded Lviv. I pass a couple of stalls selling second-hand books and jewellery, some smart-looking shops and cafes and an impressive, ornate Greek Catholic Cathedral with white marble walls and copper domes. I come to a much larger square. Off to the left is the grand Roman façade of the theatre, a huge tarmac apron spread before its steps. I'm hungry. I retrace my steps and stop at the Café Europe where I eat a large lunch of borscht, lamb cutlets, potatoes, cucumbers and carrot & cabbage salad. It's delicious and very cheap, for me. I'm a rich tourist.

This trip's the wrong way round. I should be with my relatives first. The theatre festival should come later, but I'm obliged to attend. I want to and the Scottish Arts Council has been kind enough to pay for my attendance. I ring Mykola and Xenia and we manage a basic conversation. I'm in no fit state to visit them, so I promise to go tomorrow. The hangover is gradually improving, but it's still all I can manage to get back to the hotel, where I lie down for another hour before the commencement of the day's performances and the subsequent cultural celebration, or piss-up.

When I rise, I make my way to the Young People's Theatre, its façade decorated with metallic birds and a figure who could be Pinocchio. The auditorium seats 300 and it's full for the afternoon presentation of *Marriage Play* by Edward Albee, presented by the Dramski Theatre of Skopje, Macedonia. The play is a profound, unsentimental dissection of marriage and mid-life crisis. It's given an excellent production. The two actors received an award for their outstanding work at the end of the festival.

After the performance, I have time to grab something to eat before sitting down in the main auditorium of the Shevchenko Theatre for *It Was Not To Be* by the Ukrainian dramatist Mychaylo Staritsky. This is the main presentation by the host company and the first Ukrainian play I have ever seen. Written at the turn of the last century, it's a moving story of two young lovers and the loss of innocence. Mychaylo is the son of wealthy, educated Ukrainian landowners with aspirations for greater wealth and social position. They speak in Russian and French, scorning the Ukrainian of the peasants. Mychaylo is idealistic, hoping for a more egalitarian society. He wears peasant clothes and speaks in their language. For this, he is mocked by his family.

Katerina is a peasant's daughter, beautiful and demure, aware of her low position in the social structure. She has a suitor, a peasant boy Dymytro. Convention demands that they should marry. But Mychaylo and Katerina fall in love. News of the affair spreads quickly through the community. Mychaylo's parents want to send him away to St. Petersburg. Katerina's mother warns her to keep away from Mychaylo and that she should be content with Dymytro, but Katerina becomes pregnant to Mychaylo. She doesn't tell him. The censure of his family and the larger community begins to wear Mychaylo down. He tells Katerina that they must meet only in secret. This angers her and she believes that he is ashamed to be seen with her. She becomes depressed. Mychaylo's cousin tells him that he can persuade his parents to accept Katerina and that it will be easier for him to do so if Mychaylo leaves for St. Petersburg. Mychaylo agrees, desperate for a resolution. Instead, the cousin offers Katerina money to leave the region for good. With Mychaylo gone, she plunges into despair and commits suicide.

Written towards the end of Stanislavski's tenure at the Moscow Arts Theatre where his work with Anton Chekhov had become famous, the play draws on Chekhov's naturalistic style and puts it firmly in a Ukrainian setting, acutely satirising the efforts of the Ukrainian bourgeoisie to mimic their aristocratic Russian rulers. There is a clear political aspect to the play as it focusses on these tensions and on the class divide with a Ukrainian nationalist slant. Staritsky obviously felt great warmth towards the Ukrainian peasantry, although their portrayal is not sentimental: their condemnation of the lovers is as strong as that of the rich family and Katerina's mother forcefully attempts to maintain the status quo by urging Dymytro's suit.

It's a well-structured play, given a powerful production by Slava Kila, the most impressive I saw at the Ternopil Theatre Festival. The acting of the large ensemble is uniformly excellent, muscular and spontaneous. It includes beautifully choreographed sequences depicting peasant life. Andriy Malinovitch and Svitlana Prokpova are outstanding as the lovers. A simple and effective set featured a sloping scrim backdrop, backlit for strikingly poignant scenes where the shadows of peasant children at play and girls dancing provide a counterpoint to the main action. A skeletal, solitary tree and an upright spiked pole, around which haystacks are built, complete the set.

The production is marred, however, by an aspect of life here which I can't relate to, arising in a sub-plot: the subject of anti-semitism. Mychaylo's father wants to get his hands on the land of two small independent Ukrainian farmers. He goes about this in league with a Jewish middleman, a greedy, conniving character. At another point in the play, the estate manager picks up a cigarette butt and sniffs it. 'Jew!' he says, crushing it with his boot, to which many people in the audience laugh.

In conversation after the production, members of the company are unwilling to accept that there is anti-semitism in the play, saying that it simply offers a truthful portrayal of the position of Jews as middlemen in Ukrainian society at that time and that this should be understood in its context. Nevertheless, when I ask one of the actors if there are any Jews working at the theatre, I'm told that there aren't and that if there were, they wouldn't admit to being Jewish. The Ternopil Theatre aspires to take its work abroad. This production could sit comfortably in the programme of any International Theatre Festival in Western Europe, but for its derisory attitude towards Jews.

19: Mykola

Sweet, stewed coffee poured with a ladle and a sweet bread bun. The *Staro Misti* of Ternopil, the Old Town. The hospitality is overwhelming at the nightly receptions of the Ternopil Vodka Festival, sorry *Theatre* Festival. Toasting into the small hours. *Kielbasa*, smoked salmon, pickled cauliflower, roast chicken, cucumbers, tomatoes and peppers, all to absorb the alcohol, water and beer to dilute it!

I met Roman, standing in for Sasha, our usual interpreter. Roman has a Canadian wife. He lived and worked there, legally, for nearly three years before they threw him out. His lawyers said he'd be back within three months. That was nearly two years ago. The Canadian authorities demand proof that his marriage is genuine, not a convenience to enable him to gain citizenship. How can they prove they love each other when they are forced apart? Repeated applications? $800 spent on phone calls in a few months? A baby?

Roman won't make his wife pregnant when he doesn't know if he'll be there to support her and he doesn't want his child brought up here in Ukraine, which is riddled with corruption and where healthcare, education and other public services are poor. He told me of a friend whose baby had a haematoma.

He had no money and the doctor refused to operate until he found some cash. It's a straightforward operation. In the end, Roman's friend told the doctor 'I love my child and you love yours. If my child dies, one of yours will too.' The doctor performed the operation immediately.

Roman works in a sauna. He and six or seven of his friends and acquaintances, all in their mid- to late-20s, hire the place for two hours every Saturday morning. Today is Saturday, so I go with him, fuzzy from too much alcohol and too little sleep. It's a brand new private facility, run by another friend. It's well appointed and clean, but expensive for ordinary people. It might function as a knocking shop, though I saw no signs of that. There are a couple of his old schoolmates here. Roman was once a wrestler and the others he met through wrestling.

We sit in the steam room and slap our bodies with bunches of birch and oak twigs, use the plunge pool and the showers and sit in the lounge, watching Champions League highlights (in English), drinking beer and herbal tea, smoking and chatting. England, Scotland, football, politics, gangsters. I ask if there are a lot of gangsters here. They laugh. One of the group, a small, dark-eyed, garrulous joker, gestures towards himself and a couple of his friends. 'Yes, you're looking at some!' Everyone laughs. When we leave, Roman tells me that the joke is, in fact, the truth. The joker and his two friends are part of a gang which runs a protection racket.

We walk back to the hotel where I expect to meet Bogdan, but I've missed him. A chambermaid tells me he's been twice. He's left a plastic bag containing three huge red apples for me. I wait for an hour. No sign, so I take a taxi to a large 1970s apartment block on the edge of town, the home of Mykola and Xenia. While Xenia busies herself, putting the final touches to lunch, eager to please me and short of breath, I sit with Mykola. He is dignified and quiet, full of good humour, happy to welcome me. He is also partially deaf, blind in one eye and showing signs of frailty, but he retains an upright posture and a very firm handshake. The living room walls are draped in tapestries, flower patterns and geometric peasant designs, all made by Xenia, family photographs and two of their favourite politicians, the nationalists Julia Tymoshenko and Viktor Yushchenko. A young man enters the flat, Marion the downstairs neighbour, a joiner who has a little English. We talk.

Mykola and Xenia Baldys, Ternopil 2003

Marion's English is really very limited, not much better than my Ukrainian. Mykola shows me a tome which details histories of all the villages in the *oblast*. A few pages cover my father's village, Gnilowody, a name which translates as Rotten Water, 8km from Podhajce. After the war, the Soviets renamed it Hvardiskoye, which means 'garrison town,' due to the fact that soldiers were stationed there at the time. It has since reverted to its original name. He and Xenia name my father's family, his mother Zofia, who was Mykola's aunt, his father Andrzej, and Kazik, Adam and Emilia, his brothers and sister.

Zofia, like Mykola and Bogdan, was born in the neighbouring village of Mozoliwka. Emilia had married Pavlo Tischaniuk, a Ukrainian farmer. They had a son, Teodosiy.

Then we talk about the war. Mykola presents me with a sheet of A4 paper, detailing what he knows. With Marion, he then tries to explain what it says. They slowly reveal a very different story to the one my father told me, a story which stuns me.

According to Mykola, my father was never in the Polish Army. He trained as a tailor, first in Mozoliwka, then in Podhajce, until 1940.

'Then he was drafted into the Soviet Army.'

'The Soviet Army? You're telling me that my father was in the Soviet Army?'

'Yes.'

Mykola looks to Marion for further translation. 'In army of General Vlasov, commander.'

Mykola turns to look intently at me with his piercing blue eyes.

'Vlasov?'

'*Tak*. In Vlasov Army, Russian Army.'

'My father was in General Vlasov's Russian Army?'

'*Tak, i Vlasov do Polsci i Niemcem.*' He looks to Marion. 'Er, Vlasov, to...Poland, Germany.'

'Right, Vlasov...how do you mean Poland and Germany?'

Marion doesn't answer. He is busily trying to translate the next sentence on Mykola's testament. 'Er....1944, August 1944, Soviet front River Strypa.'

'*Piat kilometr Hnilowody.*'

'Five kilometre from Gnilowody.'

'Uh-huh...River Strypa.'

'Your father in Germany in 1944.'

'What, he was in Germany in 1944?' I'm reeling.

'Yes, and then in August on front on River Strypa.'

'Was he a prisoner?' I still can't absorb what they are telling me.

'*Ostarbeiter*.' The name given by the Germans to forced labourers from the Soviet Union. 'Then on the front'.

'*Gorace kartoffle*! The potatoes are hot!' Xenia's intervention brings an abrupt halt to our progress.

'I met your mother in Poland. She was very delicate and slim, and beautiful. Is she still?'

'Yes, now not so slim.'

'Your father and his brother liked a drink. Your mother is the same age as me. Anyway, the potatoes are hot! Time to eat.'

The afternoon continues as we turn to the delicious food and drink. We laugh and joke about our few shared memories of family and, by going over Mykola's statement, I absorb the essentials. My father was drafted into the Soviet Army under Vlasov, was captured by the Germans, worked as a forced labourer in Germany, then fought for the Germans from summer 1944 here in Ukraine and during the German retreat. Vlasov is famous for being a turncoat, the highest ranking Soviet Officer to change sides. He surrendered his army to the Germans near Leningrad in 1941 and towards the end of the war led some of it against the Soviets, retreating all the way to Czechoslovakia. According to Mykola, my father was in a German Army unit which paused for a few weeks near Gnilowody, on the Strypa River, and my father managed to visit his family then, late at night. It was a very dangerous time. Mykola's statement finally declares that this story was related to him by the man himself, by my father, when Mykola and Xenia met my parents in Poland in 1982.

If this is true, and I can't think Mykola would have any reason to lie to me, then my father's story is a complete fabrication. He told me that he had escaped from the Soviet Union through Stalin's amnesty for Polish prisoners of war. Over

100,000 Polish soldiers escaped this way, along with around 30,000 Polish women and children, sailing across the Caspian Sea to Tehran. The soldiers were led by the Polish General Anders and became known as 'Anders Army'. Could my father have simply absorbed the facts of Anders Army and then imaginatively adopted that army's story as his own?

And if he had done this, what did he really do in the war?

If Mykola doesn't have a motive for lying, my father did: fear. In Britain, Poles who fought on the German side kept quiet about it. They had been on the losing side and were afraid of being perceived and persecuted as Nazis or Nazi sympathisers. As tension between the western powers and the Soviet Union grew to hostility in the years following the war, membership of the Red Army could also have been viewed with suspicion. One of the myriad brutalities of World War Two was that the vast majority of soldiers in my father's position had little choice but to do as they were ordered. The alternative was almost certain execution, either summarily or drawn out through the starved, frozen labour of the Soviet *Gulag* or the German *lager*.

But to have lived for decades with the pretence that he fought in the Polish Army and latterly the British Army, to have immersed himself in it to the extent that he could describe the journey in detail over a couple of hours, to deceive his own children and maintain the pretence with friends and acquaintances, customers and colleagues, takes determination and discipline. But then, as I reflect, there are a number of sketchy aspects to his story.

He was always vague about where the Russians took him to work; there's actually very little detail about the journey to Egypt and the period he claimed to have spent in North Africa. But there is a lot about Italy, especially about his girlfriend there and her father. Didn't he speak Italian? Yes, he did. What exactly happened to Vlasov's Army when it was captured by the Allies in 1945? Could it be that non-Russians in that army were taken west by the British and put to work in the Italian occupation? I recalled my chance encounter with the Ukrainian Paul Batyr as he was cutting his lawn in Lochend in Edinburgh. After his surrender, he was sent to work in Italy.

As I try to absorb Mykola's revelations, he produces a book about the Ukrainian Partisan Army's history during the war. I'm unaware of the existence of such an army, but quickly understand that it was established to fight for Ukrainian independence. I realise that there has to be a lot more to it than that and curse my ignorance. The book contains photographs of smiling bands of soldiers posing in front of their forest hideouts or on the march, leading horses with machine guns strapped to their backs. Mykola turns to pages which list the names of the dead and points to one of them. '*Tvoy kuzyn*. Your cousin.' There on the page is Teodosiy's name, killed by the Russians in 1944 at the age of 17 for his membership of the UPA.

I leave their house in a daze, full of good food and home-made vodka. Mykola accompanies me to a bus stop and sees me on to a packed minibus, telling the driver where I'm going. He waves me off with a smile and for a moment I wonder what his own war story was, but only for a moment. I'm upset, baffled, moved and angry. Why didn't dad tell me at least? Was he so afraid that he distrusted his own son? Did he think I'd condemn him, or was he driven by guilt? What horrors had he been witness to, or even been a party to? Now, I couldn't exclude even the worst possibilities. Now, there was a void in his history: those awful years of 1940-45. And that void could be filled with any number experiences endured by those unfortunate enough to be in the eye of the storm, in Central and Eastern Europe. Settling in a foreign country at the end of the war gave him the opportunity to wipe the slate clean, to go back to Year Zero, and that's what he did.

He lived quietly and worked hard, putting everything into his new life and his family, looking after us with a great deal of love and humour. Only from time to time, when *All Our Yesterdays*, or *The World At War* or other evocations of the war were on TV, would I catch him wiping away a tear or, in the dead of night, when I'd hear him, muffled through the thin wall between our bedrooms, half-awake and restless or talking anxiously in his sleep, were hints of the turmoil and the shock of his war revealed to me. These thoughts race through my head as the minibus speeds through the streets of Ternopil, eventually depositing me in the city centre. I make my way once more to the theatre.

The show is *The Lady with the Little Dog* by Anton Chekhov presented by Theatre Atsurko na Zdorovska. This is another fine two-handed production for a man and a woman, an adaptation of one of Chekhov's most famous short stories. It tells of an affair between Gurov, a rich, married womaniser and Anna Sergeyevna, a newly-married young woman. Both are unhappy with their marriages. Despite her shame and his self-loathing, they come to understand that they have truly fallen in love with each other and that 'the most complicated and difficult part was only just beginning.'

The short, simple production had a cumulative power as the characters' desire for each other and the strictures of their society reached a level of unbearable tension. This was acting of the highest order, both actors completely in tune with each other's rhythm and pitch, giving the production the quality of a complex musical duet.

After a short break, I'm back in the Schevchenko Theatre for *Love & Intrigue* by Freidrich Schiller, presented by the Ivano-Frankivsk Theatre, one of Schiller's great *cris-de-coeur* for the right of the individual to live his own life, free from the constraints of arbitrary authority. But the quality of the production doesn't meet the demands of the play, and my thoughts return to Mykola's testimony and those vexing new questions.

Afterwards, I attend a more subdued celebration than those of the previous evenings. The members of the Ivano-Frankivsk Theatre are quiet. Only three of them have turned up, clearly unhappy with their production and its reception. Two of them are a couple with a little boy, so have to leave early. The party breaks up quickly and I'm happy to hit the sack, exhausted, amazed by the day's revelations, anticipating the discoveries which tomorrow will bring.

20: Pidhaitsi

I wake up and decide to go for a run. It's a beautiful, crisp Sunday morning and I could do with a sweat. I jog out of the hotel along a paved walkway and on to the promenade by the lake. Men and boys of all ages lean over the iron rail and fish. There's a haze over the water. Back in the hotel, I shower, get dressed and walk out into the square in front of the hotel. A wedding party is having a photo session in front of the statue of Halitsky on his rearing horse, the groom in a pale green suit, the bride in white. Forty metres away, there's another wedding party doing the same thing and through the trees by the road, another appears to be readying itself for photos. People mill about the cathedral entrance.

Inside, there's a kind of ordered chaos. Another wedding ceremony is underway. People who are clearly not guests watch, while others are occupied with their own private prayers in groups to the right and left. A small queue has formed in front of a statue of the Virgin Mary, each person in turn murmuring a devotion, making the sign of the cross and kissing the statue's feet. More leave and others arrive. Another wedding party waits its turn. Coloured light streams through the stained glass windows and I gaze up at the domed ceiling, covered in a vivid painting of a firmament populated by saints, angels and the Lord himself.

I eat another lunch in the Café Europe and wander towards the theatre, keeping to the tourist beat. A large crowd is forming, some holding flags, and a PA system has been set up on the theatre steps. This is the beginning of a nationalist rally, a protest against any moves towards reunification with Russia and against corruption within the government. There are many Ukrainian flags, the Ukrainian Youth Association, a group of bemedalled army veterans, some in their 80s, and a mobile radio van. Many people are strolling about in their Sunday best, feeding pigeons but there to lend their support. The Ukrainian anthem blares out and a speech begins, calling for democracy and the impeachment of President Kuczma. The speaker describes him as a Russian stooge, and that Ukraine is in danger of going down the road of neighbouring Belarus, now ruled by the proto-Soviet authoritarian Lukashenko. I wander among the crowd of around 3,000 to the back of the gathering, where temporary hoardings have been erected. They bear articles, slogans and posters. One of the posters shows a cartoon, a giant boot kicking the backside of a caricatured Rabbi, the sort of thing you would have found in Nazi Germany.

In the evening, the theatre festival concludes with an awards ceremony which features performances by well-known Ukrainian opera singers accompanied by the Ternopil orchestra and an energetic young dance troupe. Most of the participating companies receive awards; there is a high degree of mutual respect which has already been much in evidence at the nightly receptions. With money very tight here, the festival is a notable achievement. Most members of visiting companies could only stay for one night or even had to head home immediately after their performance. I have been treated with great hospitality and warmth. There is a genuine curiosity about my work and my own Polish and Ukrainian background.

After the closing toasts at the final festival reception, I retire with my colleagues from Liverpool and a couple of Ukrainian friends to our hotel to prolong the party for a while. Not long after we've settled down in one of our rooms, I answer the phone. A woman's voice, in English:

'Good evening. Would you like me and my friends to join you? We could drink tea together.'

'Er...that's very nice of you to ask, but we're very tired, so, er, no thanks.'

'Oh, that's a shame. Are you sure?'

'Yes, thanks for calling. Good night.'

'Good night'.

I guess they're looking for a different kind of cultural connection. 'Drinking tea' is it. Quite witty, really.

Bleary eyed, I check out of the hotel at 11.00am, looking for Xenia in the foyer. I'd arranged to meet her there as she wanted to make sure I got safely on to the Podhajce bus. There's no sign of her, so I make my way out on to the wide pavement and find her waiting there. A woman comes through the hotel doors just behind me. By a series of nods and winks and the few Ukrainain and Polish words we can muster in common, Xenia asks me if I've spent the night with the woman. She is quite forthright about it.

'You and her...' (pointing)

'Uh-huh?' (pointing up at the hotel)

'Sleep with her? And....mm-mm-mm?'

Initially, I'm quite lost for words. I've never been asked such a question by anyone, let alone a 75-year-old woman I barely know. Then I let out a little nervous laugh, and assure her that I haven't mm-mm-mmed.

'Ah... no, not at all!'

She is delighted and relieved. She opens out her arms towards me and says, 'Lovely boy!' Then, confidentially, 'The going rate is $30, you know.'

When I visit her, the following Thursday, I discover that her own daughter, who she hasn't seen for 15 years, had gone into prostitution, leaving Xenia a granddaughter to look after. 'My daughter sticks like a bone in my throat,' she tells me.

We catch a bus to the bus station, where Mykola is waiting for us, and sit for half an hour in front of stalls selling doughnuts, fruit and household goods until my next bus arrives. Mykola gives me a carrier bag full of sandwiches and little cucumbers, the first for my journey, the second a gift for Bogdan and Hala. They lead me through the milling terminal and its exhaust fumes to the bus, a 16-seater, making sure the driver knows where I'm going. It fills within ten minutes, mainly women passengers laden with shopping from the nearby market. Xenia and Mykola stand stoically smiling by my window until the bus finally moves off, then they wave.

I'm relieved to be on my way to Podhajce at last, free from the enjoyable, relentless diversion of the theatre festival. We bump along, past fields and woods, horse-drawn carts and gaggles of geese, stopping at villages and hamlets and at the head of dirt tracks which lead to other villages and hamlets. The land looks fertile and forlorn, with much of it fallow.

The 45km journey takes 90 minutes. We pass a lake and the rolls of the landscape become more pronounced, almost hilly. Then we dip down into a valley, cross the Strypa river, where the front had halted all those years and tears ago and enter Podhajce. The bus stops at a neglected shell of a station and I get off with the remaining passengers to find Bogdan waiting. He takes my hand and gives me a hug and a little grim smile. He doesn't smile much, a bit more when he's drinking. We walk up a hill along a lane which had been laid with tarmac perhaps 25 years before, but which is now rutted and potholed, to the main street. The place is very quiet. Bogdan greets the few passers-by, who are clearly curious about me. We pass a large yellow church which looks across the valley, turn down another little lane and arrive through a gate in a picket fence. Across the yard, through another fence, hens peck and scrape. Bogdan's house is in front of us, with concrete steps leading up to the door. Another house lies close to the left and in its doorway sits an old lady. Bogdan introduces me to her.

This is Wlodzmierza, his 92-year-old Polish neighbour, who looks 20 years younger. She has a generous, long face with high cheekbones and dark brown hair with few signs of grey. At 92, surely it's dyed! I dally for a moment after greeting her and she smiles warmly. Bogdan ushers me into the house with a hint of impatience, leading me through a conservatory into a series of rooms, first the little dining room, then a lounge and finally, through double glass doors, a second lounge, which is to be my room. A folding bed settee has been made up.

Houseplants taller than me stand on either side of a table covered in a lace cloth. Soft, misty light streams through the long net curtains. An old black and white TV stands on a sideboard, and above it hangs a picture of a traditional rural idyll: two young peasant couples canoodling by a stream. Cross-stitch tapestries are hung on the walls and a large carved stag sits on top of a tall, glass-fronted cabinet full of crystal bowls and glasses. Bogdan calls me back into the dining room and opens an adjoining door to reveal the bathroom. He demonstrates the fact that the cistern isn't operational and shows me a little bucket for flushing water down the toilet after use.

Hala, Bogdan's wife, arrives home, accompanied by Tania, their daughter, who's about ten years younger than me. Hala is full of welcoming smiles, a robust, tanned wee woman who gets busy with the lunch preparations. Tania is only stopping by to meet me before heading back to the pharmacy where she's working. I'm somewhat relieved to listen to Hala's unselfconscious chatting, the perfect foil to the taciturn Bogdan, as she quizzes me about my stay so far and my family, not worrying too much that I understand only about 20% of what she is saying to me. I busily search for words in my phrasebook, which I use constantly throughout my visit. Hala has been busy in the kitchen before my arrival and soon we sit down to delicious Ukrainian borscht, *vareniki*, sausage, ham and various salads and pickles. And, of course, *horilka*. After the boozy theatre festival, my stay in Pidhaitsi (the Ukrainian name for Podhajce) is to continue in a similar vein. I learn quickly from Hala that Bogdan is supposed to be curtailing his vodka intake for health reasons. He is clearly a tippler, though, and he uses my stay as the perfect excuse for daily celebration. The *horilka* is produced at breakfast, lunch and dinner: one or two at breakfast, one or two at lunch and quite a bit more in the evenings, always accompanied by food.

After lunch, Bogdan indicates that he wants to take me for a walk. We stroll through the town's main drag, past the colourful Ukrainian Orthodox church and the impressive, newly built Greek Catholic church. It's quiet, with a few women walking by carrying shopping bags and several groups of idle men smoking and chatting. Bogdan exchanges brief greetings with everyone we pass. I am gazed at.

For most of the '70s and '80s, Bogdan had been the town's head man, the Party Secretary. He appears to have retained a significant degree of respect. We walk on up a hill, past a large stone bust of Shevchenko set in a little garden by a gable end on which is painted a mural of the poet of the nation as a *kobzar*, an itinerant Ukrainian bard who sang and played the *kobza*, the traditional stringed instrument which has the same significance in Ukraine as a symbol of national identity as bagpipes do in Scotland.

Eventually we come to a large cemetery. Bogdan leads me through a forest of gravestones and stone and metal crosses, many of the latter painted blue and white. The more modern gravestones display oval ceramic photographic images of the deceased. He stops at a gravestone and tells me that an uncle and aunt of his are buried here, a great uncle and aunt of mine, my grandmother's sister and her husband, whose name was Ovshanetski. Their son has ended up in New York State. We walk on through the cemetery and downhill again along a rough road with large houses on either side. At the foot of the road there is a fence and a statue of Lesia Ukrainska, another national poet and heroine.

Behind the fence lies Pidhaitsi's Jewish cemetery.

This cemetery is untended, a large rectangular field of many grey, weathered headstones and large spaces where only long stone stumps remain. A few cows are grazing in a corner, tended by a wizened *babcha* who sits on one of the stones clutching a willow branch and watching us. It looks like the grazing is what keeps the grass short here. The headstones lean at different, crazy angles, some lie flat on the ground, a few remain upright, many have been removed, leaving only the stumps.

I imagine the malicious chaos of hatred which produced this jumble of desolation and desecration and see how it clearly ran out of energy. Somehow, this cemetery still exists. After all the destruction and the murder, this exhausted town has left these stones alone for nearly 60 years. Little has been done by way of restoration or care, but by the same token, when the destruction finally stopped, the cemetery was left in peace. The dates on the stones go right up to 1939, a few even beyond that, 1940, 1941. That is the latest date I find.

It's taking me some time to get used to the fact that although the Russian occupation began in autumn 1939, the full-scale war in this part of the world started in '41. Such vast death and destruction occurred over just four years. Four truly apocalyptic years. Later, I discovered that the Pidhaitsi Jews, the great majority of the town's population, and those Jews from the surrounding villages, had been forced into a ghetto in a small part of the town in 1941. Those who survived it were murdered by the Nazis in 1943. They were marched out of town to a spot just over the brow of the hill opposite, just out of sight, and there shot in the head, falling into the pit which had been dug for them. Around 60 out of a Jewish population of over 3,500 survived the war.

Before the war, in the early evening, the young people provided Pidhaitsi with an unstaged show on the 'Corso,' as the pavement surrounding the marketplace was called. It was full of groups of boys and girls in an informal parade of courtship, a non-stop fashion show with young couples walking hand-in-hand. Because of this show, some people called Pidhaitsi the 'Paris of Galicia'.

After the war, some of the stones used to repair the Corso were the tombstones of Jews, taken from the Jewish cemetery.

This was the reason for the stumps.

Bogdan leads me to a far corner of the cemetery. Here, there are a couple of mounds, possibly the site of a mass grave, flanking a modern memorial stone. An inscription in Hebrew and Ukrainian or Russian reads:

'For our parents, children, brethren and sisters,
the saints of our town, who perished
during the Holocaust by the Nazi oppressor.
May God revenge their blood.
Earth, do not cover their blood.'
The Community of Pidhaitsi 1941-43

We walk on down the hill and come upon a huge ruin next to a dilapidated metal sign which rustily proclaims that a market had once been held here. The ruin was the town's main synagogue, its sheer size, along with that of the cemetery, a

Jewish Cemetery, Pidhaitsi 2003

testament to the size of Pidhaitsi's exterminated Jewish population and the significance of Jewish culture to this region. Two decaying, monumental memorials to the death of a people, in the heart of a living town. I wonder whether the quiet, subdued atmosphere of the place is influenced by their presence, if the overwhelming brutality of the war years, coupled with decades of Soviet repression and the subsequent post-communist capitalist economic shock treatment, have left Pidhaitsi in a state of collective concussion.

Further down the hill, Bogdan leads me to a third such memorial, another mighty ruin, the former Polish Catholic church. I had seen it as the bus entered the town, a ghostly sentinel from the past greeting Pidhaitsi's visitors from Ternopil. Like the synagogue, this is a crumbling shell, left alone to preach its silent commentary on the history of this place, testifying that once, Poles lived here.

Our walk is a sobering introduction to Pidhaitsi, something which Bogdan clearly felt compelled to give me. It firmly places my visit in its context: the war and its consequences, the effect

Polish Catholic Church, Pidhaitsi 2003

of the past upon the present. Without a common language, Bogdan has eloquently explained through this walk exactly where I am and the burden of history which the town's inhabitants live with every day.

The old Polish woman Wlodzimierza is sitting on her porch when we return. I sit with her for a while. She is one of only five Poles who stayed in Pidhaitsi after the Polish population was deported west by the Soviets early in 1945, to Silesia and Pomerania, from the land the Poles forfeited to the Soviets to the land forfeited by the Germans to the Poles. Wlodzimierza and her mother couldn't bear the prospect of leaving their home. They had always had good neighbours, and despite some intimidation during the immediate post-war years, her life in the town has been tolerable. She shows me an old book about the region and turns to pages about Pidhaitsi. It displays a statistical table from 1900: 600 houses, population 5,646 comprising 760 Poles, 1,007 Ukrainians and 3,879 Jews.

Wlodzimierza had a brother, now dead, who settled in South

Wales after the war, working in the pits. He had been in the Polish army. Like my uncle Kazik, he had escaped the German and Soviet armies in 1939 to make his way to Britain. She had visited him once, in the late '80s during the Gorbachev thaw, and shows me photographs of their happy reunion. I think he suggested that she stay with him in Wales, but she preferred to return home, where she endured.

Filled with anticipation at the prospect of tomorrow's visit to Gnilowody, I can't sleep as I lie in my bed at Bogdan and Hala's. Dogs howl to each other across the village. They seem to give ghostly voice to the town's pain, to the dead of Pidhaitsi, a chorus of wild heralds calling from the darkness.

21: You've Come Back

Next morning, at around 11.00am, Tania's husband Taras turns up in his slightly battered Lada Niva. A slim, swarthy, handsome man, he is to be our driver for the day, which is overcast, but dry. We are going to Gnilowody, my father's birthplace. After all the years of thinking about this place, of creating pictures of it in my mind, of hesitation and procrastination over this visit and that great majority of my life when I hadn't thought about it at all, the hour has finally arrived. Will it be an anti-climax? Will we find anyone there who knew my father and his family, or will I simply meet a succession of blank, disinterested, or even resentful faces? Lesia assured me that I would be 'satisfied' by my visit, but neither she nor Bogdan had made any indication as to how.

By the time we drink coffee, smoke cigarettes and fetch Lesia from her house, its noon. Bogdan and Hala come too. It's a tight squeeze in the Niva. Throughout this day, I juggle with a stills camera, a video camera, a tape recorder and a microphone. We drive past the Polish church and turn right up a hill out of town, heading south east. Lesia prepares me.

'Once it was a very big village, a very progressive village. But now there are only old people and drunkards. All the rest went to cities.' After a few kilometres, we turn left on to a dirt track. The going is slow and bumpy, through the fields, but we don't have far to go, just three kilometres. We lurch down a little valley between sloping fields and round a bend. The trees and houses of Gnilowody appear, spread out on either side of a stream and the stagnant ponds which give the village its name, Rotten Water. Geese and ducks hurry away as we approach. Cows and a few horses graze among the little haystacks. Some of the inhabitants watch as we pass, mainly scarved *babchas* and their husbands, lifting themselves from their tasks.

We stop outside a neat, whitewashed house. A dark-eyed old woman in a white scarf, thick skirt, cardigan and Wellington boots comes out to greet us, accompanied by a rosy-cheeked younger woman with short hair who wears black jeans and a sweater. Bogdan takes charge, having clearly arranged this meeting. The old woman is named Tekla. A few years after my aunt Emilia (Milanja) died, at the age of 55 in 1961, her husband Pavlo took Tekla as his second wife. The younger woman is their daughter Milanja, named after my aunt. She explains that she was given my aunt's name to honour her memory. She has travelled from Ternopil for the day and is to be our guide.

Tekla chats away, adding her own warm comments about Aunt Emilia as she and Milanja lead us into the house. They have prepared for our visit and get busy with carrying plates of delicious food into the living room where I'm urged to sit. I can't, the room is far too interesting. It's decorated in the classic Ukrainian rural style, whitewashed, with religious and family pictures adorned with patterned cloths. There is my aunt and her husband in a treated, black and white photographic portrait from around 1930, a strikingly handsome couple looking at the camera. My aunt's face and expression are particularly arresting. She is very serious, almost grim-faced, with strong features: dark hair and eyes; dark, arched eyebrows; a square wide jawline and full Cupid's-bow lips. Pavlo is also serious, but more boyish, with a look in his eyes which doesn't seem to be quite so sure or steadfast.

There is also a large portrait of my cousin, Teodosiy, which must have been made not long before his death in 1944. This one is in colour. His eyes and mouth are similar to Milanja's, though his face is rounder like his father's. He wears a dark blue coat and a green scarf. Tekla explains that when the Russians re-occupied the village in 1944, Teodosiy had been accused of helping the UPA and betraying Poles. She said that he had run away and hid in a bunker. A Russian soldier threw a grenade in after him.

Aunt Emilia and Uncle Pavlo c. 1930

Betraying Poles. As we eat and drink Tekla's vodka, and having listened to Mykola in Ternopil, I'm beginning to understand that there had been a war within a war in this region, between Poles and Ukrainians. You had to take sides, to declare yourself, or keep as quiet as you could to avoid the terror.

Teodosiy c. 1941

You needed the help of your friends and your community. Many communities were mixed, with villages of Ukrainians and Poles or Jews, while others were dominated by one ethnic group or sometimes exclusively Jewish, Ukrainian or Polish. It was similar to the situation in former Yugoslavia. Ukrainians, Poles and Jews had lived side by side in this region for centuries, while the inter-war Polish government, intent on asserting its rule here, had created new Polish settlements.

Gnilowody's Poles were in the former category. It had been a village of Poles and Ukrainians and according to my father there had been only one Jewish family. Mozolivka, my grandmother's birthplace was predominantly Ukrainian. Even though I had understood for some time now that Bogdan and Mykola were Ukrainians, that all of their family was Ukrainian, I was only beginning to come to terms with the fact that (of course, you fool) my grandmother was Ukrainian. My father had never mentioned it. He did tell me that she followed the Orthodox church, so really I should have put two and two together, but he was so firmly Polish. I had lived all my life with my Polishness. He had barely mentioned Ukrainians. On the few occasions when Ukrainians were discussed in our house, it was usually to associate them with the role of some Ukrainians as brutal guards at Auschwitz, as Nazi collaborators. I was now only beginning to understand that my father's denial of his mother's nationality went deeper, that it must have been related to what had happened here in Galicia during the war, to the conflict between the Ukrainians and the Poles.

My grandfather was a Pole married to a Ukrainian. Galicia, and Volhynia to the north, were full of such mixed marriages. Lesia explained that then, in a mixed Polish-Ukrainian family like mine, the sons were registered as Poles, the daughters as Ukrainian. So Aunt Emilia was a Ukrainian.

Through Lesia, I relate Mykola's testimony to Tekla and Emilia. Can Tekla shed any light on it? She explains that she had never met my father and his brothers, though of course she had known my grandmother, Zofia, and Emilia. Yes, she knew about Mateusz being in the Soviet Army.

We finish our lunch and Milanja ushers us out. A few of the neighbours appear and explanations are made about who I am. This generates a degree of excitement and animated conversations ensue all around me as two of the old ladies recall the Zajac family and the first of many fond and respectful memories of my grandmother are described to me.

'After the war, she lived with Milanja and Pavlo. She was very sad because her husband had died and her sons were away to the west. But she was a very kind woman. She was very religious, she always carried her rosary. After her daughter died, she lived alone and then she took in the local priest as a lodger. Everyone in the village respected her a great deal.'

Tekla and the other *babchas* study my features. One of them, rotund and laughing, puts her hand to my cheek and holds my shoulder, exclaiming her recognition, that she could see that I was a Zajac. 'They were all good-looking boys like you!'

I smile, gulp and catch my breath. She has a tear in her eye and seems delighted at the same time. So many years ago. That family. I hear mention of Kazik and Adam and explanations of where they had migrated to. They ask me if any of the brothers are still alive. Tekla and another old lady discuss Adam's visits to Gnilowody over 30 years previously as if they had been last week. A horse and cart trundle past. I understand that I am standing in a rare place in Europe, a place where peasants still exist, where many basic aspects of life on the land have remained unchanged for centuries and where the concept of time and place is quite different. And I am being welcomed as one of theirs. It doesn't matter that I have never set foot in the place, that I have only set foot in Ukraine a week earlier, I am one of theirs. My Polishness seems to be an irrelevance, or perhaps that is ameliorated by my Ukrainianness, my Ukrainian grandmother. As these thoughts are racing through my mind, I let them go. It doesn't matter. What matters is what is happening here and now, in front of me. I can reflect on it later.

Milanja leads us away from this little crowd. One or two of the neighbours decide to accompany us. Our visit is clearly something of an event. Lesia sticks by my side, assiduously translating as we walk through the village. Taras remains a little apart from us, watching and listening. I'm eagerly trying to absorb every moment: the images and sounds of the village, the new people, the words which are pouring from them. I am also trying to exploit my technical aids, switching from the video camera to the tape recorder to the stills camera as I converse in my rudimentary Ukrainian/Polish and in English. My head is spinning.

We turn up a sloping track which leads to an avenue of silver birch trees at the back of the village. The cemetery lies at the end of the avenue and we follow Milanja through the gate. Most of the graves are lying to the right. Other, older ones are scattered haphazardly to the left. We arrive at a grave with a rectangular stone border. At its head lies a rough stone plinth topped with a cross. It is about 2 metres in height and has been freshly painted silver by Milanja, before Easter. Sprucing up graves at Easter is a tradition here. There is no inscription. 'This is your grandmother's grave.'

I stand for a few quiet moments, thinking of Zofia, alone in her final years. The absence of an inscription seems to emphasise this for me, though it puzzles me. A wave of sadness heaves through me. My visit suddenly feels futile, 40 years too late. I should have known her when I was a child. And I feel anger, anger at being denied that knowledge by a cold ideology, by the triumph of fear. I don't cry, though I come close. This anonymous grave is all that's left of her here. Zofia Zajac, my fairytale granny, who once really did exist.

I photograph Zofia's grave and resolve to pay for an inscription on the stone. Milanja leads us to Emilia's grave. This one has an inscription carved into an inlaid blue heart, in Ukrainian, with a blue painted angel at its head. Emilia had died of heart disease. I recalled my parents had told me of a letter they had received from Emilia, around the time of my birth, 1959. In it, she explained her illness and requested that they send drugs for her which they couldn't get in the Soviet Union. Of course, they sent them. About three months later, they were returned by the Soviet authorities with the explanation that the Soviet medical services had no need of drugs from the west, that theirs were more than a match for anything to be found in Britain.

'Where's Andrzej's grave, my grandfather's grave? *Gdzie jest dzadzki grob?*'

Lesia repeats the question in Ukrainian. Milanja looks at Bogdan. She doesn't know. Neither does anyone else. They discuss the issue.

'Isn't it here?' Lesia points vaguely towards the area at the other end of the cemetery where there are only a few graves and patches of clear grass. 'No one is sure, but they say it might be over there. Your grandfather died just after the war when people had very little, so maybe his grave is not marked. It could be somewhere else.' 'Where?' 'They don't know.' I frown. This doesn't seem to make sense.

I was told by my father that my grandfather had died in 1947 or 1948, though I didn't know the cause. There certainly would have been a great deal of hardship at that time. Collectivisation had been imposed on the community. The farmers had been dispossessed of their land. Our farm had been the largest in Gnilowody. Andrzej had been an influential man in the village. I couldn't understand why no one knew where he was buried, or why some kind of headstone or cross hadn't been erected after his death when times were better. By the end of the day, I began to understand a little more. I take a photograph of the vacant patch of the cemetery where Andrzej's remains possibly lie and we walk on.

The houses of Gnilowody are spread over an area of roughly one kilometre by 500 metres, bisected by the stream and its ponds. The houses lie on natural terraces above the waters. They are square and usually single-storeyed, with typically blue paintwork, sometimes with stencilled decorative patterns around windows and cornerstones. It is a fertile place, teeming with ducks, geese and hens, fruit trees and vegetable gardens. We walk down from the cemetery and stop outside one of the houses. 'This is where your family lived. Their house isn't here any more. This one was built maybe 30 years ago.'

I look at the replacement and try to see its predecessor. I only find the deep sense of absence which had first gripped me in the cemetery. I feel as if I am trying to pull myself out of a vacuum. I look across to the other side of the water, at the view my father would have seen every day when he looked out of his front window, at the places where he would have jumped across the stream and played, at the trees by the nearby pond. I imagine him running about in his shirt and shorts on a warm summer's day with Kazik and wee Adam trying to keep up, breaking branches to make fishing rods or bows and arrows, tormenting the fowl, throwing stones at a floating target. I remember his stories of making dominoes and explosions, of the village idiot and Wawolka the storyteller spae wife. Once upon a time those stories were real, they lived here.

Milanja has been told by her mother that there are a couple of old women in the village who knew my father's family quite well. As she leads us through the village, she makes enquiries of the older men and women we meet as she isn't sure exactly who or where these old women are. Eventually, we arrive on the other side of the water at the house of one of them, Olga Kindzierska. Her husband comes out to talk to us, a boyish, rosy-cheeked old man whose mind is wandering a little. He is friendly, but his memory has gone. He ushers us towards the house and we walk into the muddy yard, scattering the chickens. A lean-to protects a large stack of hay from the rain. He calls for Olga at the door and she comes out of the house.

She is a thin, gentle old peasant lady with delicate features. Quite beautiful. Her face is tanned and weather-beaten, with high cheekbones and forehead, a small mouth, an aquiline nose and clear, pale blue eyes. Her hands tell of a lifetime of work on the land. Her voice is high-pitched and soft. Born in 1925, she is 77 years old and has all her wits about her. At once, an animated conversation takes place. I switch on my tape recorder.

'The Zajac family? Which Zajac family? Ah-ha, yes, of course I remember them. And this is Kazik's son? No, Mateusz's son, I see. From Scotland? Mateusz lived there after the war? Ah-ha. And Kazik did too?' She looks at me with wonderment, smiling, remembering her youth. 'You look like your father, I can see it. He was very handsome! And you've come back.'

I've come back, to a place I've never been to before.

22: Olga

Olga Kindzierska 2003

Then she starts talking as if her childhood recollections are of recent events, which, in the minds of the old, is what they can seem like, and which, in the scale of time, they are.

'Yes. There was Kazik and Mateusz and Milanja and Adam. Their parents were good people. Very important in the village. They had the biggest farm. About 40 hectares, many cows and horses. I went to school with Adam.' She laughs when she recalls Adam. 'He was always getting up to something. Practical jokes. Pulling the girls' pigtails in class, emptying the teacher's inkwell, tying a tin can to the back of someone's cart. He was a wild one, but very popular. I didn't know Mateusz so well. I think he must have started his tailoring work when I was about 10 or 11, he was 5 or 6 years older than me. And Kazik was a very kind man, and respected by everyone. He was a civil servant and then he was an officer in the Polish Army. There was a horse which went wild once. It kicked me and knocked me out. I was lying there in the field and the horse could have trampled me. But Kazik caught that horse and calmed it down, so he saved me. He always brought flowers for his mother when he visited. I remember he promised that he would bring seeds and plant flowers for me. But then the Russians came.

'And then, of course, there was the scandal in the village, when your father got a girl pregnant. And he said the baby wasn't his, but it was his and his parents and the elders discussed the matter and the result was they said he must marry her. And so there was a wedding, a short wedding. It was 1940. And a few months later, the baby was born, a little girl.'

I'm standing in front of her holding my microphone as the tape runs. Lesia translates Olga's words for me. Lesia, Olga, Bogdan, Taras and the accompanying villagers all seem to be watching me, waiting for my response. Or at least, that's what it feels like, as time seems to slow down and stretch for this moment as I absorb what she is telling me.

So this is why I have come. This is the purpose of my visit. It has all been leading to this moment. A wave of mild nausea overtakes me, I am mentally winded, my brain seems to simultaneously empty itself of everything and fill itself with the image of Olga's mouth uttering her revelation and what I can only inadequately describe as the essence of my relationship with my father. The sound of his voice, his smiling eyes, his big gentle hands, his slick-backed hair, the tweeds, threads and cloths which surrounded him, his drive, always forward. After a few seconds, I answer, automatically.

'Right...and...and what was the woman's name?'

Olga realises that this is new information to me. There is a look of compassion and perhaps mild alarm in her eyes.

'Laska, Anna Laska.'

'Anna Laska. Right...and what was the baby's name?'

'I think it was Irka, no? Yes, Irka, Irena. Irena.'

'Irena.'

I nod and smile weakly, trying to absorb what Olga has just told me. There is a silence. I am breathing quite hard and I think I have turned a little pale. Lesia intervenes.

'Are you all right Matthew?'

'Yes, don't worry, I'm OK.' I gather myself. Olga carries on.

'After the wedding, your father lived with Anna and her parents and worked in Pidhaitsi. And then he was taken away by the Russian Army. Your grandparents loved the baby very much. Sometimes she would stay with them when Anna had to work in the fields. Your grandmother was very kind to her.'

'So where are Anna and Irena now?'

'I don't know. Nearly all the Poles left here in 1945. Not all of them. My husband is Polish. And there are still one or two relatives of Anna Laska's here. You could ask them.' She gives Lesia and Bogdan directions. I press Olga's hands to mine, thanking her as I am led away. She smiles at me kindly and wishes me well.

Thoughts race through my mind. I have a half sister. She's called Irena. She must be 62 or 63. My parents didn't marry until 1955 even though they'd been together since 1948. They were always very secretive about the date of their marriage. It only came out when my oldest sister needed her birth certificate to get a passport in the late '60s. That must be why they didn't marry until then, because he was already married when they met. They always insisted that it was to do with him losing his papers during the war. I remembered my Scottish granny telling me how they had eloped, with my father turning up at her door several weeks later to announce that they had got married in secret. Secrets. It was all too clear to me now that my father had lived with many secrets until he died. My mother was still living with them.

We walk to another part of the village. Families are working in their gardens and we stop by one of them and a man in his sixties greets us. Yes, he knew Anna Laska, he was her cousin, Zinoviy Buhaj. Buhaj. My father's cousin in New York State was Anna Buhaj. The same explanations of who we are and why we are there ensue. A neat, fresh-faced woman in a black scarf comes forward, Zinoviy's daughter Olga Zenov. They tell us that Anna and Irena had visited Gnilowody three times, the last time a few years ago. They had received a letter from Poland a month ago which said that Anna was ill, that she couldn't walk. Olga thinks that Irena is living in France, married to a rich businessman. She smiles at me. Yes, she has an address for Anna, but it is at her apartment in Ternopil. Lesia takes her details and we arrange to visit her in a couple of days.

We drive back to Pidhaitsi. There is a subdued atmosphere in the car.

'Well, I didn't expect that.'

Lesia smiles. 'You see, life was very hard then for everyone. A lot of bad things happened. And your father never told you about any of this?'

'No. Nothing.'

'These times were very painful. Your father was just trying to survive them like everyone else.'

'I know.'

23: The Meaning of Ancestry

I sit in Bogdan and Hala's living room in the morning. Bogdan switches on the radio before going to the post office. The radio is always tuned to the live broadcast from the Ukrainian Rada (parliament) in Kyiv. At this time of day, haranguing speeches are made. After each portentous statement, which seems to last about 15 seconds, there's a pause, then a declining octave of electronic notes plays at a ponderous pace. This goes on for a good hour. Clearly, it's a regular procedure, this chant of the lawmakers, but it mystifies me.

I finish my diary entry for the previous day, the day of revelation, and speculate about Irena. Is she alive? Is Anna alive? Anna. She has the same Christian name as my mother. Is that simply a coincidence? Or did my father see something of his first wife in his second? Did he see the second Anna as a sign of some kind of salvation after his years of fear and hardship? I will never know the answers to these questions and really, they don't matter. What's done is done. He was a loving husband and his love for my mother was fully reciprocated. They both looked forward.

The fact of Irena's existence has overwhelmed me so much, that I had almost forgotten another startling story told to me on my visit to Gnilowody. I can't even remember who told it, whether the teller was a man or a woman. It was certainly one of the old folk we had met on our pilgrimage round the village. The day had been so dream-like I almost doubted that I had heard it, but it was there in my head and I did not invent it.

When my father was conscripted by the Soviets in 1940, there were two or three other young men from the village who were taken with him. One of them returned several years after the war had ended. He had been taken prisoner by the Germans in 1941. With repatriation, he suffered the fate of virtually all Soviet survivors of the German labour camps, another prison sentence, in a Soviet labour camp, years in the Gulag branded as a coward or a collaborator. This was official policy. This man, whose name I wasn't told, had been in my father's unit.

Not long after the Nazi invasion of the Soviet Union in 1941, they were captured and deposited in one of the hundreds of makeshift prison camps the Germans set up. Their invasion had been much more successful than they had anticipated. The Soviets were completely unprepared for it and as a result, over one million Soviet soldiers were captured within a month. The Germans were also completely unprepared for such a huge quantity of prisoners. Not that the Nazi command cared. Most of their prison camps were no more than open fields surrounded by barbed wire and guards, with no shelter, no toilets and worst of all, no food. Hundreds of thousands of these prisoners died of starvation.

The last the returning man had seen of my father was in one of these camps. He was starving, at death's door and the man thought he must have died too. As we know, he didn't. Some time in autumn '41, the Nazi command decided that they were wasting a good source of slave labour by allowing these prisoners to die, so they began to feed them and set them to work. I had known that my father suffered starvation in

214

the war. He once told me about eating seagulls in Italy and Kazik's wife Alice had told me that when she first met my father after his arrival in Glasgow, she had found him more than once in her kitchen wolfing down a whole jar of jam. He always ate quickly and wouldn't tolerate his children leaving anything on their plate.

I leave these thoughts and walk through Pidhaitsi to Lesia's school. I have agreed to give a talk to her English students. So I spend an hour with around 50 Ukrainian young people, aged between 11 and 18, telling them about Scotland, the UK, the Queen and life as an actor. I sing them 'Wild Mountain Thyme' and answer their numerous questions. Their English is excellent and their questions intelligent, even from the 11-year-olds. I think that here lies the hope of Ukraine.

It's a misty morning when we leave Pidhaitsi, heading for Ternopil. Lesia's brother, Hrihoriy, has organised our transport, with a friendly local driver named Levko. The sun breaks through during the journey as we drive through the vast expanse of arable land, the endless Ukrainian fields, masked at times by screens of trees, the sunlight flickering through their yellow leaves. I have four things to do on this day: get the address of my father's first wife; visit Mykola and Xenia; do some shopping; meet Roman and take copies of his immigration information as I've offered to write to the Queen on his behalf!

We arrive in Ternopil mid-morning, stopping first at the huge market by the bus station, a warren of covered stalls, prefabricated box-like shop units and larger stores. Lesia wants to buy light bulbs and we stop at an electrical stall. It turns out that she knows the stallholder. He's a friend of a journalist who was recently murdered in Kyiv, at the behest of President Kuczma some allege. The journalist was from this region, a nationalist sympathiser. The stallholder has photographs of his funeral, held in his home village. There are hundreds of mourners in a long procession led by priests and others carrying religious banners.

We drive into the city centre, where I buy carved wooden plates, a few boxes of chocolates and CDs for my daughters, Sugababes, Dido, Avril Lavigne and some Ukrainian music recommended by Lesia. Then off to a suburb, searching for the home of Olga Zenov, the relative of Anna Laska, whom we'd met in Gnilowody. Her apartment is in a large block, one of several in another Soviet scheme. When she opens the door to her flat, I don't recognise Olga at once. In Gnilowody, she'd worn a black headscarf which had covered her hair. Now her head is uncovered and her hair is not black, as I had expected, but completely, prematurely grey. Inside, her flat is tidy, clean and comfortable, decorated and furnished with the now-familiar tapestry hangings, white lace, net curtains and dark wooden chests and display cabinets.

We don't stay long. We take the details of Anna Laska's address. She has married again and is now called Kotek. She and her husband Jan are living in a Polish town called Mieszkowice. Olga wishes us luck. I thank her and we smile warmly at each other. She's reluctant to accept a box of chocolates. She protests that she has done nothing to deserve them.

We find Levko parked across the wide boulevard opposite a line of street traders, some working out of vans and small trucks, others sitting on stools with their goods spread out in front of them on crates, rugs or simply the grass: shoes, vegetables, toiletries, second-hand clothes and electrical goods, eggs, chickens, preserves and pickles.

Lesia has expressed some scepticism about the value of a second visit to see Mykola and Xenia, influenced, I expect, by Bogdan. She is disappointed by the brevity of Mykola's written account of his memories of my father and believes he has little more to tell us. I'm not concerned about this as I'm keen to

216

see them again, irrespective of what I might or might not find out. They're pleased to see me, though Xenia seems tired or disappointed, I can't work out which. Is it the effort required to entertain me again, or that I haven't visited enough. She'd expressed bitterness towards Bogdan on my first visit, complaining that when an American cousin had visited, a member of the family whose grave we had visited in Pidhaitsi on my first day there, Bogdan had snaffled the greater portion of the dollars he'd left for them. Mykola, on the other hand, is even-tempered, never wavering from the smiling, rather dignified, warm and amused demeanour he'd first met me with at the railway station.

After ten minutes or so, Xenia's mood lightens. At first, I'd thought it best not to stay too long, but now Xenia has roused herself into the hospitable old lady she is, applying herself to the task of providing us with lunch. When she hears that Levko is downstairs, waiting in the car, she urges us to fetch him, which I do. We sit down and eat delicious *plov*, along with the usual spread of cold meats, salads, pickle and bread and Mykola's excellent *samohon* (home-made vodka). I switch on the tape recorder and we go through the story once more.

This time, Mykola states that Pavlo, my aunt Milanja's husband, had also told him of my father's visit to Gnilowody in 1944, that Pavlo had seen him. But we had found no living witness to this in Gnilowody. Mykola knows about Anna Laska and the child Irena. He describes my father as an intelligent man who always thought before he spoke when Mykola probed him about his wartime experience at their 1982 meeting. His probing didn't appear to reveal any more than what Mykola had already told me. He says that my father preferred to change the subject, that he avoided going too deeply into details.

We talk about the Polish-Ukrainian conflict. Xenia asserts that there was none of this in Gnilowody and Mozoliwka. I was to discover later that this was not true. Xenia's own village, to the east of Pidhaitsi, experienced it. Her father, a Ukrainian, had hidden his Polish friends in his cellar. It was these Poles who she and Mykola were visiting in Zielona Gora in 1982.

Mykola's brother Teodosiy had spent 25 years as a prisoner in Siberia for his membership of the SS Halychyna Division. He had worked in a power plant there for most of his sentence. When he was finally released, he was forbidden from living in his home region, so he settled in Chernivtsi, 200km southeast of Ternopil. I was to discover later that Mykola had also been in the Halychyna Division. I was told that he had escaped the wrath of the Soviet authorities through the efforts of his first wife, a party member whom he had married shortly after the war ended.

Again, our time is too short. I've arranged a meeting with Roman at 2.30. I am already late. Xenia produces a stack of chocolate bars and a wonderfully kitsch tapestry picture of two grey and black kittens on a sky blue background, which she has made since our last meeting and sewn on to a square of pale green satin to make a cushion cover. She also gives me a little icon of the Virgin Mary for luck and to protect me from evil. Mykola presents me with a bottle of his five-year-old *samohon*. He then goes to his little greenhouse on the verandah and picks the single, perfect lemon which hangs from his tree. He gives it to Lesia, who is delighted. Xenia urges me to return, calling me a 'fine boy'. We hug and kiss, look into each other's eyes, and part.

I see Roman from a distance, standing in the square in front of the theatre with the actor Yuri. He hands me a sheaf of papers: copies of a letter from the Canadian Embassy in Kyiv rejecting his application for residency, his marriage certificate, a letter from his wife and a testimonial from a Canadian woman he'd worked for. I will use these for the letter I'll write to the Queen on his behalf. Mychaylo wants to see me, so we go to his office in the theatre. He wants to know more about me, about my response to the festival and about what possibilities there are for future co-operation. He tells me that the next time he sees me it will be on a stage. We discuss the anti-semitism issue and he offers the apologia offered by others. 'You must understand this is our history, these social relations, but we're not anti-semitic now.' I'd raised this with five or six people during the course of my stay. Usually I was met with a degree of amusement and the inference that I was taking it all too seriously, that it was just a joke, a reflection of the past. One person seemed offended, not because I was suggesting she was anti-semitic, but because I had failed to grasp that an anti-semitic attitude was only logical, even natural for a Ukrainian in the light of history and contemporary politics in the country.

I explain to Mychaylo that although I admire his company's production of the Staritsky play and that I believe it would stand up well against the work of the best companies in Britain, the play's casual anti-semitism would be unacceptable there. I welcome the opportunity to be frank with him in the sober atmosphere of an ordinary working day. He is clearly recovering from the intensity of the festival. As the lynchpin of the event, the Schevchenko Theatre's dynamo, I have developed an admiration for Mychaylo. He has a strong desire for recognition, not for himself, but for his company's work, which he sees as part of the Ukrainian renaissance taking place as Ukraine realises its independence. I hope he gets it and along with it, over time, a shedding of the brutalised mentality which still afflicts many people in Eastern Europe, the combination of naivety, lack of sophistication, xenophobia and venality produced by a history of physical hardship, subjugation and terror.

I take Roman and Yuri for a beer outside the Café Europe for my last hour in Ternopil. I wonder if Roman will see

Canada again. I gaze once more with grateful astonishment as one statuesque beauty after another passes by. The three of us don't say much, subdued by the impending farewell. Roman and Yuri hope I'll return. I say that when I do, I hope Roman won't be here.

I spend the evening eating and drinking with Bogdan and Hala and their friends Miroslav and Ola, Lesia's parents. Later, Hala shows me the Baldys family tree, starting at Bogdan's grandparents, my great-grandparents Gerasimus and Karolina. They had 8 children, 4 girls and 4 boys, including my grandmother Zofia.

Hala asks me if I want to wash my feet. She provides a basin of hot water and pulls down the loo seat for me to sit on. She scrubs my socks while I wash my feet and then brush my teeth. Its strange and touching to share such intimacy when we've known each other for only four days, but Hala is a practical woman and now I'm family. My employment of Levko as a driver proves to be a sore point with Bogdan. He is angry that this was arranged without his knowledge. He would have asked Taras to do it, thus fulfilling his familial duty to me and also keeping my money in the family.

Lying in the fold-down bed settee as Pidhaitsi's dogs howl in the night, I dream that my grandfather is not, in fact, a Pole, but an Iraqi related to Saddam Hussein! I've seen only one photograph of him, towards the end of his life, thin-faced and staring, with a thick, Saddam-like moustache. There is a voice in the dream telling me this, whose I don't know. It's a comical suggestion, one which mocks my search for information. But in a way, it's also pertinent. His identity, and that of so many of the dead, particularly here where so many have died in the chaos of war, is buried. Yes, he was a Pole, a rich farmer from Gnilowody, son of an earlier Mateusz, but for me now, that's as far as it goes. For all I know, he could have been a relative of Saddam, Queen Victoria, Charlie Chaplin or anyone else you care to mention. Is there a point where the extended branches of a family tree become meaningless? Or is the real meaning of ancestry the fact that each of us is ultimately connected with every other human being?

24: Communing with my Ghosts

My grandmother Zofia Zajac, nee Baldys c.1925

Today Taras is our driver once more. Lesia takes me to the registrar's office in Terebovlia, about 35km to the east. She has arranged an appointment there for us to explore its archive. We are met by the registrar, a garrulous woman in her fifties with a careless glamour, smart and made up, but not worried about creasing her clothes or ruffling her hair as she focusses on her job. She rifles through her records and goes back to 1905, where she finds the record of my grandparents' marriage, which took place in Mozoliwka. We find out that four years later, in 1909, Andrzej's mother, Catharina died at the age of 75. She must have been Ukrainian too, to be in these records. Then on through all the Zajac children the registrar can find from 1905 to around 1924. There are around 25 of them from the Gnilowody area, from several Zajac families, but no boys.

These are the Ukrainian registers, so all of the recorded births from mixed Polish-Ukrainian marriages are for daughters who would be raised as Ukrainians. My father and his brothers will be in a Polish register somewhere, if it still exists. I'm still getting used to this peculiarity. There is Emilia, born in 1906. And I discover that there were two other daughters born to Zofia and Andrzej, two more sisters, two more aunts of mine: Anna, born in 1910, who died of chickenpox at the age of 12 on the 3rd of September 1922, and Maria, who was born on the 2nd of April 1921, and who died four years later, on the 2nd of June 1925, cause unknown. Anna and Maria were never mentioned by my father. What heartbreak for Zofia, Andrzej and their surviving children. It's clear from looking through these registers that infant mortality was common then.

I'm determined to visit Gnilowody again under my own steam. I made enquiries earlier in the week about getting hold of a bike. Lesia's brother Hrihoriy, has a friend, Oleg Cyganovich, who has two bikes. Oleg has agreed to go with me. He's a boyish 41-year-old, unmarried. For the past few years, he's made a living by working in Poland for three months or so then living off the proceeds with his mother in Pidhaitsi for the rest of the year. We've agreed to meet at 10.00am outside the Kalba family shop in the centre of the town. I get there ten minutes early and its drizzling. Hrihoriy and a few others are already there, ready to start a day's labouring.

Though Hrihoriy is only back home from Kyiv for a few days, he seems happy at the prospect of the work in hand. They're digging the foundations for a new building, a shop with a doctor's surgery above it. It's next to the existing shop on a site which was blown up during the war. It's a dog of a task: there are large blocks of masonry and metal which have been buried just below the surface for 60 years. These must be dug out and removed. They've already dug a rectangular trench about 80cm deep.

Oleg arrives, without the bikes and dressed for labouring. He hasn't expected me to turn up, with the weather looking bad. Hrihoriy tries to dissuade me. 'It's cold and wet out in the fields.' But it's my last day. We stand around while they joke about the idea. Bogdan has already intimated that he thinks I'm daft. I join in the joke, but I won't budge. They relent and Oleg nips off to his house. He returns about 20 minutes later, sitting on one bike and pulling the other by his side. By this time, Miroslav has turned up, as amused by the whole venture as everyone else. Wouldn't I rather 'trinken schnapps'?

Hrihoriy then decides he's going to come, or perhaps his father tells him to accompany me, so we go down to his parents' house, where he changes. His bike is in a bit of a state. It looks like it hasn't been ridden for months, the gears are dodgy, so there's a further delay while Oleg fetches a neighbour's bike. And then they decide this one's worse so they return it. Hrihoriy has wrapped up in four layers of sporty clothes. He carries a black plastic bag, which I assume contains food. It's 11 o'clock by the time we get moving. But then we have to go to Oleg's so Hrihoriy can borrow a pair of his trainers. We cycle the 300 metres back into the centre, by which time Bogdan is out, chatting on the pavement with his pals and watching the world go by. After a few salutations, we're finally off.

Going down the steep hill into the river valley to leave the little town, I quickly discover that my brakes are almost non-existent and very noisy, but I'm delighted to be out on the road. It's quite a climb after that and I power on, welcoming the opportunity to exercise after over a week of excessive eating and drinking. I look back. Oleg and Hrihoriy are 300 metres behind me, walking their bikes up the hill. I stop and wait for them. We pass a neglected old Soviet war memorial, an inscribed concrete block on a patch of scrubby grass attended by a couple of foraging chickens. We climb another hill, passing a horse-drawn cart very slowly, and then we leave the road, veering off to the left, by an old collective farm headquarters.

A group of workers are haymaking. Oleg and Hrihoriy ask the way, shouting across the field. We carry on and pass another group digging up beets. We check the way again. We're on a rutted track. We freewheel down to a T junction and I find I'm miles ahead again. The beet diggers are in the distance and I get my video camera out. Hrihoriy takes this as a cue. 'Hello from the Ukrainian-Scottish expedition to Hnilowody!' His shouts attract the attention of an old man who appears out of the wood beside the road. He looks like he lives in there. He's stocky, with a huge round ruddy face and laugh lines round his eyes so deep you could plant potatoes in them. His hands are encrusted in dirt, pudgy, with fingers as thick as sausages. We ask him the way too. He's jolly and interested in our trip. Hrihoriy reaches into his plastic bag and produces two copies of a newspaper he works on, *Miska Brama*, a regular publication full of news and historical reminiscences. His company publishes copies specifically for each of the numerous *raions* (small administrative districts) of Western Ukraine. He gives the copies to the old man. Hrihoriy has decided to use our excursion to spread the word. '*Miska Brama* is a patriotic nationalist newspaper. In Hnilowody, I know that all the people there are patriotic nationalists.'

'*Prosto, prosto, prosto!*' is the direction we need to follow, which seems simple enough. It is. We maintain a roughly straight line east for seven or eight kilometres. The terrain is rolling arable land, with few trees and little birdsong. Much of it is fallow. In places, the track is strewn with the detritus of harvested maize. We pass another group of workers bent to the beets. We also pass a couple of primitive concrete crosses, one of them cracked and crooked. Hrihoriy alerts us to them, and he and Oleg remove their baseball caps. I'm not wearing a hat, so it's not an issue.

After half an hour or so, we're in a shallow valley. A little line of trees becomes visible in the distance and below it, a building or two. This is Gnilowody. We're approaching from a different direction, the direction my father would have taken from Pidhaitsi on foot, on horseback or on the sleigh. I recall his story about being chased by the wolves. That was on this route. It takes me a few moments to realise that the line of trees is the one I walked through a few days previously, the one leading to the cemetery. The terrain opens out as we reach the village. The track curves to the left over a boggy patch, and round to the right to become the main street. We pause, a couple of hundred metres short of the first house. It's quiet, save for several groups of ducks and geese waddling about among the haystacks and the grazing cows. An old woman in a headscarf walks hand-in-hand with a child over the hill to our right. A horse and cart, driven by a man in a flat cap, pulls out of the village along a track to our left. It could be any time. Another track comes over the hill on our right to converge with ours, the one we took in the car a few days previously.

We trundle on. There aren't many people about, it's Saturday lunchtime. A couple of boys play with a ball. A spunky little girl on a scooter, wearing white with a white ribbon in her blonde ponytail and dark, wire-frame glasses, asks me who I am. Her mucky little sister toddles about in a T-shirt, nothing else, still amazed at the wonder of walking. We see more children and I'm heartened. This seems to contradict Lesia's assertion that Gnilowody is moribund, like so many of Ukraine's villages, populated only by old people and alcoholics. But then it is Saturday. Maybe these are the children of sons and daughters visiting from the city.

Hrihoriy hails a burly, bearded man and explains who we are. We smoke a cigarette and saunter along to the centre of the village and the pretty, wooden, Orthodox church. Its little silver domes look as if they have been wrapped in tin foil. The man fetches a small, lively woman of around 35. She opens up the church for us. Inside, it's a delightful grotto of colour and sparkling metal. The walls are covered with icons which have the traditional, geometric tapestry cloths hung about them. The altar is festooned with crosses and candles. Metal rings hold banner poles in place at the end of each pew, the banners protected by orange floral sleeves. I turn my video camera in a circle and there, in a corner, is a painted inscription, dated 1884.

My understanding of the Cyrillic alphabet has developed sufficiently for me to recognise my own name. The inscription is referring to the earlier Mateusz Zajac, my great-grandfather, the former head man of the village.

Hrihoriy's English isn't great, but he tries to translate. 'It says that Matvi Zajac looked after this church…' 'So he was like a caretaker? Like this woman today, making sure it's kept well, cleaned, that the building is repaired?' 'Maybe, maybe no.' 'So he was like an elder, a leading member of the church congregation?' 'Yes, I think so.' 'But why is there this sign with his name on it? There must be a lot of people like him who have looked after the church. And I was told he was a Lutheran.' 'He must have been special to the church. Maybe

227

he gave it a lot of money. Your family was rich here.' 'Has this always been an Orthodox church?' 'I think so.'

My father only ever mentioned one church, and that Orthodox and Catholic priests would visit on alternate Sundays, so he attended both services. 'Maybe that's true.' Of course, Orthodox to Hrihoriy is Ukrainian or Russian Orthodox, not Greek Catholic, which observes Orthodox ritual but recognises the Pope as head of the church, the Western Ukrainian hybrid which my grandmother followed.

I make a donation to the church, we kiss the altar and thank the woman, who smiles and wishes us well. Hrihoriy wants his picture taken in front of the church for his newspaper, so I oblige. The bearded man leads us along the road then hurries off. Several people with shopping bags are hanging around and then a bus appears. 'It's the Ternopil bus.' The people get on and the bearded man now reappears from a lane. This time he is accompanied by a tall man in his fifties. This is the caretaker of the other church, the grander, stone-built Greek Catholic church. He opens up and we enter. The walls of the nave are painted pale yellow. The tall, narrow windows are stained with squares and triangles of red, blue, green and yellow. Soft afternoon light filters through and becomes sea-green, dreamlike and submarine. Here too are icons and traditional tapestries, sun-ray crosses and candles, but with more space between them.

'Before the war, this was the Polish Roman Catholic Church. This was the church your father and his family would have come to. It was built in 1935. Between 1945 and 1989, it was the headquarters of the *kolkhoz*.'

Like the Orthodox church, this one is beautifully kept. Ukrainian exiles in the US sent large sums of money to restore it during the early '90s. Its religious artefacts, the icons and crosses, the chalices and banners, are new or imported from other churches. There is little or nothing from the pre-war Polish church other than the building itself, which is unchanged.

228

As I am told of its pre-war status by the caretaker through Hrihoriy, I picture my father with his father and brothers, his mother and sister standing next to me. Not exactly a picture, more an imagined presence, which is almost tangible, the pale green dream light and the impression of silent figures standing respectfully between the pews, facing forward, eyes open: the strong features of Emilia, who I never met, prominent among them, the portrait of her with Pavlo, which I'd seen in Tekla's house still strong in my mind; their son Teodosiy, my partisan cousin; the frail grandfather Andrzej, still tall, with his dark head of hair, but with a slight stoop in his shoulders, his head leaning forward; my grandmother Zofia, strong and kind with her handsome, generous, stoical face; the three brothers, Adam, Kazik and Mateusz, the ones who would be scattered; the boy Adam, the wild one who was the natural farmer, the civil servant Kazik, sober and responsible, and my father Mateusz, the young apprentice tailor who dreamed of making it in Warsaw, the one who caused the scandal.

My ghosts in their home, here in this church, the only building left standing where they would have gathered.

Mateusz, Kazik and Adam c. 1963

25: Departure

Our time has run out. I want to visit Olga and Tekla. I want to re-visit the cemetery. I'd have liked to have seen Anna Laska's relatives. I have so many more questions: what was Olga's school like? How many pupils? How many teachers? What languages were spoken at school? Are there any Poles left in the village? Were there any Jews here? How many local people did my grandparents employ? Michael Boklach! He lived in Newton Mearns in Glasgow. We visited him and his family there a few times. He worked for my grandfather at times. But he's dead now too. What did Anna Laska look like? What was her personality? When did she and Irena leave for Poland? How many others members of my family lived locally? Where did my grandfather's brothers live? Did he have any sisters? How long had Zajacs lived here? Did anyone else know of my father's 'visit' in 1944? But we have to go. I make another donation. Hrihoriy dictates an announcement about my visit and donation to the caretaker, to be made at the following morning's service.

On our way out of the village, back the way we came, we pause to watch a woman milking a cow. Hrihoriy hands a few more newspapers to the woman's mother and neighbor.

Then we're off over the fields, passing the crosses and a few workers on their way home, finally freewheeling down the hill and across the river into Pidhaitsi.

As we walk up the steep hill to the main street, we talk about a beer, but choose instead to climb further uphill, past the cemetery to the football ground on the edge of town. And there we ignore torrential rain and have a kickabout. Hrihoriy has told me of Oleg's footballing prowess. He once played for Berezhany, I guess the equivalent of Ayr United or Darlington. And it shows. There are exceptionally gifted professional foot-ballers, like Pele, Zidane and Messi, and then there are the rest and for these players, the line between the top flight and the lower leagues can be very fine. Oleg strikes me as one of these players: he might have made it into the top teams in Ukraine, but for one reason or another, he didn't.

I'm due back with Hala and Bogdan, and still the rain comes down, the sky weeping its apology for the driest summer they've had in years. I clutch the pathetic, whining brakes as we make our way downhill again to Hrihoriy's house. I say goodbye to him after we exchange addresses and then I pop into the Kalba shop and buy three bottles of *horilka*. I give one to Oleg. We cycle down the street and at the point where we are to part, he asks me to wait. He runs down the lane to his house and returns with gifts for me: an old football pennant and a photograph of him in his trunks, standing on a beach by the Sea of Azov. He walks with me round to Bogdan's house and we shake hands.

My final evening with Bogdan and Hala is subdued by my impending departure. I wash my hair and my feet and I pack. They press gifts upon me, *horilka*, chocolates for my children, a set of golden tumblers, a ceramic decanter and one of Hala's home-made tapestries. We eat and drink a few toasts to each other, a safe journey and my return one day. The normally surly Bogdan surprises me by breaking into song – *Kawa, Vodka I Zona* – Coffee, Vodka and a Woman.

Bogdan and his family, Pidhaitsi 2003 Bogdan far left, Hala 2nd right

I'm tired. The daily round of heaps of food and drink, the constant effort to bridge the language barrier, the desire to respect my hosts by accepting their generous hospitality and the struggle to understand my father's past and my connection to it is a combination which has worn me out. I'm leaving with an experience which is to take some time to fully digest. Both my physical and mental digestive systems have been under a lot of strain.

We drive to Lviv, leaving at 8.30am. It was supposed to be 8.00, but Taras was a little late. Then we have to drive a kilometre out of town in the wrong direction to fill the tank and after that we pause back in Pidhaitsi to pick up Lesia and her heavy bag, loaded with jars of mushrooms, oil, sausage, fruit and vegetables for her son Nazar, a forestry student in the city. She normally sends a weekly package of food to him by bus. Bogdan is with us too, the old man determined to fulfil his familial duty and see me safely through the check-in gate.

Taras coaxes his old Niva into life with the throttle. It strains to pull its heavy load up the hill out of town and we're away. Soon, we're in beautiful rolling countryside, vivid in the autumn sun, passing forests, leaves burnished all shades of yellow, orange, green and red, fields, ploughed and fallow, small groups of cows, hardly herds, often tended by an old man or woman stoically sitting by them as they graze. Sometimes we see two or three people moving their cattle, an old man, his son and grandson, and others moving into woods to gather mushrooms. Taras has to veer to avoid gaggles of geese on the road several times. There is a whole set of hazards: the geese, hens, cows, horse-drawn carts, sometimes followed by tethered foals, roadside produce sellers, little boys on bicycles which are far too big for them, crumbling tarmac, subsidence and potholes.

Taking the shortest route, we pass through the village of Brudanka, which roughly translates as 'muddy village,' where the road is a long succession of giant puddles, ruts and holes. The village is about one kilometre from end to end. It takes us nearly ten minutes to pass through. We pause to have a look at a stationary bus in the middle of the road, its sump spurting oil back into the deep hole which was responsible for piercing it. The driver looks on, resigned and helpless. I'm glad of my lift – it's the Pidhaitsi-Lviv bus. After a few more kilometres, it's Ivanovka and the same story, bar another stricken bus. Taras takes it all in his stride, knowing what to expect. Lesia is rueful when she asks me if such roads exist in Britain. She knows that my answer will be no.

After a couple of hours, we're skirting the south of Lviv. It looks like a huge white Lego fortress, a massive Soviet housing scheme on the horizon seems to encircle the city. We turn north into an arterial road which takes us between the massive blocks and, in spite of their concrete brutalism, they're teeming with life. Shops and kiosks line the thoroughfare, people come and go, wait for buses and just get on with their daily lives. The large spaces around the blocks are green and tree-lined with very little litter about and the buildings themselves are in a reasonable state of repair. I expected something altogether grimmer and as the blocks give way to older terraces, detached houses, petrol stations, supermarkets, shops, it becomes clear that Lviv is far from depressed.

The old cobbled streets of the centre are very bumpy and I marvel again at the fact that the tramlines remain smooth and intact. The centre itself was untouched by serious fighting during World War II. It is dominated by 18th and 19th century architecture, crowned by the stunning neo-classical opera house. A few hundred metres away, down the boulevard, stands a new monument, a 6-metre bronze statue of Shevchenko, the bard, standing before a sweeping bronze relief, a representation of the Ukrainian people. We walk through a little arts and crafts market and I buy a few souvenirs, feeling rushed by the watchful eyes of Bogdan, who's eager to get to the airport.

First though, we have to deliver Lesia's bag of food to Nazar. We drive to quite a well-heeled neighbourhood and park behind Nazar's hall of residence. I carry the bag for Lesia and we find Nazar's room in a dimly-lit corridor. It's simply furnished, around 3m x 4m with four narrow beds. Nazar greets us cheerfully, the food is unpacked and stored, Lesia collects the empty jars from Nazar's previous delivery and we all go down to Taras and Bogdan. The Niva won't start. I don't want to miss my plane. We push it and that gets it going.

Twenty minutes later, we're at the airport. Lesia and Nazar photograph us. I reach the check-in. Bogdan gives me my rucksack. We shake hands and kiss, saying nothing. I can't say anything. We just look at each other with misty eyes. I blow a kiss to Lesia and Taras and I'm away. The security man takes a cursory look through my rucksack and I deposit my holdall with a baggage handler who takes me into a corner and tries to wheedle dollars or euros out of me in return for nothing as far as I can tell. I'm exasperated, but I want no complications passing through to the departure lounge. I give him 50 *hrivny*. He shakes my hand. It's my last act in Ukraine before I board the plane.

A few hours later the rain pelts down as we board the plane in Warsaw. In the consumerist limbo of Warsaw Airport, I wonder about my journey into the past and my experience of the present in Ukraine. How do the two relate? I have often asked myself this question, answering glibly, 'Without an understanding of the past, an understanding of the present is impossible.' I do believe this but, as I've witnessed the desire to strive towards prosperity, barely nascent in Ukraine, in full stride in Poland, I question my purpose. Is it relevant only to me, when the ostensible vision of those around me, here in Eastern Europe, particularly the young and early middle-aged, is to move forward, forward, forward?

PART SIX
Irena

26: Search

So my father was never in the Polish Army. During the period when he said he'd been in the Polish Army, captured by the Soviets and sent to Uzbekistan, he was actually continuing his work, learning his trade as a tailor under the Russian occupation until he was conscripted by the Soviets. I now had the testimonies of two people, Olga and Mykola, along with the photograph of Dad in a Soviet uniform. Some time after his conscription, he had married Anna Laska and Irena was born. Then he was possibly at the Front to resist the German invasion of 1941. There was the story of his capture by the Germans and his starvation in a German POW camp, that he had become a forced labourer in Germany, and the story of his presence on the front near Gnilowody in 1944 as a soldier in the German Army, which Mykola asserted was Dad's own account, backed up by Uncle Pavlo. This period, '41-'44, was when he said he had taken the journey of General Anders' Army out of the Soviet east to Persia, North Africa and Italy.

It was all so sketchy. I needed more hard facts. I continued my search. I wrote to the Polish Army Archive: as I expected, it had no record of him being in the 51st Infantry Regiment. I wrote to the Germany Army Archive: they too had no record of a Mateusz Zajac. I thought he might have given a false name. I tried Mateusz Baldys, but no luck with that. I wrote to the Russian Army archive: they asked me to specify which unit he had been in. It may be that with some comprehensive detective work, I could establish which Soviet Army units were recruiting in the Podhajce region in 1940, but that would entail a prohibitively expensive and quite possibly fruitless trip to Russia, so for now that was a dead end too. I wrote to the Red Cross Tracing Service to see if they had a record of him as a displaced person. That source may yet come up with an answer although, with a huge backlog of enquiries, the waiting time can be more than 8 years.

I listened to the tapes again with a more forensic ear. The pauses for thought, the hesitations, the struggles with names, places and dates took on new meaning. I checked the date of Stalin's declaration of the amnesty for Polish POWs. It was 30th July 1941, not the beginning of 1942 as my father said. I found the exact location of Proskurov, the town where he said he'd found the Polish officer after the escape he had claimed he made from Uzbekistan. Proskurov is now called Khmelnitsky. It's in Ukraine, a small city around 3000 kilometres from Uzbekistan. It's only 180 kilometres east of Gnilowody. It was under German occupation during the period in question, impossible as a place of Polish recruitment. He could only have been in Proskurov as a Soviet defender, a German occupier or a fugitive from either the Soviets or the Germans.

All this research was carried out in parallel with what had become my new, overriding priority: finding Irena.

Edinburgh, Scotland 25th October 2003

Droga Pani Anna,

I am the son of Mateusz Zajac, from Gnilowody. A few

weeks ago, I visited my father's birthplace for the first time and discovered that he had been married to you before the war and that you had a daughter, Irena. This was a shock for me: my parents never told me or either of my two sisters about this.

Mateusz died in 1992. He was a wonderful father to me, but I have been full of questions since this revelation, none of which he can answer.

A lady called Olga Zenov, who I think is related to you and who lives in Tarnopol, gave me your address. Another, much older Olga, who was at school with my father's younger brother, Adam, told me the story of your first marriage.

I would very much like to meet you. I quite understand if you do not wish to revisit the past, so please do not feel obliged to meet me. However, I do feel an obligation to Irena, to tell her about her father and his life after the war. I would be very grateful if you would send me her address.

The upheavals of the war caused scars and shocks which, in some cases, have still not completely healed. My father lived a very quiet life in the north of Scotland, running a small, successful business as a tailor. He held things together for himself and his family here. I always knew there were experiences which he didn't want to recount. My curiosity arises from a need to understand him and the events he lived through in order to understand my own identity. It's taken a long time for me to begin exploring this in depth. I visited my Aunt Aniela in Augustow last year. I'd last visited her in 1990, when her husband Adam was still alive. Adam died in 1996 and the oldest brother, Kazik, died in Glasgow in 1988. Aniela gave me an address for Bogdan Baldys, my father's cousin in Podhajce. I didn't know he was still alive and I contacted him earlier this year and visited him a few weeks ago. That journey has led me to write this letter.

I do hope that you will want to reply, particularly in view of my relationship as a half-brother to Irena. I hope you are in good health. Best wishes to you and your husband.

Czekam na szybka odpowiedz.
Najlepsze zyczenia.
Matthew Zajac

Gdansk, Poland @wp.pl 12th November 2003

We've just received your letter about Ukraine. I must say that it is quite shocking! You can be sure that we will do as much as we can to help you solve this problem. I'll translate your letter for Aniela as soon as possible.

Love, Ula, Wojtek & Janusz

Augustow, Poland 2nd December 2003

Dear Matthew and family,

Wojtusz has translated your letter to me, so I'm replying. I'm feeling very poorly, my heart is failing, but I'm still on my feet. I may live until Christmas, but being 82 years old I feel I have managed to live long enough.

Now as far as your father was concerned, we knew everything. The fact that he had been in the Russian army was not his fault and if he hadn't gone into hiding they would have exiled him to Siberia and he would have perished there, because those who were from here and were hiding not wanting to join the army were caught by the Russians and transported to Siberia and murdered there.

And the fact he had been married – he always maintained that the child was not his, but how much truth there is in it – is unknown. But he was a very good man always helping other people and us, as much as he could. He had one weakness, namely he liked women, but I can't say a bad word about him. And later he took our son Jurek and saved him from the communists. And he was helping us and we were sending 400 zlotys every month to granny via Moscow and she had more money than those in the kolkhoz.

And there was nothing to go back to Ukraine for, because the Russians had invaded it.

Your father was a very decent man. You can be proud of your father. And you can always come to Poland, both to Gdansk and Augustow. There is enough to eat and a place to sleep.

All the best,
Aniela

Pidhaitsi 23rd December 2003

Dear Matthew,

Many thanks for the letter you've written and for the photos. They are great. We've already been waiting for your letter. Many times Bogdan asked me if you called and so did my students. Bogdan thought something was wrong when you were here. He was so happy receiving your letter. His granddaughter translated for him and in the evening he came to my parents with this letter and asked me to translate again.

We are glad that you liked the trip. As to my going to Hnilowody, I think I'll do it after Christmas. First, I'll have more free time. Second, maybe roads will freeze a little bit because now it's practically impossible to get there except on a horse. I'll ask some of my friends to take me there. As to your father's visit to the village during the war, Tekla doesn't know about it, we asked her. Maybe Olga knows.

Have you already had information from the British Army Records? What about Irena? Did Anna Laska answer you? And how is your mother? What was her reaction when you told her all these things? Don't you think that it was your parents' secret and they didn't want you to know about his past?

All the best,
Lesia Kalba

I needed to see his British Army Record. In order to do that, I needed to get my mother's written permission. She refused to give it. She told me that she couldn't understand why I needed to see it, why I needed to dig up all that old stuff. She told me that I should show more respect to my dead father, who had been such a good man, who had given me so much. She suggested I was simply looking to exploit his life. But in her heart, she understood that a child has the right to know his father. She knew that I loved and respected him and though she was afraid for herself, for what might be discovered, for what I might expose, for what her community of friends in Inverness might think should unpalatable facts become known, she relented. After many months and several attempts at persuasion, she wrote her letter of authorisation.

Edinburgh 30th August 2004

Droga Pani Anna,

It's nearly ten months since I wrote to you. I'm writing again in the hope that you will receive this letter and feel able to reply. I hope you'll understand that I feel compelled to persist.

If you received my first letter, you'll know that I would like to contact Irena. Please understand that I simply want to tell her about her father. I'm sure she must be curious. I would be delighted to meet her.

I was in Poland for a holiday with my family in July, visiting my aunt Aniela in Augustow. It did occur to me that I could drive to Mieszkowice and pay you a visit, but I don't want to do that without an invitation from you. I would be grateful and thrilled to meet you.

I know you must have had a difficult time during the war and that my father's behaviour towards you may not have been as good as it should have been. I hope you can understand my need to know his buried history and that you'll decide that you want to help me. Please understand also that I do appreciate how sensitive this subject is. I have no intention of causing you and Irena any upset or embarrassment. I do believe that reaching out like this can be a very constructive and positive act. Please get in touch.

Ministry of Defence, Ruislip, Middlesex
11th February 2005

Dear Mr. Zajac,

Thank you for your recent letter and enclosures and in reply please find a statement of service for your late father as requested.

In Poland, he was called up from the Polish Army reserve on 20th August 1939, and with the 51st Infantry Regiment, he fought against the Nazi invasion.

There are now two conflicting statements as to his actions between 1940 and 1945. These statements were made by your father, first on enlistment in the British Army in Italy and then in the Polish Resettlement Corps in the UK. There is no way we are able to confirm either of them:

According to the first statement, he was conscripted and served in the Soviet Red Army from May 1940 to December 1943 and then he was in the German Army from July 1944 to 7th May 1945, the day Germany surrendered.

According to the second statement, he was deported as forced labour to work in a sawmill in Germany from 1939 to 1943. He was then in the former USSR as a soldier from 1943 to 1944 and in Germany as a prisoner of war from 1944 to 1945.

I can confirm the following particulars of the British military service of 30086980 – Private Mateusz Zajac:

Service in Italy with the Polish Forces under British Command from 3 June 1945 to 17 March 1947. Finally discharged 4 October 1948. Conduct: good.

So now I had incontrovertible evidence that my father was never in Anders' Army, never in Persia, North Africa and the invasion of Italy. To have joined up with the British Army in June 1945 in Italy, a month after the German surrender, he must either have gone through a displaced person's camp, probably in Germany, or been captured as an enemy soldier and identified as a Pole before transfer to the Polish 2nd Corps, or both.

The two conflicting statements came from his own mouth. The first is clearer than the second and, in my view, much closer to the truth. The first was made on enlistment on June 3rd 1945, the second nearly two years later, on March 18th 1947 on enlistment into the Polish Resettlement Corps. He had had nearly two years to learn of the war's outcome, the new political settlement, and the beginnings of the Cold War. By the time of this second statement, he would have known that a return to Poland was out of the question. As a former member of the Red Army who had fallen into the hands of the Germans, and then as a former member of the German Army, there would have been only one destination for him at the hands of the Communist authorities: the gulag. His only option was to settle in the west, among a population which had fought Germany and which was becoming increasingly hostile towards the Soviet Union. Out of fear and the survival instinct which had kept him alive during the war, he had begun to construct his new post-war identity in his new refuge. Why would he want people in Britain to know he had fought in the armies of both these enemy powers?

His admission of membership of the Red Army in his British Army Record simply confirmed the photographic evidence and the accounts of Mykola and Olga. His admission of membership of the German Army also confirmed Mykola's claims, though there is confusion about the dates. Aniela's letter of 2nd December 2003 provides a possible explanation of his movement from the Soviets to the Germans: 'The fact that he had been in the Russian army was not his fault and if he hadn't gone into hiding they would have exiled him to Siberia and he would have perished there, because those who were from here and were hiding not wanting to join the army were caught by the Russians and transported to Siberia and murdered there.'

However, there is no hard evidence that he did desert, go into hiding and eventually join up with the Germans, by coercion or voluntarily. There is also no hard evidence to support Mykola's claim of capture by the Germans as part of Vlasov's army near Leningrad, although there was the story of the soldier who retuned to Gnilowody, who had last seen my father starving in a German POW camp in 1941. Maybe he was in one of these camps, maybe he wasn't. But this much was clear: his movements and actions for over four years, from spring 1941 to June 1945, remained almost completely unknown.

27: Approach

Pidhaitsi 17th February 2005

Dear Matthew,

Firstly, please accept my apologies for taking so long to write to you. Just before the new year, I fell down and had a fracture in my right hand, so I had a kind of 'break'!

As I've already told you on the phone, I was in Hnilowody twice: in spring with Hryts and in autumn with my husband. I had a talk with Olga. We also spoke with two other old women, trying to know something about your father's visit to Hnilowody in 1944. But no one knows about it. You see, it was a difficult time. People were afraid of everything. Even if he was there, he tried to be inconspicuous, not to cause trouble to his family.

Olga gave me two addresses and here's what she told me:

1. Laska, Maria. She was a girlfriend of Adam Zajac, your uncle Adam.

2. *Szarejko, Stefania. She was Anna Laska's friend.*

Maybe they will help you.

As to your grandfather's grave, nobody knows anything about it. But Olga promised to try to find out. Have you already persuaded your mother to give you permission to look at your father's army records? I think you can get a lot of information there.

Now some words about us. We had a stressful time at the end of the year. I mean an Orange Revolution. Thank you for supporting us. With all good reason, I can say that World History has never witnessed such a kind of protest. Thousands of people, standing shoulder to shoulder in the square crying out 'We are together! We are numerous! No one can conquer us!' A blissful aura reigned about the square. Just think about it! Such a huge crowd of people, it was rather cold, but they stood there day and night. One had to see it. It was neither a revolution nor an upheaval. Revolution brings heavy fighting, radical changes, bloodshed. But this was a peaceful protest of the people who want to live in justice. We support Yushchenko with all our heart and we are glad that Ukraine has a president like him. It's high time...I guess we have been waiting too long for that moment in Ukrainian history.

I hope to hear from you soon, not like I do it and trust that you are well.

Love,
Lesia

Edinburgh 1st March 2005

Dear Pana Szarejko,

I have been given your address by Olga Kindzierska, who I met when I visited Gnilowody, near Podhajce. I was there in September 2003.

My name is Matthew Zajac. I am the son of Mateusz Zajac, also from Gnilowody. Perhaps you remember him. He had two brothers, Adam & Kazik and an older sister, Emilia. He died in 1992. He married Anna Laska around 1939. They had a little daughter, who I believe is called Irena. When I visited Gnilowody, Olga told me about my father's marriage to Anna and their daughter. It was the first I had heard of it.

I would like to contact Irena and Anna. I was given an address for Anna in Mieszkowice, but I have had no reply to my letters. I don't mean to rake up painful memories, and I quite understand if Anna has no wish to meet me, but I feel an obligation to tell Irena about her father. She may want to know about him.

I understand you are Anna's friend. I am writing to you now to ask you to help me, if you feel you can. Please talk to Anna. I am quite prepared to come to Poland to meet her. I mean no harm and simply see this contact as a way of healing the wounds of the past. I would very much like to meet my half-sister Irena.

My father settled in Scotland after the war. He married another Anna, my mother, and had four children. We grew up in Inverness in the north of Scotland where my father had a tailoring business. I work as an actor and director, mainly in the theatre and occasionally in film and television.

I would be very grateful if you would help me. Please reply.

Yours sincerely,
Matthew Zajac

Szczecin, Poland 18th March 2005

Dear Mr. Matthew,

Thank you for your letter. I receive it 15th March a few days ago. How glad I am that you write to me. When I read your letter I was surprise and understand all. That is all true what said Olga to you. I remember your all family, your father (he was very tall) and brothers Adam and Kazik. I visited Gnilowody in 2002, you in 2003, why write to me so late? I can help you because my first name is also Laska. When your father married with Anna I was there with my parents. Please await for my long letter. I will write soon. Bye.

Stefania

Szczecin 6th April 2005

Dear Matthew,

Irena is very sick on the heart. She is 63 years old and her mother Anna is 84 years old and she is also sick. They have very hard problems and great terrible. Irena has husband and three children, they all have own family. Now Irena two weeks ago went to hospital. When she go back home I don't know.

251

I call to Irena but she was in hospital. I speaking with her daughter Mirka. She is teacher. I think that she write a letter to you soon.

Anna has also husband. He is a good man, he take care of her. She is very tired by life and sick now.

In Polska we have a very great mourning. I think that you and your family are seeing on TV. We all cried for St. Papa (Pope John Paul II).

Excuse me that I do so many mistake, but I many words forget and many years I don't write in English language. Do you understand my letter? Matthew please me answer! I give address to Irena. In holiday I want to go by train to Mieszkowice to meet Irena and Anna. It is 90km.

Good luck and goodbye,
Stefania

28: Contact

Mieszkowice 17th April 2005

Dear Mr. Matthew,

I am your sister, Irena. I am very happy to learn that I have a brother who wants to meet me. I never imagined that any member of my father's new family would like to contact me. The only things that remind me of my father are his photo and a dress, which he sent to me in Mieszkowice, when I was a little girl. Besides, he has appeared in my dreams, however in each dream he was trying to run away from me.

I was born on the 2nd of February 1941. I don't really remember my father as he had been transferred to the Eastern Front soon after I was born. He was captured by the Germans. In 1944 he sent a letter to my mother Anna posted from Germany, in which he was asking her to visit him there as he was unable to come back. Anna wanted to go, but she had me and her parents to take care of. Even Mateusz's father dissuaded her from her journey to Germany.

After that, we had to leave Gnilowody and move to Podhajce as in summer of 1944 Ukrainian nationalists started to slaughter Polish people. We barely survived, hiding from the Ukrainian bandits, my mother forced to labour for the Germans digging trenches, then hiding from the Russians as they looted and raped. We were suffering from starvation. I temporarily lost my eyesight. In 1945, we were deported to Western Poland. The journey took six months. My mother carried my father's sewing machine with her, for his return.

In 1948 my father sent a letter saying that he had settled in Britain and asking for a divorce. He also sent the dress for me which I remember to this day. From that time on we lost contact with him. My mother never spoke badly of him. She always said he was a good man. She loved him very much.

I am very glad that you have made contact, because it helps me to believe that not everything connected with my father has to be painful. I hope that a prospective meeting and an honest conversation will help both sides.

With kind regards,
Irena

Edinburgh 6th May 2005

Dear Irena,

This is my first letter to you. I didn't know whether I would ever get the opportunity to send it.

I hope you are recovering well from your operation. I am very sorry that it has taken me a long time to reply in person. I have been extremely busy, working away from home on a new theatre production. Finally managing to make contact with you has also stunned me. I am very pleased! Thank you very much for sending the photographs. They are quite moving to me – I gaze at them in wonder! You look like a warm friendly woman. I think I am like that too. As you probably know, I first tried contacting Anna in autumn 2003, and had no idea if I had the correct address, or that you even lived in Mieszkowice. Someone in Gnilowody thought that you lived in France!

I am so sorry that you never knew our father. If it's any consolation, I can tell you many things about his life in Scotland and how he was as a father to me and my sisters. I realise that this is a delicate and potentially painful relationship to open up but, as I said in my letters to Anna, I feel compelled to give you the opportunity to know something of your father and, perhaps, develop a new relationship with a new branch of your family! Strange indeed! My visit to Gnilowody in 2003 taught me that my father kept a number of important facts from me. I went there because I was curious about his life before the war. I had recorded conversations with him about his life in 1988, knowing that one day I would want to write about him. I discovered that there was a lot more that I didn't know: that his mother was Ukrainian (he never told me); that he had been in the Soviet Army; and, most important of all, I was told by Olga in Gnilowody that he had been married and had a daughter. After my letters to Anna didn't reach her, I asked a friend I'd made in Podhajce, Lesia Kalba, to visit Olga again to see if she could give us any more help. She gave Lesia addresses for Stefania Szarejko and Maria Laska, as you know...

Irena, I know that all this has happened at a bad time

for you, when you need rest and peace to recover. I hope you aren't finding it too stressful. I really do have the best intentions. I would like to come and visit you and your family, Stefania and, of course, your mother, but I don't want to do it until you are well enough. Please let me know what is best. I can come very soon.

You know much better than I ever will how difficult the war years were. You, your mother and father were survivors and for that I am thankful. I don't understand why he never contacted you, although I can guess at reasons. There is much to be talked about and it will be best to meet face to face.

With best wishes,
Matthew

He had been in Germany in 1944. He had sent Anna a letter from there asking her to come and join him. Maybe he was working in a sawmill there at *that* time. He certainly felt settled enough to ask her to undertake the risky journey to Germany. Or maybe he was undergoing military training, or carrying out military duties in Germany. There is a multitude of possibilities. With the letter from Germany providing the only hard evidence of his whereabouts from spring 1941 to his enlistment with the British army in June 1945, four years are unaccounted for. One can't even discount the darkest possibilities. He could have become a Nazi. He could have participated in war crimes. I would be amazed if that turned out to be the case as there was never anything in his behaviour to suggest he harboured those repugnant secrets or beliefs, but when one knows *nothing* of his actions during this period, *anything* becomes possible. Did he ever go into hiding? Was he taken prisoner by the Germans? Did he simply come out of hiding to volunteer for the Germans? My efforts with the German, Russian and Polish military archives were fruitless. I think I will never know more than the sketchy facts I have. The real story of his life during those four years will remain unknown. Perhaps it doesn't matter. My father was just one of the millions tossed about by the merciless currents of the war. He was just lucky to survive it all and to retain the strength of character to build a decent life for himself in the aftermath.

Edinburgh 6th May 2005

Dear Stefania,

Thank you so much for your letter of 22nd April. I am very glad that I was given your address: you have been the key which has opened the door to Anna and Irena. And its great that you can speak English! I think I understand everything that you have written to me, so don't worry about your grammar etc.

I must admit that the whole process of discovering that my father was married before and had a daughter, the subsequent attempts to contact Anna and finally making contact has been quite strange. Sometimes it feels like a dream. In fact, life can feel like a dream or an invention when I consider the secrets which my father concealed and lived with for most of his adult life. But you, Anna, Irena and Mirka are all real people and so am I and there is a blood relationship which is also real!

Thank you too for inviting me to Szczecin, and for Anna's invitation to Mieszkowice. Irena and Mirka have also invited me. I think I'll be coming quite soon. I have sent an email to Irena saying that I will wait to see how she feels about a visit as she must recover from her time in hospital, so when I come is dependent on Irena's health.

There is much to say about my father and his life. I realise that it is a very sensitive subject and that Anna and Irena may feel a lot of bitterness towards him. I don't understand why he never contacted them and I can't excuse it. It is shameful, even though they were forced apart by extraordinary circumstances. He was a very good father to me. I loved him very much. He was popular, generous and hard working. He rarely talked about the war, although as I grew up I became aware that it clearly had a profound effect on him which he didn't always conceal. He did tell me a story of what happened to him during the war which I have since discovered is nearly all a fabrication.

You told me that Anna's husband did not give her a letter I sent. Does this mean that I had the correct address for Anna? Perhaps Jan thought it would be too upsetting for Anna.

I enjoyed reading about you and your life. I too love singing songs, so perhaps we can sing a few when we meet! It sounds like you lead a very active life now that you have retired. That will keep you young!

I very much look forward to meeting you. Please pass on my regards to your family and to Anna

Best wishes,
Matthew

29: Irena

Irena and Anna 1948 Irena wears the dress my father gave her

August 24th 2005. Newcastle to Berlin. I'm going to Poland again, but not to Gdansk or Augustow, Krakow or Warsaw. I'll stay the night in Berlin. Tomorrow I'll drive 100 kilometres, just across the border, to Mieszkowice. I'm due to arrive at Irena's house at lunchtime.

A thick invisible presence will accompany me, accompanies me now. He will hover at my shoulder as I leave the plane. He may need to talk to me in the dead of night. He will fill the space I'm not occupying in the little hire car. He will harry me and urge me on as I leave Berlin. He will grow restless at the border at Frankfurt-Oder, where we crossed on childhood holidays, turning south towards Uncle Adam's, never north to drive the 40 kilometres to Mieszkowice.

He will grow fearful, grief-stricken and numb as I approach Mieszkowice, ask for directions and find Irena's house. He will follow me, perhaps at a distance as I approach it.

He will be afraid when Irena appears. He will place himself between us as we meet each other's eyes, as we hold each other's hands and, as we embrace, he will engulf us.

I drove into the square at the centre of the little town of Mieszkowice and parked the car. It was cool, clear and sunny. Climbing out, I scanned the people going about their business, looking for Piotr, Irena's grandson, who I had exchanged text messages with as I approached the town. There was a young man across the road, slightly swarthy, with close-cropped hair, looking out. He spotted me and the German number plates on the hire car. I waved tentatively. It was him. We crossed towards each other and shook hands. His English was halting. He got into the car with me and he led us through an archway into a yard behind the shops on the square. I parked and got out. Three women, a man, a teenage girl and a boy were standing on a stone stairway which led up to apartments. The oldest woman was at the top of the stairs. We didn't say much as we approached each other. Perhaps we didn't say anything.

We just fixed our eyes on each other and pulled ourselves towards each other. And he was there somehow, as we embraced and held each other, and cried.

'Moj brodzy. Moj brodzy.' My brother. My brother.

I ate and drank with them. Irena admonished her husband Czeslaw for the frequency with which he refilled the vodka glasses. I joked with Mirka and her sister Beata and her children Piotr, Sabina and Wojtek. We gazed with wonder at each other. Irena smiling with her dark eyes. My translator Piotr sat by my side. He stayed with me like this for virtually every waking hour I was in Mieszkowice.

Irena told me that she had met Uncle Adam by chance at a party in Zielona Gora when she was 18 years old, in 1959, the year I was born. They were in a room full of people. One of Irena's friends pointed across the room and said 'You see that man? That's your uncle.' She approached him and introduced herself. She asked him to tell her father about her. She gave him her address, asking that he pass it on to Dad and urge him to write to her. He said he would, but she never heard a thing from either of them. Maybe Adam never passed on her message. Maybe our father chose to ignore it.

I was taken to Anna's house. Jan opened the door to us, a small, compact and strong old boy, clear-eyed and with a benign smile. It was a small, simple apartment on the ground floor. He ushered us into the little, windowless hallway where shadowy light spilled in from the neighbouring rooms, and there she was, a small white-haired old woman, slightly bent from all her years of work, with arresting blue eyes and the face of an angelic pixie. Like an aged, girlish, Slavic Audrey Hepburn.

She took me in with those wide blue eyes as she held my hands, starting to talk softly to me and I felt as though she was transporting me back in time. Slowly, it became apparent that, for her, it was as if he had walked through her door after

Jan and Anna Kotek, nee Laska 2005

an absence of 64 years. She didn't see me, she saw him. She treated me like I was him, for the two hours of my first meeting with her, and for my subsequent meetings with her during my four days in Mieszkowice. I think she saw me from time to time, but most of the time she gave free rein to the heady dream which my presence engendered for her. The dream which she had over and over again during those terrible years, that he had come back. And now I was here, she asked me why *I* had never come back, it was so good to see me again. She stroked my face, asking me if I would take her with me. She stroked my leg with her strong, gentle hands. Working hands, worn hands, translucent skin. She whispered sweet nothings across the room, she winked at me, she held my hand in hers. It was as if she was twenty again, as if we were courting, as if I had just come across the stream from the house in Gnilowody to her house, or as if we had returned together from a walk in the fields. Those warm summer days of bucolic pleasure when they loved together. When Irena was conceived. Mateusz and Anna. Anna Laska.

I stayed with Beata, Irena's youngest daughter, a late child, only 26, and her husband Marcin. His father, like most of Mieszkowice's older generation, was also from Galicia. There were others in the town from Gnilowody. I met Praxheda, another tiny old woman, wiry, dark-haired, 93 and garrulous. She attended the wedding of Anna and Mateusz. A short wedding, because of the straitened circumstances of the Soviet occupation, only two days. The dancing was in a big barn and in the yard in front of it. They played all the dances, Oberek, Mazur, Polka, Sznej Polka, Kozak... With a fearful look in her eyes and a wailing voice, Praxedha told me of the executions she had witnessed in Gnilowody in 1944, Polish men who had been laid face down on the ground by the *banderovci*, their hands tied behind their backs, their heads pulled up by the hair, their throats cut. That method saved bullets.

I dined with Mirka and her family and met her brother Marek and his family, my niece and nephew, though only a few years younger than me. Mirka took me to a print shop in a neighbouring town to copy some old photographs belonging to Anna and Irena. She presented them to me in an album: Irena's wedding in 1961; her confirmation photo when she was 12; with teenage friends at a funfair; Mirka, Marek and Beata as children in the 1960s; Anna on the street in Mieszkowice around 1950, fresh-faced and recovered from the war.

There were also two photos of my father, both from Podhajce in 1938. In one, he sits in the centre of a small group, fellow apprentices at the tailoring school, three young women in coats with fur collars and fashionable little round hats and a melancholy young man, dark hair neatly parted. My father wears a pin-striped, double-breasted jacket with wide, wing lapels, a shirt and a tie. He fixes the camera with a serious look. The second photograph is of a much larger group, the whole tailoring school I think, 70-80 people, the majority men, in front of Podhajce's Polish Catholic church, using what appears to be the steps and lower structure of a war memorial to create a pyramid shape for the group. A grandee sits at the centre of the front row, wearing a voluminous fur-collared coat and a Homburg. There are a few other senior-looking folk on either side of him and a couple of the young women in the first picture, and at one end sits my father, clearly taller than everyone else, in a smart dark short coat, scarf, shirt and tie, baggy trousers with turn-ups and a flat cap. Nearly all the men wear flat caps. He looks very serious and handsome, with his high cheekbones and slightly slanted, Slavic eyes. His big hands rest on his knees. His shoes are shiny. He was always pretty smart.

I wonder how many of this group survived the onslaught which was about to engulf them. How many of them ended up in the Podhajce ghetto? Around 70% of the town's population was Jewish, and in those days, 90% of Galicia's tailors were Jewish, so it's likely that most of this group perished. Which of them ended up dying on a battlefield, labouring on the permafrost, hiding in a cellar, starving in a camp, collaborating to save his skin, protecting a neighbour, spitting at a victim, looting a corpse, being raped, joining the partisans, surviving? I know the fate of only one.

Stefania arrived from Szczecin, a bundle of energy and enthusiasm, delighted to have been the one who had brought us together. We all dined together in the open air at the family allotment, a couple of acres of orchards, vegetable gardens and beehives, tended by Jan. He proudly showed me his vats of delicious honey, collected at different times of the season, from different flowers. We drank Jan's excellent *bimber*. I was welcomed with open arms into this family and though I was the special guest, I quickly became familiar to them as we laughed and celebrated. Irena and her family accepted me without question, looked after me, pulled my leg, the long-lost brother from Scotland.

Tailoring school group, Podhajce 1938. My father is on the front row, far left

We visited a museum and war cemetery by the Oder, a few kilometres from Mieszkowice, a bridgehead for the Soviet Army as they advanced towards Berlin. We swam in the nearby Lake Moryn. We visited Stefania in Szczecin and had a tour of a fire station, where Mirka's husband Marek, a witty French speaker, was assistant chief. Irena and I did ordinary things together. Visited the shops, went for a walk, ate together. But because of who we were and how we had come to meet and the aching gulf of time and experience which was behind us, to simply sit at a table together was a moment to treasure. Many questions remained unanswered, but somehow they had ceased to matter.

When the time of my departure came, the women were full of tears. So was I. With the faithful Piotr by my side, Beata and Mirka took me to Anna. I was still a ghost to her. I hugged her to my chest as I said goodbye and as she withdrew from me, she let out a primal cry, a searing wail of loss from the pit of her stomach, from the core of her being, from decades ago. He was leaving her again. It sent her crashing to the floor. When I left, she lost consciousness for two days.

Irena held on to me, and I to her. She said that now I was a part of her, that my family was her family. She urged me to return. I promised I would. They watched in silence as I got into the car, and waved as I pulled away. I guided the car out of Mieszkowice and drove on a straight road through fields. After a few kilometres, I had to stop, to cry until I was exhausted by crying. Through a lifetime of separation and ignorance, through the juddering echoes of that great war and the fragile threads which survived the destruction of people, families and places, and through this son's search for his father, some reparation had been made. I didn't really know what I had been looking for, but now, at last, I knew I had found it.

Me and Irena, Loch Ness 2006

EPILOGUE

In the years since my first meeting with Irena, my father's story has had more impact than I could ever have imagined. I now have wonderful new relatives and friends in Mieszkowice, as well as Pidhaitsi, Ternopil and Lviv. I visit them when I can, though not as often as I'd like. Irena and her family have shown me nothing but generosity and love. In addition to this, the success of my play has taken the story into the public realm and the response of the public has been quite overwhelming.

I had never intended the play to be in any way fictional – it was written from direct experience, with only a couple of short sequences taking imaginative leaps, based on the stories I'd heard of my father going into hiding and starving in the German POW camp. I didn't want to create characters I didn't know, perhaps because I didn't trust myself to do it convincingly. I felt it was appropriate to use the artifice of the play's construction, without any further fictionalisation. I wanted the fewest possible barriers between the audience and the truth of the story. It seemed clear to me that there should be only two characters, me and him, and that I should play them both. I also didn't want to be alone on stage. Not because I was afraid of that, I have done it before, but because I felt the need for richer contextual and emotional possibilities than a lone presence could offer. There had to be music and there had to be a musician. The violin is the quintessential instrument of Eastern European and Scottish folk music, so a violinist it was.

The play kind of wrote itself. It has elements contained in this book – my father's account of his life, my discovery of some of the truth. I already had so much material: the transcriptions, the war record, letters and diary entries from my travels. And I read around the subject: Primo Levi, Norman Davies, Anthony Beevor, Orlando Figes; Waldemar Lotnik's autobiographical account of his young life as a Polish partisan in Volhynia, *Nine Lives*; Kate Brown's fascinating study of nationality and identity in the region immediately to the east of Galicia during the first two decades after the Russian revolution, *A Biography of No Place*; Joseph Roth's bittersweet elegy for Austro-Hungary, *The Radetzky March*; Shimon Redlich's moving and illuminating account of his formerly multi-ethnic Galician town during the inter-war years, which was only 30 kilometres from Gnilowody, *Together and Apart in Brzezany*. I trawled websites and found one on Podhajce's Jewish past which showed photographs of existing houses and details of former Jewish owners. The extraordinary website *jewishgen.org* contains a chapter for each of the lost communities, so there is a Podhajce chapter full of memoirs of survivors. I did write a substantial amount, but a large part of the process was collating and ordering material, giving the story shape and dramatic rhythm. Having spent nearly 20 years to arrive at the point of creation, it didn't take much more than a week to put the text together.

I met the play's director, Ben Harrison, in 2006. He was immediately interested in the story. Even though I had met him only once for about 45 minutes, the way he engaged with it, coupled with his own adventurous work with his company, Grid Iron, told me that he was the right person for the job. With Dogstar regular Jonny Hardie and with Gavin Marwick, I was blessed with two of Scotland's finest fiddlers. One fiddler would never be enough, as musos always have several irons in the fire, with bands, recording and writing commissions, so we had two in rehearsal. So far, one of them has always been available when needed.

With editorial advice from Ben, a rehearsal draft was ready at the beginning of 2008. We spent a week in March experimenting with the script and production ideas. More edits were made and a few elements of the script were re-ordered. At the end of the week, we presented a staged reading of the script, with music, to an invited audience of fourteen people at Theatre Workshop in Edinburgh. It worked, and for the first time, we began to understand that we might have something quite special in our hands. I don't mean to sound conceited, I'm simply reflecting on how it felt at the time, for us and for those fourteen.

There's a lot of information to absorb in 75 minutes of the performance. I wanted to use some of the video and stills I had gathered and I felt that the audience would need further illumination through the presentation of maps and the routes of journeys. We also needed the projection of translations of the Polish songs and passages in Polish, Russian, German and Ukrainian. Ben had done some work with the video artist Tim Reid, so he pulled him on board. I had described the setting as a tailor's workshop, which is where I had recorded my father's words. Ali Maclaurin designed a set which evoked much more than just the workshop. She created a dream-like playing space of grey, blue and white, with a tapered backdrop of clothing, some of which spilled on to the floorcloth, pressed into it. The texture of the painted clothes played with the video images which were projected on to them. Fabric, and fabrication, became a central metaphor. The clothes were ever present, powerfully evoking the dead, all those souls who were absent, whose stories were embodied in my father's story. Kai Fischer's subtle lighting and Timothy Brinkhurst's sound design completed the assemblage.

After a couple of preview performances at the Arches Theatre in Glasgow, *The Tailor of Inverness* opened at the 2008 Edinburgh Fringe Festival at the Assembly Rooms. After 5 days, the show was a sell-out. Word-of-mouth can be very powerful at the Fringe. We were awarded a Scotsman Fringe First at the end of the first week. Critics and public alike raved about the show. I was receiving letters and cards on a daily basis from audience members who felt compelled to write. Like me, some were sons or daughters of Poles. One woman told me that I was 'telling the story of every Polish family'. Another said that for fifty years she had never believed that it would be possible to encapsulate this experience on a stage. The show won two more awards. It was exhilarating, humbling and exhausting. One of our awards took the show to the Adelaide Fringe Festival for a month early in 2009. The Adelaide audience embraced the show in the same way as the Edinburgh one, with many of the city's Eastern European community attending. I was invited to the Polish club by a marvellous old Ukrainian academic and radio presenter, Myk Mykyta, and Gavin and I were driven to Polish Hill River Museum, the site of the earliest Polish settlement in South Australia, 130 kilometres north of the city.

We toured Scotland twice that year, with most performances sold out. We took the show to Sweden too, playing at the inaugural Skelleftea Storytelling Festival and at Umea University, both in the north of the country. In early summer the Scottish theatre critics named me best actor for my performance in the show. This was flattering, though somewhat ironic when you consider that for half the performance I play myself.

In the autumn of 2010, Dogstar took the play to Poland, Ukraine and Germany. To coincide with our Ukrainian performances, the play was translated by Svitlana Shilpchenko and published in the literary magazine *Vsesvit (The Whole World)*. My cousin Ula's son, Wojtek Wozniak, provided us with an excellent Polish translation and we presented the show on this tour with a complete projected translation for our Ukrainian and Polish audiences.

It seemed right to me to take the story back to its origins, but I was nervous about how it would be received. I was conscious that it could be viewed as a presumptuous act, for a foreigner to have the gall to tell Poles and Ukrainians their own story. But my previous trips to Ukraine in particular had told me that this was a story which had rarely been expressed on a public platform. The shock of the war and the subsequent 45-year Soviet stasis retained their grip. The fear of speaking out which was endemic to the old Stalinist culture meant that many people, particularly in the older generations, still had a policeman in their head.

The show was included in the programmes of two major theatre festivals, Konfrontacje Teatralne (Theatre Confrontations) in Lublin and the Zoloty Lev (Golden Lion) Festival in Lviv. I met the Scottish academic Robert Brown through the Ukrainian Club in Edinburgh. He was involved in charitable work in orphanages in Ukraine and he put me in touch with his Ukrainian colleague Valeriy Fen. Valeriy organised two performances for us at Lutsk University in Volhynia. I also made a speculative phone call to Kyiv Mohyla University and was answered by a secretary who spoke no English. Fortunately, a law student who did speak good English happened to be passing by the secretary's desk and she turned out to have a passion for theatre. Her name was Oksana Ivantsiv and she became the show's promoter in Kyiv. I also wanted to present the show in Pidhaitsi, so Lesia arranged a performance in the town's social club. I discussed a presentation in Mieszkowice with Irena's family, but they felt that the personal exposure would be too difficult for Irena and Anna. Instead, I arranged a performance with Zielona Gora University, 130 kilometres south of Mieszkowice.

We experienced a comedy of errors and obstruction at the Polish/Ukrainian border, which initially resulted in us being barred from taking our van into Ukraine. This led to us spending the whole night at the border and the organisers of the Golden Lion Festival sending their own van over for us to transfer the essentials of our set and equipment into this van. We eventually arrived in Lviv only five hours before the first performance, having had no sleep. Adrenalin kept us going and the packed audience gave the show a rapturous reception and a standing ovation. The same happened with our second performance the next day. I received several gifts from audience members.

Unfortunately, the delays caused at the border crossing, which continued when we returned to make another attempt to get the van across, caused the cancellation of our Pidhaitsi performance. This was a huge disappointment. For me, it was our most important performance in Ukraine. But the remainder of the tour went well. In Lutsk, a former Polish city, an audience of over 400 was initially quite restless, but it fell silent as I mentioned the Soviets for the first time. I found this quite disturbing. The play is not exactly positive about the role of the Russians and as I performed the show, I wondered if I was offending anyone. If I was, I never heard about it. I think this sudden concentration was another manifestation of the old taboos, that one couldn't talk openly about such things as the Soviet annexation of Eastern Poland and the Gulag, and here was a Scottish theatre company doing just that. The Lutsk audience gave the show another standing ovation as did all our audiences in Ukraine. A young Jewish student came up to me afterwards, barely able to talk. He took my hand and mumbled his thanks before darting away. I wanted to have a conversation with him, but I was besieged by other people. Although the play is not directly about the *Shoah*, it was impossible for me to ignore it as a fundamental part of the story. So the vibrant pre-war Jewish culture of Pidhaitsi and the fate of its people are described, including the two little boys who were at school with my father, Lipko and Muinka, represented by two white shirts.

We played for three nights in Kyiv, in a studio theatre at the university. Oksana had worked energetically to generate an audience, with the help of her enthusiastic friends. It was refreshing to meet these intelligent young Ukrainians. We stayed in Podol, a lively, cosmopolitan neighbourhood next to the wide River Dnieper. If you visit Ukraine and stay only in the centre of Kyiv, you might get the impression that Ukraine is much richer than it really is. There are designer shops, smartly-dressed urbanites and endless rows of black SUVs with tinted windows parked on the roadsides, the conveyances of members of the oligarchy or of organised crime. We visited Bulgakov's house and the impressive Great Patriotic War Museum, its exhibition unchanged since the Soviet era, perhaps because it quite justifiably emphasises the enormous scale of human sacrifice which took place.

We had full houses in Lublin and Zielona Gora. These audiences responded warmly, but there were no standing ovations. We travelled to the outskirts of Lublin to take a grim walk through Majdanek, the intact concentration camp, now a museum. We held a discussion after the show in Zielona Gora where one of the university's professors questioned my even-handed description of the Ukrainian-Polish conflict, asserting that the Ukrainians bore a far greater responsibility for atrocities. Perhaps this explained the more reserved reaction in Poland. But these were still special performances, and there were numerous expressions of thanks and appreciation. The Zielona Gora performance was particularly special for me as this was the one which was attended by Irena and her family. They had already read a translation of the play and seen a DVD of an earlier performance. They were pleased at the play's success, but I think they were even more pleased just to see me.

We travelled on to Berlin for a successful week at the English Theatre. German audiences have embraced the play too. Since then, it has been presented in Kiel and Dresden in Germany. Our first US performances took place at the University of Massachusetts in February 2012. We got a standing ovation there too, and we were already looking forward to further touring in Denmark, Sweden, Ireland and the UK during 2013.

A month after the 2008 Edinburgh Fringe, I received an email from a woman called Hela Deacon. Hela lives in the East Midlands. She hadn't seen the show, but she had read about it after googling Gnilowody with a cousin who was visiting from Poland. She felt she had to contact me because her mother, whose maiden name was Olszewska, had been from the village and her father was from Podhajce. Her Uncle Janek Olszewski and his wife Jozia, both from Gnilowody, were still alive and living in a village called Lezyce, close to Zielona Gora in south-west Poland. She has several other cousins there. She knew of a family of Zajacs in Lezyce too. I recalled a visit to Lesna in the '60s from a man called Marion Zajac. He was tall and swarthy, with a gentle demeanour and slicked back hair like my dad's. I was told he had come from Zielona Gora. Hela explained that 'As to your sister in Mieszkowice, Marysia (her cousin) said that the Gnilowody village was divided between Lezyce and Mieszkowice, being told that Mieszkowice had more fertile land and was the better option.' She was referring to the deportation of the Gnilowody Poles by the Soviets at the beginning of 1945, the six-month journey taken by Irena and her mother.

The following autumn, Hela told me that a memorial to the Gnilowody Poles who died at the hands of Ukrainian militiamen during the war was to be unveiled at a ceremony in Lezyce in October. This was part of a process which was being carried out with the support of the Polish government in many of the communities which had been resettled from Ukraine, more than sixty years after those dreadful events. Any public discussion of the conflict had been banned under the communists and it was only now that a formal acknowledgement and honouring of the dead was taking place. In Ternopil in 2003, Xenia had told me that there had been no violence between Poles and Ukrainians in Gnilowody. I remembered meeting the old woman Praxedha in Mieszkowice and her eyewitness description of the execution of Poles in Gnilowody. On my second visit to the village, in October 2007, Olga Kindzierska had admitted that there had been some violence, 'but only towards a couple of Polish families, only a few were killed'.

I decided to attend the ceremony and took a flight to Berlin and a hire car to Lezyce, three hours away, driving through early morning mist and following our old holiday route south from Frankfurt Oder. I met Hela and her husband Douglas in a car park on the edge of Zielona Gora and they led me to Janek and Jozia's house. Both in their 80s, they were sprightly and very welcoming. Jozia had made fresh doughnuts. They both recognised me, a typical Zajac. They said my presence made them feel as if they were back in Gnilowody.

The memorial had been erected on a piece of ground before Lezyce's pretty little church. It consisted of four flat stones standing vertically on a plinth, angled towards each other as if in conversation or communion. The first declared their purpose, the others listed the dead, their names and ages and the dates when they died. Forty-five people, men, women and children, some with names which had become familiar to me

– Bokla, Olszewski, Laska. No Zajacs. There were 10 Olszewskis. Later, Hela told me that her mother was related to all of them, that she and Janek were the only members of her family to survive.

The ceremony began inside the church, with a 25-minute recital by a local choir followed by prayers and a brief sermon. There were around 175 present. There were a few old men in their Polish army uniforms, carrying banners and accompanied by a group of boy scouts. They led us out of the church and down to the memorial. There were conciliatory speeches by the mayor of Zielona Gora and a Ukrainian representative from Ternopil. An old Polish man gave a fiery speech which criticised the Ukrainians for failing to fully admit culpability. A smartly dressed man in his fifties spoke on behalf of the people of Lezyce, fighting back tears. I discovered later that his name was Rafael and that he was married to a distant cousin of mine, one of the Lezyce Zajacs. Another then read out the list of the dead. His name was Czeslaw Laska. He was also related to me. We stood in a circle round the memorial and listened to the names in the biting wind. There was a minute's silence. The priest gave his blessing and we walked to the church hall for drinks and sandwiches.

In the hall, I was introduced to Rafael's wife, Valeria and her mother Stefania, Zajacs descended from my great grand-father's brother. Stefania explained that on the day of the most extensive murdering in Gnilowody, a Ukrainian friend came from Mozoliwka, my grandmother's village, to warn her family a few hours before the Ukrainian militiamen arrived. The family fled the village and survived.

I spent the evening as a guest at Valeria's house, eating with her extended family (*my* extended family!) and trying to keep up with all these new family connections. An old photograph of my grandfather's cousin, a patriarch of this family, had pride of place on a display cabinet. He was a farmer standing in the sun before the camera in his working clothes, tall, weather-beaten and dark-haired with a bushy moustache. Very similar to the only picture I'd ever seen of my grandfather Andrzej. The photograph must have been taken around 1920. I was told that my Great Uncle Michal's children were living in Katowice, and that my Great Uncle Anton's daughters had emigrated to America before the war. A new family tree was scribbled out for me. When you start looking into these things, it can become quite overwhelming. All these relatives I never knew I had: Valeria, Stefania, Anton, Michal, Jan, Irena, Hanka, Michal, Ivan, Pela, Hanna, Maria, Antonina, Piotr, Julia, Czeslaw, Micha, Wanda, Henryk, Sabina, Franciszek, Jan, Anna, Pawel, Ludwig, Stasza, Halina, Czeslawa, Marian, Wladyslaw, Bogdan, Mykola, Mariana, Khrystyna, Ira, Tania, Beata, Mirka, Marek, Piotr, Sabina, Wojtek, Jakub, Karolina, Nikolai, Irena.

During my later visits to Mieszkowice, Pidhaitsi and Hnilowody, I gleaned information about the fate of my grandfather, Andrzej. It was never entirely clear, but it seems that he was also a victim of the Ukrainian militia. I was told that he had been badly beaten up by them, that he had never fully recovered from the beating, and that this was the cause of his death a year or two later. I was told that his marriage to my Ukrainian granny had probably prevented them from killing him. I was told that my granny had taken revenge for his beating, and maybe for the murders too, that she had informed her people in Mozoliwka who the culprits were, and that those culprits had received summary justice, that they had been executed by their own people. I was told that my grandfather's grave may not have been marked because of the extreme poverty at the war's end. It's possible that if it was marked, it was destroyed as part of the anti-Polish hatred. On my second visit to the Hnilowody cemetery, I discovered some Polish graves. Most of them had been desecrated many years before, their headstones removed. One of the few intact Polish graves was that of my great grandfather, the Mateusz Zajac whose tribute was painted on the wall of the Orthodox church. The inscriptions on what was left of the other Polish graves had been painted over. I found a large kind of medallion with a relief of Jesus beside one of them, a grave decoration, and used it to scrape away the paint, revealing a name: Anton Zajac, quite possibly my great-uncle. On a second grave, I uncovered the name of Jakub Zajac.

From both a military and political point of view, the history of Ukrainian nationalism during and after the Second World War is riddled with complexity and contradiction. When the Nazis started recruiting for their two SS Halychyna Divisions in 1943, it split the nationalist underground resistance between those who saw it as an opportunity to create a standing Ukrainian army which could resist the oncoming Soviets, and those who refused to collaborate. There was already a Ukrainian puppet administration headed by leaders who saw the Nazi occupation as their opportunity to assert statehood, however compromised. There was the Ukrainian Partisan Army (UPA) and the Organisation of Ukrainian Nationalists (OUN). A faction of the OUN, known as OUN (B) or the *banderovci,* was led by the Ukrainian hero, Stepan Bandera. There is a tendency for this name to be applied to every Ukrainian militia group of the time. Some historians argue that this is inaccurate as there were further splinter groups, factions and opportunistic groups of bandits, sometimes simply groups of thugs who bore a grudge against a neighbouring village or particular families.

There were occasions, too, when groups of Polish partisans acted independently and brutally. The thirst for revenge drove these groups to ever-increasing acts of cruelty. There are many conflicting accounts of what actually happened during the Ukrainian-Polish conflict, not helped by the fact that most information about it was heavily suppressed by both the Polish Communist and Soviet governments as a way of trying to suppress nationalism. Fighting continued sporadically for years after the war, between Poles and Ukrainians and between Ukrainians and the Soviet Army. Indeed, I've been told that the Soviets only succeeded in putting an end to violent Ukrainian nationalist resistance in Western Ukraine as late as 1960. What is clear is that the fighting and terror during 1943-44 was savage and often indiscriminate and that the Ukrainians had the upper hand, especially those who were sanctioned by the Nazi occupiers.

On a visit to Pidhaitsi in June 2008, I stayed with Bogdan's daughter Tania and her family. Her house was on the opposite side of the valley from the main part of the town, high on the valley slope. Tania's 18-year-old daughter Khrystyna took me for a walk one morning through the fields behind the house. We walked over the brow of the hill, just beyond the view of the town, passing a statue of a saint which commemorated a battle which had been fought there between the Poles and the Mongols. Khrystyna led me to two grassy mounds, guarded by a few shrubs and a couple of trees. These are the mass graves of the Pidhaitsi Jews. The survivors of the ghetto had been marched to this hidden field in 1943 to be murdered, each child, woman and man shot in the head to fall into the freshly-dug pit. The mound suggests that the bodies piled too high, that the pit wasn't deep enough to contain them. The second mound marks the grave of the Jewish administrators of the ghetto, those who had collaborated, believing it might save them. They had followed the first group. A memorial stone stood by the first grave. There was none by the second.

As with Pidhaitsi's Jewish cemetery, I was reminded that, for all the casual anti-semitism I had encountered during my visits to Ukraine, communities such as Pidhaitsi's still manage to retain some degree of respect for the remaining physical evidence of their murdered heritage. Occasionally, a party of Jews or Poles will visit Pidhaitsi to walk the streets and visit the Jewish cemetery, the mass graves, the ruined synagogue and the Polish church. They are the survivors, the children, the descendants of those who once lived there. Like me, they have come to remember.

ACKNOWLEDGEMENTS

There are many people who have been essential in helping me to complete this book. Most of them feature in it. My aunt, Aniela Zajac set me on the trail to Ukraine. Bogdan and Hala Baldys were my hosts on my first trip to Ukraine and Lesia Kalba was my vital translator. The hospitable Mykola and Xenia Baldys, Olga Kindzierska and Olga Zenov provided me with crucial details. Taras Teslyak was our patient driver. Stefania Szarejko put me in touch with Irena and her mother. Piotr Butrymowski translated for me on my first trip to Mieszkowice and Beata and Marcin Mokrzyccy, and Mirka and Marek Butrymowski were my generous hosts. I must also thank, in Ukraine, Tania, Khrystyna & Marianna Teslyak, Tekla & Milanja Tischanyuk, Hrihoriy Kalba, Oleg Cyganovich, Sasha Papusha, Mychaylo Forgel, Ira Dzadukevich, Iryna Suharska, Vasyl Kalba. In Poland, Ula & Janusz Wozniak and Wojtek Wozniak for additional translation work, Marek & Ula Bogucki. In Berlin, Tom Morrison, Klaus Mummenbrauer and Johannes Steinbruckner. In England, Barbara Kroll at the British Army Archive, Hela & Douglas Deacon. In Scotland, Lallie, Pip & Steve Wilson and Maria Gibbs.

I must also thank those who enabled the theatre production

of *The Tailor of Inverness*. The creative team: Ben Harrison, Jonny Hardie, Gavin Marwick, Ali Maclaurin, Tim Reid, Timothy Brinkhurst, Kai Fischer, Sholto Bruce, Laura Edwards, John Spiers, Karen Sutherland, Laurence Winram, Angela Cran, Catherine MacNeil, Liz Smith, John Gordon and Hamish MacDonald. Judith Docherty of Grid Iron and Mary Shields. The Scottish Arts Council/Creative Scotland and the Hugh Fraser Foundation for financial support, Hi Arts and Highlands & Islands Enterprise.

Finally, I must thank Virginia Radcliffe and my daughters Ruby and Iona for living with me through it all. And for opening their doors to me, I thank Anna and Jan Kotek and, of course, my half-sister Irena Bogucka and her husband Czeslaw.

GLOSSARY

Polish/Ukrainian

Gnilowody/Hnilowody pron. Gneelovody/Hneelovody

Podhajce/Pidhaitsi

Tarnopol/Ternopil

Brzezany/Berezany

Lwow/Lviv

Galicia/Halychyna

Arbeit Macht Frei – work makes you free

babcha – grandmother, old woman

banderovci – Ukrainian militia men, the name derives from the UPA leader Stepan Bandera, though the name banderovci is often used by Poles as a blanket term, whether a militia member or group followed Bandera or not.

barszcz – beetroot soup

bigos – Polish hunter's stew with pork, sausage, sauerkraut

bimber – Polish home-made vodka

Czekam na szybka odpowiedz.- I await your reply

croft – very small Scottish farm

donner und blitzen – thunder & lightning

golabki – parcels of cabbage containing a mixture of rice, herbs and meat with a tomato sauce

gulag – the vast network of Soviet labour camps

Hannukah – Jewish festival of light held for 8 days towards the end of the year

horilka – vodka

hrivny – Ukrainian currency

Hutsuls – indigenous people of the Eastern Carpathian Mountains

jutro – tomorrow (Polish)

kasha – buckwheat

kielbasa – sausage

kolkhoz – collective farm

kompot – fruit cordial

lager – German prison camp

lederhosen – traditional German leather short trousers or dungarees

Lesna – pron. Leshna

Luger – German handgun

March March Dabrowski – Polish national anthem

Najlepsze zyczenia – best wishes

Niemcy/em – Germany/German

NKVD – Soviet Secret Police during the Stalin period, ideology enforcers

oblast – Ukrainian (and Russian) administrative county
Ostarbeiter – lit. Eastern worker – the name given by the Nazis to forced labourers from Russia, Ukraine and Belarus

pierogi – traditional flour dumplings with various fillings

placki – potato rissoles

plov – Ukrainian rice and chicken dish

Proskurov – pre-war name of present-day city of Khmelnitsky, Western Ukraine

prosto – straight ahead

rastplatz – literally rest place – motorway lay-by

samohon – Ukrainian home-made vodka

Shoah – the Hebrew term for the Holocaust, literally 'calamity'

spae wife – Scottish Highland term for soothsayer, wise woman

Sto Lat – One Hundred Years – Polish celebratory song

tak – yes

Untermenschen – subhumans – Nazi term for non-Aryans

vareniki – Ukrainian name for pierogi, see above

voivod – Polish administrative county volksdeutsch – people considered by the Nazi authorities to qualify as having ethnic German identity

zloty – Polish currency

zurek – sour ryemeal soup